THE MASARYKS

Zbyněk Zeman

THE MASARYKS

The Making of Czechoslovakia

WEIDENFELD AND NICOLSON
LONDON

Weidenfeld and Nicolson
11 St John's Hill London SW11

ISBN 0 297 77096 9

Printed in Great Britain by
Willmer Brothers Limited, Birkenhead

For Adam

Contents

Introduction

THIS dual biography ends with the statement that Jan Masaryk, the son of the founder and the first president of Czechoslovakia, was the heir to a name charged with historic meaning, but that the meaning was not read in the same way even by all the Czechs and Slovaks, and by others less so. Thirty years after Jan Masaryk's death this is still the case.

As recently as 1972 a closely argued analysis was published in English, advancing the theory that Jan Masaryk was murdered by his Communist adversaries. Jan Masaryk's death seems to have retained its fascination. Thomas Masaryk, on the other hand, is half-forgotten in the West. The last full-length biography of President Masaryk was published in 1960.

Between the two wars it was Thomas Masaryk who had stood at the centre of attention. He was seen, by his English-speaking biographers and other interpreters of his life, as a 'professor-politician'. From there, it was only a short step to the view of him as 'philosopher-king' or, as his son eventually came to see him, 'scholar-saint'.

The people who wrote about Masaryk in English were mostly academics themselves. In a lecture delivered at the University of Liverpool in 1932, for instance, Nowell Smith, the headmaster of Sherborne School, put the matter quite bluntly: 'I believe Masaryk to be one of the best and greatest men who have lived upon this planet. I will not waste time by arguing about degrees of comparison.' At London University, Sir Robert Birley, headmaster of Eton College, said on the centenary of Masaryk's birth in 1950: 'He is great for what he did and what he stood for in his personal life, which was indistinguishable from his public life, rather than for what he wrote and said. Essentially his great achievement was to live a life honestly based on moral ideas amid the strains and stresses of politics.'

D. A. Lowrie, an American biographer of Thomas Masaryk, also conceded that 'his weapons were those of the spirit: truth and justice'.[1] But Lowrie translated the Masaryk myth into the terms of American legends, with titles such as *From Log-Cabin to the White House*. They extolled men who had 'started life as poor, ignorant folk in the backwoods and had climbed the ladder of life by heroic work and powerful character until they came to preside over the life of their nation. This man, Thomas Masaryk, had, I reflected, done all that.'

Out of so much praise in the West a curiously flat person emerged. The philosopher-king, the coachman's son who made good, the politician who hardly ever put a foot wrong. It is perhaps not surprising that Thomas Masaryk is half-forgotten, and that much of the writing about him throws little light on the reasons for the highly charged significance of the name.

In their own country the two Masaryks have been the subjects of much controversy. It was sometimes contained between the covers of august academic periodicals; in the main it was political, public and violent. The hard lines of that debate, up to the death of Jan Masaryk, are sketched out in this book. But the controversy continued after 1948. There was, in the first place, a reaction against the view of Thomas Masaryk as the sole begetter of the Czechoslovak republic; a continuation of the pre-war argument, carried on by historians rather than politicians.

Some of the Communist historians perhaps took their disregard for the role of Masaryk in the construction of the state too far. There was also a political consideration: the need to dismantle the Masaryk myth, and diminish the memories of Czechoslovakia's links with the West.

Then the collections of documents appeared, in 1953 and 1954: papers from Masaryk's private archives, which were meant to demonstrate that in politics Masaryk belonged to the other side of the barricade. That he had plotted against Lenin and the Soviet regime and against the socialists in Czechoslovakia; that bankers were his best friends; and that his presidency was a very expensive affair indeed. Despite their clearcut political purpose, the documents are well-edited and valuable sources on a part of Masaryk's political life.[2]

In the years 1967–9 a few studies of Masaryk and his policies appeared in Prague, in particular a biography of Masaryk as a philosopher, and a study of his activities in the First World War. The latter book, *Bez legend* by Karel Pichlík,[3] is excellent, and draws heavily on the Masaryk archive. It continues a tradition of political and historical writing in Czech which was established between the two wars, but has hardly found its way into English at all.

On the political side, Ferdinand Peroutka's monumental *Budování státu* (The Building of the State) gives a sharp insight into the early years of the Czechoslovak republic, by a sympathetic contemporary observer. In the field of historical research, Zdeněk Nejedlý's four-volume biography of young Masaryk could hardly be more comprehensive. It tells the reader what books people read, what the ancestry of Masaryk's wife was, how Masaryk met and parted from his friends.

Both books were completed shortly before the outbreak of the Second World War. Peroutka, who now lives in exile in the United States, has recently started revising his book for a new edition; Nejedlý died in Prague in 1962, the deputy prime minister in the Czechoslovak government and the president of the Academy of Sciences. Nejedlý was a pupil of Masaryk who became a Communist and a critic of Masaryk's foreign policy; perhaps one flaw of the biography he wrote is that it is too deferential towards his former teacher.

In 1968 the Masaryk issue became fissionable material. After many years of official silence and disapproval the death of Jan Masaryk and the life and work of Thomas became the object of great public interest. Students made the pilgrimage to Lány, the cemetery where both the Masaryks, as well as Charlotte, the President's wife, are buried. Early in April a students' magazine examined the death of Jan Masaryk in an article based on a Western source of doubtful quality, and called for an official inquiry.

Soon after the military action against Czechoslovakia in August 1968, a radio station in central Bohemia, sponsored by the Warsaw Pact forces, broadcast a programme on Thomas Masaryk's role in the intervention against the Soviet Union, and in the assassination attempt on Lenin in 1918.

The view of Masaryk as 'philosopher-king' did not quite fit into the Russian scheme of things; the Russians had never had their own, say, Mr Lowrie, to make Masaryk understandable to them in simple terms. On both sides there was general incomprehension and, sometimes, hostility. Masaryk had failed to admire Tsarist Russia or to welcome Lenin's revolution. After the First World War, he reminded Beneš, his foreign minister, 'Do not forget, the Bolsheviks are Jesuits'; he told his son that Russia was an 'Asiatic state'. Many Russian refugees came to Prague after 1918; one of the most prominent of them, Boris Savinkov, the revolutionary, terrorist and novelist, and one of Masaryk's protégés, chose to denounce Masaryk at his trial in Moscow in August 1924.

And what is true of Thomas Masaryk also applies to his son. He was, very simply, the heir to a name with a much better reputation in the West than in the East. But he himself had not been the maker of that reputation, and his brief political life was both aided and in the end broken by it.

In English, Jan was better served by his friends than his father had been by his biographers. Mrs Marcia Davenport, the American novelist, and Sir Robert Bruce Lockhart have written personal memoirs of Jan Masaryk which are more revealing than all the biographies in English put together – perhaps with the exception of Paul Selver's biography, published in 1940, which is very good on Masaryk's early years. But in a way Mrs Davenport and Sir Robert had an easier task than the biographers of Thomas Masaryk: they wrote of the last years of a person who was perhaps less complicated and certainly less political than his father.

Between them the lives of the two Masaryks spanned almost a century – 1850–1948 – and one of them made an important contribution to the shaping of a part of that century. In the eastern part of Europe the Masaryk issue is still very much alive. It has caused much controversy. But controversy is a matter of the postures men choose to take up, often an affair remaining on the surface. Underneath the controversy, and the historical events which caused it, the common life of the country continues. Its continuity and unity often remain hidden from the view of the casual observer. The names, for instance, of Masaryk, of his fiercest political adversary, Kramář, of Masaryk's pupil, biographer and critic, Nejedlý, may all be found on the title page of a collection of essays, published in Prague in 1925. They are reminiscences of Lev Tolstoy and of his house at Yasnaya Polyana.

In the First World War Thomas Masaryk taught at the University of London; during the Second World War, Zděnek Nejedlý was at the University of Moscow. One of his pupils there, Ivan Ivanovich Udaltsov, became, as the counsellor at the Soviet Embassy to Prague, one of the most important links between the two capitals. There now exist many connections between Moscow and Prague; in a way, the hopes of the Czech Panslavs of the nineteenth century have come true.

Masaryk had, of course, envisaged a Czechoslovak state strongly linked with the West: this book examines the reasons why such an alignment could not be maintained. That there should be a Czechoslovakia was Masaryk's first objective; for more than half a century the Czechs and the Slovaks have been estimating the price they have to pay for their common state.

26 August 1975

1

Young Masaryk

On 19 January 1876 Thomas Masaryk applied for admission to the final examinations in philosophy at Vienna University. He enclosed a *curriculum vitae,* which opened with the sentence: 'Pindar advises us that the beginning of every enterprise should be magnificent – if you are embarking on an enterprise, make its appearance shine from afar.' A brief but comprehensive autobiography followed, written in German in neat and angular hand, with frequent erasures and a large ink blot.

The *curriculum* had been written in August 1875, when Masaryk was staying with his parents in Moravia during the summer vacation. Originally it was not drafted for an official purpose. In a retrospective mood, Masaryk was writing his first autobiography for himself. It is a revealing document about the first twenty-five years of his life and about the author himself.[1]

Born in a small country town in Moravia – 7 March 1850 – I was in my early youth carefully brought up and tended by my good mother, to whose self-sacrificing love I owe everything: sweet hours of domestic love and peace will for ever be my pleasantest memories; love for my parents and siblings, two brothers, has often been the only, but rich, source of consolation in my troubled hours. When I was six I came to a village (Čejkovice) where I acquired in the first form the basic beginnings of knowledge; fortunately, as a friend of the son of a high imperial official, I also shared private tuition with him, while at the same time I made good progress in German, a language not entirely foreign to me – my mother was German – but I was decidedly less fluent in it than in Czech [– or rather Slovak]. (*Author's note*: the significant passages which Masaryk struck out are given here in square brackets.) In addition, I read books for children by Nieritz and Schmidt; a detailed history of Bohemia and Hungary sparked off my love for the past of my country, which I got to know well from some statistics and old atlases; at that time I started a list of Austria's towns, and busied myself in my spare time with the invention of a language which was to be intelligible to everyone: its alphabet was based on numbers. I read a lot about ancient knights and my friend and I used to imitate them: we were given a donkey each and a colourful uniform, and we set out, every Sunday, as 'generals' to play gay military games with our peers; when the games were forbidden after an accident, we invaded a deserted Jesuit monastery as 'penitents' and amused ourselves with sermons, celebrating masses, and other church ceremonies.

When I was nine I lost my friend and returned to school; here, to the great joy of my parents, I became the star pupil. During one exam we read an article called 'Beyond the Stars', and I was asked to explain it; the memory of my recently deceased sister made me cry a lot, and I could not go on; the inspector, a deacon, liked that. After the examination he asked for my mother and implored her that my parents should let me become a 'village teacher'; the outcome was that I was sent to school in Hustopeče.

To remind me of my childhood room, which was also my 'study', I asked my teacher for a book, which he lent me: it was *Physiognomy* for teachers, after Lavater, which contained some nonsense concerning skulls. I learned that book almost by heart; I checked the length of my school-fellows' fingers, and the shape of their chins. I tried all the theories on my school-fellows, and the result was that I could not find a friend to my taste, and they avoided me for my curious behaviour.

Since we were taught in German at school, I had to learn almost everything by heart, and my memory as well as fluency in the language benefited; I became the top pupil in the first years. All the time, I had no friends and saved myself from moral corruption, which affected my school-fellows; *Physiognomy* was my only entertainment in this unfriendly foreign country.

After two years I returned home to 'practise' (*Author's note*: to become a pupil-teacher), ie to be taught music by the village master, and to teach children; at that time people were admitted to teachers' training colleges only when they were sixteen years old, and I therefore had to wait for four years; no one was of course concerned with what I would forget by then; I therefore became apprenticed, only to leave again after two months; because I could not stand 'practising' all day, alternating with the master's wife's two brats.

My father was then very busy with the supervision of a large farm; and because I could not go on studying, because of financial difficulties, I had to choose different work. Time passed and I found myself in the company of depraved 'ex-students'; [even now I thank God that he preserved my moral purity; a certain modesty, which had become my habit in H, restrained me from excesses which were, at least then and there, the rule with young people; I cannot say whether I would not have died without the intervention of my decisive father;] and for a long time all my thoughts and acts centred on play-acting and other similar time-wasting entertainments.

So I was woken up by my father at midnight, and had to get dressed, and off we were to Vienna; my good mother accompanied me all the way there, and took me, having got an introduction from an acquaintance, to a lock-smith, where I was supposed to spend four years before becoming a master. My mother left, and I remained in my green 'locksmith's apron', standing in the workshop, making plans for the future. The noise of the city, relationships with my new 'comrades', very soon became unbearable for me; bookshops were my only joy, where I sneaked to during the lunch break – I ate little, sometimes nothing at all – to read the titles of the books, remember them and during working hours speculate about their probable contents; in the evenings I read in my own books, or studied Stieler's atlas, finally to find the page with my own country on it – tears interrupted this pastime, and night after night I cried myself to sleep.

I thought about changing my job; I visited a bookseller and asked for clerical work, or something like that, but I was sternly told off; perhaps I would have become reconciled to my fate had a certain detail not put me off: a fellow-boarder stole all my books including *Physiognomy,* and sold them; from that moment I could no longer stand it; I knew clearly that I would have to do something for my intellect, that I also needed something for my mind – and returned home. My father was beside himself over the 'shame' which I caused him by my second 'change'; and acting on the advice of an 'expert', a barber, he apprenticed me to a smith, so that I could later enter a veterinary institute. I shall pass those six months in silence: suffice it to say that I was very often slapped by farm-hands who were under the supervision of my father, when I put a hoof-nail in the wrong way, so that they would let me know what it meant to be a 'spoilt student'; the proverb 'cobbler stick to your last' was heard by me and my father very often from an envious and malicious mob.

One autumn morning I walked, as usual, to get two buckets of water from a nearby well; when I returned to the smithy I noticed that a certain gentleman was watching me steadily for a long time, and when I looked more carefully I recognized my former piano teacher: the buckets fell out of my hands, and I walked like a machine with my head down, away to the nearby hills, to think about my fate and to cry.

In order to be brief, I shall simply say that after a few days I fortunately became an assistant master, to the father of my former piano teacher, and that I started on my former profession with great zeal, because I saw, in my progress up to date, the finger of God, which seemed to beckon me to the originally determined aim by the most varied paths.

As an assistant master I had nothing free apart from my lodgings and my meals were brought to me by my mother, who walked an hour every day; here and there grateful farmers remembered me with a piece of meat or a bottle of wine etc; I very soon gained the sympathy of my pupils and their parents, though I had to take a lot of rudeness from the older boys at the beginning, because it was difficult for them to call their former school-mate 'Sir' – I was of course much older, but they remained in an elementary school, in the same form, for six to seven years. As a recent 'spoilt smith's apprentice' or, as they used to say in that part of the world 'Mr Preceptor', I had a

lot to do, because I had to look after the two classes; apart
from that, I had to perform the organist's duties in the church
and, when necessary, fill in at funerals etc, and then I had to
return the clerical robes to my boss, who occupied himself
exclusively as the notary public, a fairly profitable line; otherwise I was expected to kiss the hands of 'her ladyship', the
senior master's wife, and of the 'young miss', a duty which
I very soon substituted by only bending my back, to the utter
disgust of my elevated ladies: to sum up – I did not like the
house, and this dislike naturally affected my job, which was
inside and outside the house; my restless spirit found no rest
in the day-to-day, routine teaching of the same things; and
displeasure was expressed in a higher place with my innovations.

For instance, I began to teach some natural history, geography,
etc, but I was in the end completely forbidden to do so, because
several cautious mothers complained to the deacon that 'their
children have to learn such silly pieces', which 'no clever person
can ever need'; but on the whole the peasants were on my side,
and they honoured me with a visit to my lodgings, and asked
me to go on teaching a great deal, so that one day Čejkovice
would see 'many of my pupils become corporals with the
military'; our measure of the master's ability was the way he
used the rod, or, when a more sophisticated criterion was
applied, according to the number of corporals supplied by the
village; on this occasion – it was a market day – every emissary
put a mouldy old penny on my table 'for improvement'! But
enough of this.

For church ceremonies, I had no Latin; and there was another
thing: in the derelict Jesuit library, to which I had access,
I found among other books a seventeenth-century catechism
which stimulated me to learn eagerly; in that bulky volume there
were scattered many axioms by learned men of old and, because
they were given in the original language, I could not understand
them, and those written in Greek I could not even read; I was
sorry about that, and started thinking about learning those languages. I was enthusiastic about this, and visited the local priest,
PS, who found my intention very praiseworthy, and willingly
promised me his support; he gave me an old dictionary straightaway, which from that moment on I started to learn by heart,

Principio de nacionalismo

so as to go through, with this vocabulary, the Latin quotations and books. But this priest was not on very good terms with the teacher; the teacher representing the German, and the priest the national, side: I knew nothing then about either side, but after some time I was won over for the 'national cause', though at the same time I lost the favour of my superior. [(At this point, Masaryk provided an explanatory footnote.) Only by study and the proper understanding of Roman history did my view of 'nationality' develop in such a way that I now understand Cicero's opinions and on the whole agree with Mill, who expresses his opinions in his *Logic*, volume VI, chapter 10.] I took little notice of him because I was very enthusiastic and then I decided, despite my advanced age, to finish my school studies. I used the first opportunity to thank the headmaster, who cursed me on my way.

I therefore studied Latin, enrolling as a private pupil at Strážnice, and then passed my exam very successfully. I was interested, at the time, in controversial religious questions, because I wanted to dedicate myself to the path of faith. Mr s, did not, being well intentioned, make a firm believer of his protégé, who even succeeded in converting a Protestant woman (a married lady from Mohuč, Mrs bvc) to the Catholic faith; [from that time I retained a certain predilection for the faith of my childhood, and of my youth, and a certain distaste for Protestant rebels and Catholic defectors; for that reason I later became very fond of Comte's writings, but we must not anticipate.]

During the vacation I went, like other poor students, 'journeying', and I brought back six gulden, and went to be matriculated in Brno, accompanied by my good mother. I was admitted into the second form of the German grammar school, with ready cash of 70x (*Author's note*: 'x' of Masaryk's German original was translated as crowns into Czech by Doležal, the editor of the document: but the crown replaced the gulden as the currency unit in Austria-Hungary only in 1892.) – the amount left after I had bought the most necessary books and things. In the first half I lived in unspeakable poverty; at the end of the year I was top of the class, and from that moment I did well, often very well. I was asked, on the recommendation of my maths master, to the house of the local chief police superintendent, le Monnier. I am grateful to that noble man for the subsequent education of my character; I admired sciences and I gave all my spare time – and nearly all my time then was spare – to extra-mural studies; I gradually started reading German classics, of whom Lessing very fast became my favourite author, and later I went on to academic authors; I had a lot of trouble with the Humboldts, though on the whole natural science was my favourite subject.

I was not at all interested in my colleagues, bearing in mind the sentence that 'too many people are interested in the affairs of others, without looking closely at their own kidneys' (Xenophon). At that time I learned French and made a little money for the purchase of the most essential books; in my completely free moments I also put together some poems, especially at school between lessons. I had the misfortune of being taught by bad masters, with the exception of one (Mr P), and my idea of a good teacher is based on his angelic behaviour; unfortunately our schools are not very good, ie our masters are petty-minded, pedestrian scholastics; I could not disguise my aversion to them, and therefore had to suffer a lot; but I was very careful, and I learned Latin and Greek grammar; nevertheless later, St succeeded in pushing me into the third place. It did not make me feel sorry, on the contrary, it taught me something; in any case, school soon became a burden to me, but it was a means to an end, and I had to put up with it; and so I concentrated on my favourite subjects more eagerly. From natural sciences I moved on to philosophy; at that time, the burning question of Darwinism brought me into the eye of philosophical storms, and I sailed without a pilot and without a rudder, lost on the open sea of opinion.

In the year 1866 I joined a few hot-blooded youths, who set out to fight for their country; in the Pressburg hospital my bed was next to that of my friend F, the only comrade I trusted at the time; we talked about our future the whole day, and he decided to be a priest, and I wanted to be a philosopher: my friend is a priest.

My resolve was strengthened by a curious misfortune. When, after the conclusion of peace, I was returning to my parents' house, I was attacked and very seriously injured one Sunday (5 August) by a hooligan; there were many of them roaming the countryside at the time. After my return I left for Brno and went on studying, only to run into severe difficulties with the headmaster, Mr кr. The friction got worse on the arrival of an emotional master, Mr ғ, from whom I did not hide my aversion, which I expressed by gestures and even by words; and by chance, I became aware of his petty-mindedness. The difficulties continued. Then 'wretched passion' upset my balance (1868) and even threatened to upset my plans; I soon realized though, that I was about to enter wholeheartedly into an unsuitable connection, and broke off the ties [which arose out of sweet habit]. At that time my younger brother came to live with me, and I had to take care of him; he was a school boy. I received a 'veiled hint' to leave, and I asked for my leaving certificate.

In the year 1869 I left with my benefactor [who in the meanwhile was elevated to a noble rank] for Vienna [where he became the chief superintendent, and, shortly afterwards, the president of the police]. I continued my school studies in Vienna, and became absorbed in my philosophical interests. From then on I visited the university library daily, and read the writings of Lavater, Reichenbach and other philosophical nonsense. Logic and academic philosophy did not satisfy me at all; my favourite reading then was the Czech translation of Lange's *History of Materialism,* which I annotated and on which I expressed unformed views; I also read then most of the Greek and Latin classics in complete editions, as previously I had used only expurgated editions for schools.

I also learned English, because I was aware of the fact that, as a future philosopher, I had to have access to authoritative works in English.

At the university, I registered in the philological department of the Faculty of Philosophy, when my plan to be admitted to the Oriental Academy had failed. I never wanted to become a teacher, so that I would be free to pursue philosophy for myself, though not entirely on my own; however, I had to give in.

Death snatched away from me my dearly loved brother in 1873 – from that time I devoted myself entirely to philosophy, and sought and found solace in it. A month after my brother's death I buried my only and true benefactor. [Now, apart from my old parents and brother, of whom I have to take care, I have no one else in the world; the promise, which I made to myself at one time, will come true with the help of God; bearing in mind that 'everything great must be true' I want to make my way through life so that I could improve, on the way, what is in my powers to improve.]

Finally, I should like to set out the plan of my studies during the past three years, as it is entered into my university index; what I learned on my own, I should like to report on elsewhere.

There follows a long list of subjects that young Masaryk had read at Vienna University. The document is dated 25 August 1875. It was written by a thoughtful and self-centred person. Pursuit of knowledge and social advancement went hand in hand for young Masaryk; despite the opening quotation from Pindar, he was not much concerned with appearances. He handed in the document as he had first drafted it, erasures and all, with German nouns starting with a small letter and long, idiosyncratic clauses punctuated at will.

The *curriculum vitae* was written during the long university vacation, in the countryside of Masaryk's boyhood, a remote corner of south-east Moravia where the river Morava, in its lower reaches, runs alongside the border between Moravia and Slovakia. It is a flat country, from time to time ruffled by low, rolling hills. There are meadows near the river, and fields and dusty roads further away, and very few woods. In the summer, the sun scorches the fields and the roads, and slows down the river; in the winter, the river freezes over and the countryside hibernates under a thick cover of snow.

The name of the region, Slovácko, conveys its nature: not quite Slovakia, but well on the way there. It is border country, with clearly distinguishable Czech and Slovak elements dwelling side by side. Young Thomas knew well two villages within one parish which were different from each other in both dialect and costume; in Čejkovice the dress was that of Haná, of the fertile Moravian plain, and the people spoke with a soft 'r'. A few miles away in Potvorov, the villagers embroidered their clothes in soberer colours, and Masaryk would have had his name pronounced as it is today, that is in the Slovak manner. The hesitation as to the true nationality of the inhabitants of the region was reflected in Masaryk's *curriculum vitae* where, referring to the language he spoke, he struck out Slovak and substituted Czech. At that time, half-way through the nineteenth century, Slovakia proper was still a part of the kingdom of Hungary; for some thousand years it had been cut off, politically, from the Czech lands to the west. But both Hungary and Moravia were a part of the Habsburg Empire, and they had shared Habsburg rule for three centuries. Vienna, the Empire's capital, was some sixty miles to the south of the Moravian border; in the region where Masaryk was born, German and German-Jewish minorities lived side by side with the Slavs.

The small town in Moravia where Masaryk was born on 7 March 1850 was called Hodonín. All his life Masaryk felt at home in flat countryside, and found mountains oppressive. These were the cultivated, prosaic plains of small fields, rather than the limitless and romantic plains further east, suitable for the breeding of horses rather than the cultivation of vegetables.

Masaryk was born in the dead middle of the nineteenth century. Even the writer of the *Annual Register* was not certain which way the affairs of Central Europe would turn: 'It is difficult to give a clear account of the political affairs of the different Germanic kingdoms during this year, as they were in a state of great confusion.' The revolutions of 1848 gave no clear indication as to the future of Central and East Europe; they had been too easily suppressed, their objectives too varied and contradictory.

The rule of the Habsburgs in the German, Slav, Magyar and Italian provinces survived the widespread rebellion, and so did the system which Francis I had described to the French ambassador:

My peoples are strangers to each other, and it is a great advantage. They are not prone to the same sickness at the same time. In France, an outbreak of fever gets you all on the same day. I send Hungarians to Italy and Italians to Hungary. Everyone watches his neighbour. They don't understand each other and they hate each other. Order is born out of their antipathies, and universal peace out of their hatred.

Less than two years before Masaryk's birth and not very far from his birthplace, in Olomouc, Emperor Ferdinand handed over his diverse dominions to a boy of eighteen, Franz Josef. The boy knelt before his uncle, who simply said to him: 'God bless you Franzl. Be good. God will protect you. I don't mind.' The authority of the young emperor was soon re-established: he never questioned the fact that this authority was a gift from God, and he did not expect anyone else to do so. In the early years of his reign, Franz Josef I showed a marked preference for military over civilian advisers, and for military solutions. Nevertheless he gradually learned to delegate responsibility and to concede parts of his powers: he did so only when he absolutely had to, in order to preserve the unity of his empire. He had the misfortune to be the symbol of that unity at a time when it was getting less and less real.

Franz Josef died in 1916, in the middle of the Great War, two years after he had once more given way to the impulse to use military solutions, and less than two years after Masaryk had declared his own war on the Habsburg Empire. Despite the fact that the two men had a lot in common they never exchanged more than polite nods at a few receptions for parliamentary delegates.

Masaryk was twenty years younger than the head of the state he did so much to destroy. He was born on the feast of St Thomas Aquinas, and was named after the saint; the origin of the name Masaryk was Slovak, and sometimes appeared in the local records as Masařík. The village scribes, the only people who could write, approximated the way people spoke: the hard and the soft 'r' was a matter, we have seen, of some fluctuation in the region, and had its effect on the spelling of the family's name.

Masaryk's father Josef was a Slovak who had been born a serf. He was the youngest of three brothers, and went to seek employment on a large estate which belonged to the imperial and royal family. A century earlier, the estates on both sides of the Slovak-Moravian border had passed into the possession of the husband of the Empress Maria Theresa; it was a k.u.k. (*kaiserlich und königlich*) property.

When Masaryk's father was twenty-six years old he married a woman ten years his senior, on 15 August 1849. Her name was Teresie Kropatschek, and she was a cook. Her family was German

– they spelled their Czech name in the German way – from the neighbourhood of the Moravian capital, Brno. They belonged to the small town's gentry, as there had been inn-keepers and even mayors in the family.

Josef Masaryk married an older woman and he married above his station. His bride was pregnant on their wedding day. There has been speculation as to the true paternity of the Masaryks' first-born son, Thomas. His mother had worked in the Redlich household, and a certain family resemblance between Masaryk and Josef Redlich – presumably Masaryk's half-brother, who became a distinguished Austrian politician – has struck a number of writers with a taste for the more scandalous turns of history.[2]

In any case, the influence of his mother on young Thomas was decisive: she gave him much more of her time than the other two sons, Martin and Ludvík, born in 1852 and 1854. (The youngest child, a daughter, died in infancy.) Masaryk's mother was an intelligent, sensitive woman, who always dressed in town clothes; she was ambitious for her eldest son, and tenacious in her efforts to give him education. In Masaryk's autobiographical fragments there are only occasional references to his father, who was taught to read and write late in life by his eldest son.

Young Masaryk was a thoughtful boy, and the influence on him of the countryside and of its inhabitants can be traced more easily than the influence of his parents. The difference, for instance, between the peasants and the other inhabitants of the region was among Masaryk's early memories: a striking difference, involving class as well as nationality. In those remote Moravian villages of Masaryk's youth the peasants were Slav, and their masters German. Young Masaryk witnessed the feasts following shoots on the imperial estates: Slav beaters were given the remains of the food. Their hatred for their masters did not stop them fighting over the food; they were especially fond of macaroni, and called them 'tubes'. Masaryk observed the estate managers and their bailiffs, the tough NCOs of the semi-feudal society, tease and torture the peasants and their subordinates, including his father, and his helplessness made him cry with fury.

Nevertheless the social and national differences were reflected inside the Masaryk family: the children spoke Slovak to their father, but prayed in German with their mother; later, Thomas corresponded with her in German. She did, in the end, learn quite good 'Moravian'. She was a strict Catholic, and the religion and its priests were an important feature of Thomas's life. In Čejkovice, one of the villages where Josef Masaryk was sent to serve his masters, a local priest, Father Sátora, played an important role in Thomas's boyhood. Sátora was a complex person. A popular preacher, he had several children living in and out of the parish; from time to time, he made abject but energetic confession of his sins from the pulpit. Masaryk acted as Sátora's acolyte at the mass on Sundays; he was aware that Sátora, as a Czech, was having difficulties with his superior, as well as the local headmaster, who were both German.

National and religious differences (a number of Jews and Protestants lived in the parish) occupied young Thomas's inquiring mind. The problems of his native region made a deep impression on his thinking; nevertheless the *curriculum vitae* made it quite clear that his main difficulties lay elsewhere, and were of an entirely practical nature.

Young Masaryk spent his childhood moving with his parents and then his two young brothers around the imperial estates in south-eastern Moravia. He was born in Hodonín, and spent a large part of his childhood (the years 1856–62) at Čejkovice. As a low-ranking employee on the estate, a groom and later a bailiff, Masaryk's father was given a flat at the farm; the manager and higher officials on the estate lived in the country house. Though young Thomas and his brothers were usually dressed differently from the peasants' children, in town clothes, it was very difficult for Josef and Teresie Masaryk to afford them a better chance in life.

This is why Masaryk's *curriculum vitae* is so breathless in places, why there are so many hints of hidden danger in it. Young Thomas wanted to break out of the system of semi-feudal hierarchy, and education was his and his mother's chosen way of doing this. But there were constant obstacles: mainly the lack of money. (There may have been some financial help from the Redlich family for Thomas's education; if there was it was not very regular.) His education was therefore interrupted, on a number of occasions: in the three final forms at school, Masaryk was three years older than the other pupils.

Perhaps with the help of his mother, young Thomas devised a way which made it possible for him to complete his studies. He learned to make himself useful in the households of his better-off pupils, and supported himself, for many years at school and then at university, as a private tutor. He must have received some encouragement to do this at home: the pattern of his connections with more fortunate children was consistent. At elementary school Masaryk had benefited from his friendship with the son of a 'high imperial official' with whom he shared private tuition. In Brno he became private tutor to the son of a high-ranking police official, his 'only and true benefactor'. Thomas was gentle with the boy, a sickly child, and Mrs le Monnier was very fond of Masaryk; when her husband was transferred to Vienna, Masaryk was asked to come with the family.

He was probably grateful for the offer: the dark hints, in the *curriculum vitae,* at the difficulties with his masters at school in Brno refer to the time just before the le Monniers' departure. Masaryk was a good student, but he could be extremely stubborn. On one occasion, he told the headmaster that, 'Whoever acts against his conscience is a scoundrel', and was nearly expelled from the school. He also formed his first emotional attachment in Brno: he fell in love with his landlady's daughter, an 'unsuitable person', as he soon decided.

In Vienna Masaryk went to one of the best schools in town. His own class at the Akademische Gymnasium was distinguished: one of the pupils, Beck, later became the prime minister and another, Klein, the minister of justice in Austria. Masaryk joined the sixth form (there were eight forms in the school) in the year 1869–70; he lived at the le Monnier house, accompanying their son Franz, who was four years younger, on the way to school.

In Vienna Masaryk's frequently interrupted education, as well as stiff competition, removed him from the top of the class. Nevertheless his education was now secure: Masaryk knew that he could at least reach matriculation level. He was almost twenty years old when he joined the sixth form in Vienna, and he soon started moving on to other things. He felt that he belonged to the university rather than to a school, and he spent a lot of time at the university library; he had a record of truancy in the seventh form.

Masaryk himself gave the reasons for his frequent absences from school when he celebrated his sixtieth birthday in 1910:

> I never had any plans for my career, I just wanted to go forward, I wanted to work, I know that, but I did not know what I wanted to become. A certain plan began crystallizing in me only when I came to Vienna, towards the end of my schooldays. I wanted to be a diplomat. That was my first ideal. In order to be a diplomat, one had to attend the Oriental Academy. They taught classical Arabic there, a native Arab taught it, and we wrote Arabic with quill pens. I should like to say that I no longer remember a single letter. I even passed the language examinations; but you know what happens at the Oriental Academy: the sons of aristocrats take everything; it is better nowadays, but then there was not a hope that I could become a diplomat. So my ideal disappeared.[3]

That was how Masaryk explained his truancy, but he said nothing about the way he dealt with his masters. He simply told the master that he would not be in on that day, as he would be occupied elsewhere; sometimes he did not bother to tell anyone at all that he would stay away from school. Though he knew that he would not be able to join the diplomatic service, Masaryk gave a lot of his time to equipping himself with foreign languages. He had learned some French and Polish in Brno; in Vienna, he began learning English and Russian. And history, philosophy, psychology and logic, probably in that order, were his favourite subjects.

Though he lived in a German town, Masaryk's life there moved mainly in Czech and Slav circles: there were enough opportunities for this in Vienna. He learned Russian by giving private lessons to a Russian student. He had known Professor Šembera, who taught Czech language and literature at the University of Vienna, when he was still at school in Brno. When he came to Vienna, and especially when he joined the university, Masaryk was a frequent guest at Šembera's house, and became very friendly with the professor's daughter. The Šembera household was the centre of Czech life in the Habsburg capital; Zdĕnka, the daughter, was a friend of Masaryk, no more.

Masaryk's sexual morality was Victorian: he was reticent about sexual matters in his youth and, above all, he feared 'impurity'. He was also cautious, perhaps timid, emotionally. In his early youth, he was accustomed only to the company of his mother, as there were no girls of his age in the family. He was first disappointed in love in Brno, when he was eighteen years old. Masaryk never made the same mistake again, and struck out 'sweet habit' from his life, as well as from his *curriculum vitae*. He experimented with friendship with women, and he regarded their company as a means for developing his own self. But he kept his distance. The Victorian morality of an industrial age, combined with Central European Catholicism, put tough restraints especially on the new members of the middle classes; Masaryk was then well on his way into that class. And at the time when he was developing his pure and functional friendships with women, Sigmund Freud – also a native of Moravia and a student at Vienna University – was becoming interested in hysteria, hypnotism and sexual aetiology.

In other respects as well, Masaryk had to be a very self-disciplined person. He had no background of family or money to fall back on. He worked very hard, looking for the subject most suited to his temperament; the range of his reading was extraordinarily wide. At university after 1872 he soon gave up reading philology, because he disliked the dry, academic treatment of classical authors; he was looking for a way which would link up his academic studies with the real world around him. The World Exhibition was then being prepared in Vienna, and he was fascinated by it. According to his *curriculum vitae*, it was the death of his brother in 1873 which finally decided Masaryk to seek solace in philosophy.

His brother Martin was a grocer by trade who was then serving with an artillery regiment in Vienna where he died of pneumonia. Thomas hated watching him die; the Roman authors he was then reading gave him no sustenance in his personal tragedy. From his own accounts, his academic studies and his personal life were always very closely linked; for this reason, he dismissed classical philology on the grounds of uselessness. Here we notice flashes of passion cutting across an otherwise controlled personality: Masaryk said that, when he returned from his brother's deathbed, he 'flung innocent Catullus, and even more innocent Tibullus and Propertius, into the corner'.

In any case neither philology nor pure academic philosophy could satisfy Masaryk's intellectual curiosity for long. At Vienna University, the leading teachers of philosophy were Thadeus Gomperz, Franz Brentano and Robert Zimmermann; Zimmermann occupied himself mainly with aesthetic theory; Brentano and Gomperz were exponents of Western, English and French philosophy. They all had one thing in common – a dislike for speculative, German philosophy – which had a profound effect on Masaryk's intellectual development. They drew Masaryk's attention to the value of positive proof and of experience, as well as to Western philosophers: Comte, Mill and Hume became the decisive influences on Masaryk. Their writings aroused his interest in sociology. Philosophy was, for Masaryk, a practical discipline, partly a solace and a guide to living, but mainly a tool for analysing the society around him. This society therefore became the main object of Masaryk's interest, a very broad subject, and suitable for a young man who wanted to keep all his options open.

At this point we approach the summer of 1875, when, during the vacation, Masaryk was drafting his *curriculum vitae*. It was to be his last university vacation, but being on vacation did not mean that Masaryk was entirely free. When Mr le Monnier died, his son was nineteen years old, and Masaryk's services were no longer required. His new post was as private tutor to Alfred and then Max Schlesinger, the sons of a director of the Vienna Anglobank. Being a private tutor meant that Masaryk was on duty during the vacation as well; Alfred sometimes went with Masaryk to Moravia, to stay with his parents.

In addition to his studies and duties as a tutor, Masaryk led an active social and political life in Vienna. He became a member of the Czech Academic Society, a students' society at the university, and, in the years 1874–5 he was its chairman. At that time Masaryk also acquired a middle name – Vlastimil, somebody who loves his country – after the manner of Czech patriots of the time. Masaryk was a popular and successful chairman, though one of his plans for the society failed: he wanted to establish a united, all-Slav club in Vienna, but the Poles objected to the proposal that Russian should become the common language of the society. The plan did not materialize.

Masaryk graduated on 10 March 1876, with a thesis entitled *Das wesen der seele bei Plato* or the nature of the soul in Plato's philosophy. Even in the title of his thesis Masaryk disregarded German orthography, and the rule that nouns should start with capital letters. By the time he graduated, Masaryk remained a Czech, though the option to adopt the ways of the culturally stronger Germans was still open to him. He was a philosopher with an interest in sociology, and he had made his first attempts at writing. He was good-looking in a full-faced, rounded way – he grew thinner as he grew older, and his face gradually lost its youthful roundness – with lively black eyes and full beard. He must have been a reliable student for middle-class mothers to trust him with their sons. His teachers at the university, especially Franz Brentano, also had a fondness for Masaryk. He was serious and hard-working, and they knew of his desire to become educated, and of its cost to him.

Masaryk had by then lived in Vienna for some seven years, but he was not particularly fond of it. He later complained, in his first book, that the whole 'rational and moral energy' of its inhabitants was taken up by nationality conflicts, and that no one in Vienna had any understanding for 'a really moral and uniform structure of social life'. Masaryk knew Vienna as a self-indulgent town, and he knew that the proverbial *Gemütlichkeit*, the cosy charm of its citizens, was a superficial quality. Underneath, national strife, social injustice, antisemitism – those phenomena, but writ large, which Masaryk had noticed in the Moravian villages in his youth – were eating away the foundations of the easy-going life.

Masaryk's way of looking at Vienna was an outsider's way: detached, cold and slightly censorious. He showed little sympathy for the town, and for the transformation it was then undergoing. When Masaryk arrived there in 1869, the Ring – the broad avenue which had replaced the old city walls, and which changed the character of the centre of the town – was only some ten years old. The disappearance of the city walls symbolized the disappearance of the fear of invasions and of sieges: the invasion which took place in the nineteenth century was of a different kind. Since early in the century, new inhabitants had been arriving from the German and Slav hinterland of the capital to its industrial suburbs. The scene was being set for the political developments of the last decades of the Empire's existence.

Masaryk was glad when he could at last leave Vienna. He failed to get a travel scholarship from the ministry of education, and, instead, he accompanied Alfred Schlesinger, who had just successfully completed his matriculation, first to Rome and then to Leipzig, for the academic year.

It was an important year for Masaryk, in every respect. Masaryk liked Leipzig with its comfortable bourgeois life and its lively university. He broadened the circle of his academic acquaintances and, from time to time, visited Wundt's seminar and psychological workshop. But his stay in Germany was marred by illness; he returned to Vienna, where his doctor diagnosed a severe 'catarrh of the stomach'. From the turn of the year 1876–7, Masaryk was miserable, and not himself. In May 1877 he complained to a friend that: 'I am writing this letter in the garden. I am mentally greatly weakened, and I get cross about every small thing, my thoughts are unsteady, like water.'[4]

There had been a sharp change from the early months of Masaryk's stay in Leipzig, when he was working hard, almost feverishly, and when he was constantly adding to his interests. In the spring of the year 1877 he was listless, went to a few lectures when he felt like it, without being able to focus his mind on anything. His illness, diagnosed as typhoid, or gastric catarrh, or possibly a kidney complaint, had drained his energies. Perhaps the long years of difficulties and self-discipline had started taking their toll. Perhaps the fact that he was a first-generation town-dweller, the first person in his family to change to a sedentary occupation, also helped to break his natural resilience.

When he was at home in Moravia Masaryk used to spend a lot of time walking, and sometimes running, through the countryside, often at night, always on his own, thinking. He was a self-centred person, and very young: he thought about himself. In Leipzig, at the lowest point of his physical and spiritual crisis, Masaryk started returning to himself. His doctor had ordered him to walk a lot; Masaryk obeyed the order. In May 1877, he got lost in a wood near Leipzig. Slowly, his native toughness started reasserting itself.

He also had the time to read novels, and read them eagerly; from his correspondence we know that he related them and their characters to himself. He read a lot of English literature. Like English philosophy, it seemed to him the most vital of all European writing, and he liked it best. He read Dickens and Thomas Moore, and he was especially captivated by a novel, first published in 1859, by Miss Dinah Maria Mulock (Mrs Craik), entitled *Life for Life*. It was an emotional and moral tale, relating the passions of the human heart to stern ideals of commitment, duty and dedication, and portrayed marriage as a step properly undertaken only from a position of perfect trust and equality between the partners. And at that time, when young Masaryk turned to introspection, he also looked at his emotional life. Again a part of his person stood aside and the examination was carried out in a cool, detached way; he was thinking more of the future than of the past. He studied women. He read J. S. Mill's *The Subjection of Women*; he borrowed Bogumil Goltz's book *On the Natural History and Characteristics of Women* (*Zur Naturgeschichte und Charakteristik der Frauen,* Leipzig, 1858). He concluded that, as far as human well-being was concerned, 'learning alone is not enough, because so many people are happy without learning; satisfaction can be achieved in other ways, honour, glory, love etc'.[5]

His Leipzig environment was also conducive to such an inquiry. The house where Masaryk and Alfred Schlesinger were staying was full of young people, and there was much talk there of love, and of its more practical aspects: of engagements and marriages. Masaryk wrote from Leipzig: 'I hear a lot here about love; there is a young man here who is very happy in his love – but I am hardly capable of this emotion, and therefore I don't seek it out. I would not reject it if I found it, but where should I look for the body, where should I look for the soul, and who gave me the right to possess a beautiful body and soul.'[6]

Masaryk had written those lines shortly before Christmas of the year 1876; six months later, his soul-searching was at an end. In the spring it became known in the Goering household where Masaryk was staying that an honoured guest would arrive from

New York. When, on 13 June 1877, Charlotte Garrigue walked into the house Masaryk was standing by a window, watching her arrive. She came from Brooklyn, and she had stayed at the same house in 1871, when she was studying music at the Leipzig Conservatoire.

Born on 20 November 1850, seven months younger than Masaryk, she was the daughter of the president of *Germania*, a New York insurance company. Her father Rudolf was a Dane, born in Copenhagen. Originally a bookseller, he had been apprenticed in Leipzig, where he had known the Goering family. A French Huguenot family, the Garrigues had left France at the end of the seventeenth century. Many of them had settled in Germany, Holland and later in Denmark; one of the families came to England, and David Garrick was its descendant.

The Brooklyn Garrigues were entirely American. Rudolf had married Charlotte Whiting in Chicago in 1847; Charlotte was their third daughter. She met Masaryk on the day of her arrival in Leipzig, at lunch. The following night he accompanied her, Mrs Goering and her handicapped daughter Hedwig to a theatre.

Charlotte arranged with Hedwig to teach her English, and Masaryk asked them if he could also take part in the lessons. They started reading Byron, and Masaryk suggested that they should read *The Subjection of Women,* as well as Henry Buckle's *History of Civilization in England.* Less than a week after Charlotte's arrival in Leipzig, she was spending most of her time with Masaryk: they usually read together in the morning, talked after lunch and went for walks in the evening.

Gradually Masaryk recovered from his depression and ill-health: 'Now, in the beautiful meadows of Albion and of free Americans I leave that soul behind and pick flowers, putting them into garlands and bunches.'[7] He came to admire Charlotte; her sensibility and her education; her approach to life. 'Her head was better than mine,' Masaryk remarked many years later, and added, 'It was characteristic that she loved mathematics. She longed for exact knowledge.'[8] He admired her practical sense. Her character was firm, and she knew what she wanted, what to do, how to behave; this impressed young Masaryk, who was used to the unemancipated, malleable womenfolk of Central Europe.

Her simplicity made him trust her, and her steady view of

the world around her added to his admiration. She had an interest
in the underprivileged, and went even further: she took their
side. As a poor boy who had been brought up and educated in a
semi-feudal society, and who had to make his own way in the
world, Masaryk was then doing little to shorten the distance
between himself and those he had left behind. Later, Charlotte
helped him change his mind and habits. As his wife, she joined the
Social Democrat Party, took part in the demonstrations for
universal suffrage in the Habsburg Empire, and shopped for her
family in a workers' co-operative store.

Anyway, in the summer of 1877 Masaryk was enchanted with
her: she liked Masaryk, and spent much of her time in his
company. He was was a direct and serious person, and a bit of
a puritan: Charlotte had been brought up in the Unitarian faith.
He had a genuine love for English and American literature. He
was good-looking, and probably very charming to her. She liked
the Slavs; during her first stay in Leipzig, a Ukrainian girl,
Kirpotina, became Charlotte's best friend. But young Masaryk
was still very uncertain of himself, his manners were sometimes
abrupt and his emotions too near the surface. He had only just
graduated, had no job and no money. As far as Charlotte was
concerned, this did not matter. She had been brought up in the
American spirit of economic optimism, and was quite able, and
old enough, to choose her own partner.

It is difficult, across the distance of a century, to discover the
reasons for two people's friendship and, still more, the true reasons
for their decisions. We know that Masaryk had discussed marriage
in the abstract with his friends and teachers; we know that
Masaryk's mother wanted him to get married soon, because, as
Thomas himself put it, she 'knew that I could not find my own
true happiness in family alone'.[9] Late in June 1877 Masaryk wrote
to a friend that he did not know what would happen and that,
because he had dedicated his life to 'my parents, my brother and
science', he was still convinced that he would die without getting
married.

He was then getting restless. Early in July he resigned his post,
as of September, with the Schlesinger family. He wanted to be free
and independent, but he did not know what he would do with
his independence; or indeed, whether he should want it. But

then an accident happened which nearly cost Masaryk his life. On 24 June a party from the Goering house went on a boat trip to a nearby village. After nine o'clock in the evening they tried to land and have a picnic on the bank. Mrs Goering, a stout lady, fifty-five years old, slipped and fell into the water. Masaryk jumped in, and it took him some time to pull her out. When they rowed back, they got caught in a storm; on the way home Masaryk passed out in the carriage, and it took him several days to recover.

Three days later Charlotte left Leipzig for the country. It is possible that her departure, and his accident, prompted Masaryk to act. He wrote Charlotte a letter about his feelings for her: her reply was cool, non-committal. Masaryk wrote another letter. Without waiting for her to reply, he left for the small spa of Elgersburg, in the Thuringian forest, where Charlotte was staying with a friend. Masaryk arrived there on Monday 6 August 1877, and the two young people spent several days walking and arguing together. They announced their engagement on Friday the same week.

He did not reflect that he was adding another responsibility to those he already had; he was overjoyed with the prospects the future opened up before him. Having agreed with Charlotte to marry her in America the following summer, he decided that he would have to finish his habilitation study – a thesis which would give him the right to lecture, though without being paid a salary, at the university – during the next academic year in Vienna.

During that year his life seemed even more unsettled than it had been before. He had nothing to live on; he considered taking on some teaching, private or at a school, or going to Prague or even emigrating. He did not like Vienna when he returned to it any more than he had done before he left it; it seemed to put too many limitations on his life.

He could no longer live at the Schlesinger's house, and he rented a room off the Landstrasse – in the east of Vienna where, according to Metternich, Asia began – and started working on his thesis. Most of his friends from his undergraduate days had left Vienna, and he also parted company with the family of Professor Šembera. He had some difficulties with the daughter of the family, and his friend, Zděnka. He had written often to her from Leipzig, and then about his affection for Charlotte. For many years his letters to

Zdĕnka Šemberová had been a rich biographical source; their correspondence now stopped for some time.

Masaryk was wrong to have regarded her only as a friend: she had, after all, thought of him as a man, and as a potential husband. Masaryk's last letter to her, of 21 September 1877, speaks of his disappointment: 'Why have you recognized my faults only now? Was it I who acted carelessly? When and where? Did I not share with you everything confidence required? Perhaps more than you shared with me. Don't be afraid of being "misused". I wanted true friendship.'[10]

Instead, Masaryk wrote to Charlotte often, almost every day. He worked hard and finished his habilitation study, *On the Principles of Sociology*, by the end of November. He submitted it, together with a very brief *curriculum vitae*, on 6 December 1877. Sometime at the beginning of February 1878, while he was still waiting for a reply from the university, Masaryk received a letter from Charlotte's father.

The accident-prone side of nineteenth-century life had started taking over Masaryk's life: after his own illness and then the river accident, now Charlotte had fallen under a carriage, and was seriously ill. Rudolf Garrigue asked Thomas to come over to New York at once. At the end of February Masaryk was on board ship *Herder*, sailing from Hamburg to New York, via Le Havre. It was a poor, uncomfortable kind of ship, and this was its last transatlantic journey; it sank on its next crossing. Masaryk's trip took seventeen days, the weather was foul, and the ship became flooded once; this time it was only the drinking water tank which burst. The ship's engineer was from Prague, and he told Masaryk a lot about the Czech colony in America.

By the time Thomas arrived in New York, Charlotte had almost recovered. Masaryk was pleased about that, and about her family. He liked her parents, and he thought that her father was 'a kind of old Viking and an American'. Apart from Charlotte there were eleven other children in the family. Masaryk considered staying in America for good, perhaps as a journalist or a university teacher. But in the end he and Charlotte decided that he should return and complete his habilitation at the university. He asked his future father-in-law whether he would give them enough money for three years, until Masaryk became financially independent. Mr

Garrigue refused, saying that he regarded it as a matter of course
that a man would not get married unless he was able to support
his family.

Masaryk did not quite agree with that view, and spent some time
on the family sofa, not talking very much and looking rather cross.
Nevertheless the two young people got married on 15 March 1878,
twice on the same day. The civil wedding took place in the morning at the Brooklyn town hall; the civil contract was consecrated,
according to the rites of the Unitarian church, in the evening, in
the family circle. The bride's father also relented: he gave the
couple 3,000 German marks and two one-way tickets to Europe,
and he promised occasional financial support. A week later,
Thomas and Charlotte Masaryk left New York on the *Suevia*, a
better class of ship than the luckless *Herder*.

Masaryk's two remaining Czech friends in Vienna expected a
'proud American woman, proud with the riches of this world'.[11]
But they soon came to like Charlotte, and Masaryk's brother,
Ludvík, became especially fond of her. They helped them settle
down, first in Masaryk's old room, and then in a small flat nearby,
in the Landstrasse itself. The Masaryks lived there modestly,
until their departure for Prague four years later. Charlotte had
some German, and she at once set out to learn Czech, a much
more difficult language. She mastered it in the end, though she
could never quite manage the feminine endings in Czech verbs.
Vacations spent at Klobouky, where Masaryk's parents lived, were
of great assistance to her in learning the language. English became
Masaryk's third language, after Czech and German; they spoke
it often at home, and it suited Masaryk's predilection for English
writing. He also got rid of his patriotic middle name, Vlastimil,
and substituted for it his wife's family name. It was as Thomas
Garrigue Masaryk that he became known, many years later, to
the world.

From their arrival in Vienna in April 1878 the Masaryks led a
life of close proximity. We know of Thomas's high regard for his
wife and for her judgement; for her part Charlotte must have
known that, in order to stay close to her husband, she would have
to share his intellectual interests. Music played an important part
in their lives; Charlotte played the piano, and Thomas the violin.
They had very few friends then, and spent most of their days

together. It was an idyllic time for them; their close bonds were loosened later, and gradually.

Though they lived very modestly, Masaryk was constantly worried about money. He was not helped by the rumours that he had made a rich marriage, rumours which overlooked the circumstances of his married life. In spite of all visible evidence, the rumour survived for a long time. Vienna bankers kept on offering to manage his wife's funds; when the Masaryks arrived at his parents' house in the summer, a delegation of local farmers begged him to finance a branch railway from Klobouky to Hustopeče. As late as 1886, when the question of Masaryk's full professorship at Prague University was discussed, the governor of Bohemia remarked, with a complete lack of precision, that 'Masaryk married rich in England'.[12]

There were other worries for young Masaryk. The university administration in Vienna had set aside his habilitation study, because they assumed that he would not come back from America. Sociology was a suspect discipline in Vienna, and Masaryk's thesis had that word in its title; it was described as Part I, and there was no other part to follow. In July 1878 Masaryk decided to cut his losses, and start all over again.

He had intended the *Principles of Sociology* to be a part of a larger study which was to treat suicide. He had interested himself in the subject for some years; now, in the summer and autumn of 1878 he very quickly wrote a book on suicide. It was submitted to the faculty of philosophy in Vienna on 14 November; after some delays, it was passed by the examiners on 7 March, Masaryk's twenty-ninth birthday. It was published, with minor corrections, as Masaryk's first book in 1881, under the title *Der Selbstmord – als soziale Massenerscheinung.*

It was an unusual subject for a thesis, an odd one for a book. There was some question whether it could be properly examined in the faculty of philosophy. It was written at a time when Masaryk's fortunes were at their lowest ebb. The money he had been given by his father-in-law in New York had run out, and since neither private lessons nor seminars on philosophy, which were then becoming fashionable with middle-class women, could support his wife and himself, Masaryk took his first job. He started supply teaching at a school, and came to dislike the job as much as he did his colleagues who, he was convinced, were narrow-minded people marking time before their retirement. He could bear it for a term, no more. His wife was then expecting her first baby, and the joy of that announcement did not lighten Masaryk's worries.

It seems that Masaryk's character made the examiners regard his thesis, and his determination to become an academic, with sympathy. The thesis, *Suicide as a Social Mass Phenomenon,* was very clearly a young man's work, and difficult to fit into any academic category. But it was open-handed and generous, and encompassed much of Masaryk's thinking at the time. He estimated that some 50,000 people died by their own hand every year, and that their number was constantly growing. He indicated that the society where these murders took place was unhealthy, and that suicide belonged to the realm of psychopathology. Suicide was for him a 'mathematical measure of the true mood of the society'.

Masaryk pointed at the restlessness of modern times, and went through its various aspects. Marriage, for instance, instead of producing harmony, drove people to suicide. Since the French Revolution, politics had added another unsettling dimension to people's lives. And so did their diverse forms of nationalism, as well as their uniform military discipline; poverty as well as riches and luxury; even education, according to Masaryk, drove people to suicide. 'Primitive' people, the author thought, did not commit suicide: it was the 'subjectivism' of civilized men that drove them to take their own lives.

According to Masaryk, early Christianity, until the end of the Middle Ages, knew no epidemics of suicide. But Renaissance and Reformation, both resisting authority, pushed the individual to the forefront. The rest of European history was, for Masaryk, a story about how 'subjectivism' developed. Schopenhauer, the sage of Frankfurt, held funeral orations over the graves of suicides, and of European civilization. Nevertheless Masaryk pointed out: 'Religion is to people what invisible smell is to a flower. If you destroy the smell, the flower will go on pleasing your eye, but it will no longer be so sweet; if you take away from man his religious feeling, you make him a being whom you can honour and perhaps admire, but not love, whole-heartedly.'

Suicide therefore was, for Masaryk, an aspect of the crisis of religious belief. Having surveyed the various Christian creeds and the ways in which their adherents were more or less prone to suicide, Masaryk gave his views on how to improve the situation:

> Almost every theorist and practitioner tries to overcome the evils of modern society by economic and political reforms. But I cannot share this hope. Political and economic conditions of people are only the visible aspects of their spiritual lives, and therefore the doctor has to look at that. The attempts and struggles of our parliamentarians, politicians and economists appear to me to be very petty; and surely, society will not be saved by political and economic concessions, large or small reforms. A few rights and a little money cannot do away with a pessimistic saturation with living.

Nor will revolutions help but, Masaryk suggested, a new religion. 'Our time is made for a new religion.'

Though Masaryk did not go into the details of this new religion, he had suggested, earlier in the book, that an almost ideal situation obtained, in this regard, in the United States. There the divorce between the Church and the State was complete; there were hundreds of religious sects there, and people with deep religious convictions. They needed, according to Masaryk, neither the clergy nor the military to keep them in order.

There was little difference between the thesis and the subsequent book. It is unthinkable that a young man nowadays could submit, and get away with, a similar study. Even for Vienna University in the 1870s the conception of Masaryk's thesis was too general, skimming over too many of his interests. Nevertheless the examiners' commission gave Masaryk credit for his courage, and for his energy.

The dissection of society by sociologists was then a comparatively new discipline, and the excitement of its pursuit concealed many of the dangers of that approach to society. Masaryk took most of his statistical material at its face value, remarking, for instance, on the low incidence of suicide in Catholic countries, without pointing out that suicide cases were likely to be hidden in statistical interstices, because of the stigma attached to the act of suicide in those countries.

Nevertheless the book faithfully reflected Masaryk's personality as well as the extent and shape of his intellectual world. He was critical of political and economic reform; there was more than a hint in the book of his search for some kind of a spiritual panacea. He gave some attention to the material world around him, but it was a remote backcloth, without any meaning to him. He asked how the body, nature and environment affect man; his answers were very sketchy, saying little to him and to the reader. Statistics were introduced to support his general thesis.

The individual was at the centre of the study, and its main stress was psychological: the spirit was decisive. It was his own world Masaryk was describing: his individual was an intellectual. He anticipated Emile Durkheim in isolating the unlimited desires and ambitions of his contemporaries, as well as their weakness and impotence. Masaryk wrote:

> The trend to suicide and nervousness, philosophical pessimism, the sentimental moans of our poets – all that is an expression of one and the same reality: a desire for peace and quiet. What an English cleric said of the Protestant attitude towards Rome, I should like to say towards the end of my deliberations about modern suicide: we are tired, we have done enough fighting.

Many other writers dealt in a similar way at that time with the desiccation and tiredness of the European soul: the *fin de siècle* was upon them. Masaryk himself was one of the new arrivals in the society of intellectuals. He too had to come to terms with the changing social and spiritual map of Europe. Its long period of peace had been accompanied by the fast growth of industries and towns; the advance of material sciences had undermined faith in the existence of God, or at least severely limited the area of operation of his grace. In this regard, Masaryk was an optimist. He thought that if philosophers thought more correctly, or people prayed better, the *malaise* he was describing would go away. He found it difficult to come to terms with secular solutions and, even more, to recognize the existence of insoluble problems.

Some months after Masaryk's thesis on suicide was passed for habilitation, he started lecturing at the University of Vienna, in the summer term of 1879. He lectured on the 'History and Critique of Pessimism', Plato's philosophy, Buckle's history, and on Comte and John Stuart Mill. Before the winter term (*Semester*; only two of them made up the academic year at continental universities) of 1882, Masaryk announced that he would lecture on 'Hume's Philosophy of Religion'. Instead, he gave an inaugural lecture on Hume at the new Czech University in Prague.

Masaryk in Prague

THE imperial decree on the establishment of a new Czech part of the University in Prague was published on 11 April 1881 and, after its passage through the two Houses of Parliament, the law was sanctioned by the emperor on 28 February 1882. On 10 September Masaryk came to Prague for good, as the newly appointed professor of philosophy at the Czech University.

The town where Masaryk arrived with his family (his daughter, Alice, had been born in May 1879, and son, Herbert, a year later) was changing fast, and in the same way as Vienna and other towns in Europe. The change was perhaps happening later, and on a smaller scale. For a few decades before 1880 Prague had been losing the features of a medieval town. Early in the nineteenth century the gates in the city walls were still being bolted for the night, and the burghers went to sleep knowing that they would be safe from invasion for another night. There were some 100,000 of them, and about 750 oil lamps flickered in the streets. Only one bridge and several ferries linked the two banks of the river Vltava, and there were four postmen to deliver those letters which were not carried by private messengers. Then, in 1841, a second bridge at last joined the bridge which had been built five centuries before, and the old town walls started being breached or pulled down to make way for railways, sanitation, and other communal necessities of modern towns.

When the Masaryks arrived in Prague in September 1882, the Czech National Theatre was almost completed and Rudolfinum, the new concert hall, was being built. The statues in the Horse Market had been replaced by trees, and the market itself was renamed Wenceslas Square, after the first Czech Christian ruler. The town was lit by gas, though the first experiments with electric lighting had been made, and there were horse-drawn trams in the streets.

The population of Prague was changing. Immigrants from the Czech countryside had been arriving in large numbers, and the villages around the city were being transformed into industrial suburbs. From 239,790 inhabitants in 1880, their number grew to 514,345 at the turn of the century. The new citizens of Prague were largely Czech: the German share in the population was thirteen per cent in 1880, and only six per cent in 1900. In other towns of Bohemia and Moravia the contest between the Germans and the Czechs was also being won by the Czechs.

Their national movement, the industrialization of the country and the development of towns went hand in hand in the nineteenth century. Though the Czechs – a Slav people, who had survived in an exposed position far advanced to the West – had behind them a long history, in their historical memories long periods of adversity were punctuated by tragedy. The deeds of their heroes hardly ever brought the nation victory, profit or joy. At the opening of the Christian era and the beginnings of their state, early in the tenth century, Ludmila, the grandmother of Prince Wenceslas, was slain at the bidding of her daughter-in-law. Wenceslas himself was murdered, by his own brother, at the door of a church. Though the prince and his grandmother were later canonized, their shadowy, reproachful figures stand at the door through which the Czechs first entered European history.

The legendary pattern of ill-luck and despair was constantly added to. Jan Hus, the follower of Wycliff, who challenged the power of the medieval Church, and who insisted that his teaching was no heresy before the Council of Constance, was burned at the stake by a decision of that Council on 6 July 1415. Religious wars lasting some eighteen years laid waste to the country, without settling its political or religious adherence. The first Habsburg, Albert (ruled 1437–9), then briefly held the crown of the Kingdom of Bohemia, though the crown did not pass into the permanent possession of the Habsburgs until 1526. Almost a century later, in 1620, the Czech estates declared their only serious rebellion against the Habsburg rule: they were defeated at the battle of White Mountain. On 21 June 1621 twenty-seven leaders of the rebellion, including three nobles, seven knights and seventeen burghers, were executed in public, outside the town hall in Prague.

In the following decades, the Jesuits made the Czechs return to the Catholic faith, while the recalcitrant Protestants went into exile. The Czech nobility became denationalized, German-speaking, and dependent on the favours of the Habsburg dynasty. The towns became German. The Czechs, who had lost their own dynasty, were deprived of their ruling class and, because of Protestant emigration, of many of their learned men. The nation and its language went into hibernation: they were pushed into the villages and the fields, unprotected by their own state and unsupported by their own learning and literature.

The Czech and the German; the Protestant and the Catholic; the lord and his vassal: the ways in which these elements fitted together, or made war on each other, were explored by the Czech historians and revivalists in the nineteenth century. They blew hard upon the embers of past glory: they were partial, in their writings, to Emperor Charles iv, who was half-Czech and who transferred the Holy Roman crown to Prague early in the fourteenth century, founded the university, and built the city's only bridge for five centuries; to Jan Žižka, the military leader of the followers of Jan Hus, who was clever at using lightly armed, highly mobile peasant armies against the monstrous, heavily armoured medieval knights. And the key figure of the Czech historical revival was of course Jan Hus, the inventor of Czech orthography, a fearless preacher who captured the imagination of the common people of Prague, the key figure in the historical writing of the Czech national revival.

The Czech national movement developed rapidly in the nineteenth century, and each of its elements left a lasting mark on Czech consciousness. The necessary concentration on the language and on the history of the nation meant that writers and historians moved into leading positions. They became the guardians of the nation's past, and of its most highly prized possession: its language. Their responsibilities assumed political dimensions, a duty which could not be borne lightly. Writing, especially of history, was for the Czechs no detached inquiry into the past: a slip of the pen, and writing could easily become treason against the nation.

František Palacký, who had reconstructed history for the Czechs, became their first member of the Upper House in Vienna in 1861. By then the German monopoly in secondary education had been broken, and the children of Czech peasants who had come to seek work in German towns were able to attend their own schools. Step by step Czech language gained admission into the administration and the courts in Bohemia and Moravia; step by step German towns in Slav countryside became Czech. But the close links between the development of industry and the Czech national movement meant that the nationalism of the Czechs, as well as of the local Germans, acquired some harsh, intolerant features.

Competition for jobs, houses, schools for the children in the fast-growing towns became a part of the clash between the Czechs and the Germans. The first riot of German workers against Czech immigrants took place in Bohemia in 1868; in the summer of 1881 a severe battle occurred between Czech and German students; in the 1880s clashes between Czech and German miners became extremely violent, and involved the throwing of home-made bombs. The fast growth of industry, especially in Prague and Pilsen, in Brno and Moravská Ostrava, was accompanied by the organization of a working-class movement in trade unions and the Social Democrat Party. By the end of the century it was clear that neither the party nor the trade unions could be run, in the Czech lands, on a regional basis, and separate Czech and German organizations developed.

Their main political struggle was with the Germans, and with the government in Vienna. While the Czechs in the second half of the nineteenth century were winning their contest with the Germans, they were doing much less well with regard to the central government. The political leadership of their movement lacked confidence, as well as political experience. It was in the hands of the new middle class. In comparison with the advantages conferred on the Hungarians by having their own aristocracy to take care of their politics, or with the Poles who had also retained their own ruling class, underpinned by a powerful national Catholic Church, the Czechs were in a weak position.

They tried to compensate for it by turning East, and looking beyond the borders of the Habsburg Empire. The pro-Russian, Panslav strand of their national revival reached far back, into the movement's very beginnings. On 11 July 1799, when the Russian

troops passed through Prague on the way to fight Napoleon's armies
in Italy, the only, recently founded, Czech newspaper announced
with joy that 'the heroic Slavs use almost the same language with
us, the Czechs'. Then there was the Slav congress in Prague in
1848, and various exhibitions, and much coming and going between
Moscow and Prague. By the end of the century, there was a pro-
Russian group of politicians in Prague, for whom the fact that
the Russians were Slavs was much more important than the way
in which the tsar ran his empire.

When Masaryk arrived in Prague in 1882, the political scene
was only partly formed, still running largely on the lines of the
early era of the national revival. The Czech Social Democrat Party
was then some four years old, and the Agrarian Party, which was
later to contend for primacy in Czech political life with the Social
Democrats, had not yet been founded. The Young and the Old
Czechs (the Young Czechs sometimes referred to themselves as
liberals) representing the initial aspirations of the nation, still
dominated its politics. They revolved round the question of 'state
rights', the degree of autonomy the Czechs could achieve in their
own lands on the basis of their historical claims.

But when their cultural aspirations entered the realm of practical
politics, their political inexperience told against them. Their timing
was bad, and sometimes they confused a firm political line with
obstinacy and plain sulking. At the crucial time, in the 1860s,
when the dynasty and the central government were rocked by
serious defeats abroad, the Czechs believed that, by ignoring the
existing political institutions, and the recent parliamentary institutions in particular, the rights which they thought were theirs
would fall into their laps. But then came the *Ausgleich*, the compromise, with the Hungarians in 1867. What the Czechs wanted,
the Hungarians got – and perhaps more.

The monarchy, as well as its Parliament, was divided into two
parts. The Austrian and the Hungarian part of the monarchy
remained linked by the person of the emperor, and by common
defence, fiscal and foreign policies, and the appropriate ministries.
The Czechs remained in the Austrian part of the empire, and there
were still the privileged Germans in Austria with whom the Czechs
had to contend for the advancement of their political rights.

It was not surprising that the Czechs remained 'passive' with

regard to the Parliament in those years that they felt too remote
from Vienna and, at the same time, too closely bound to it. The
surprising thing was that they did not opt for the easy way out.
At no point in the nineteenth century did they give up the uneven
fight, and decide that it would be easier to become German than
to remain Czech.

Masaryk had visited Prague for the first time in 1873, on his
way back from Marienbad, where he had spent the summer with
the Schlesinger family. He had not liked the town, finding it brash
and mean at the same time. To accept a job there in 1882 was
therefore a hard decision for him to make. 'My transfer from
Vienna to Prague was a new crisis for me, which I suffered in
Vienna. I was afraid of the smallness of Prague, I was a stranger
to the people and to their national life, though I had passed myself
off, from time to time, as a Czech writer.' (The last clause in the
original Czech is even more self-disparaging: 'trebaže jsem
příležitostně vystupoval jako český spisovatýlek.')[1]

But his first impression of the Czech capital in the autumn of
1882 was good, and being there proved no hardship to Masaryk
and his family. In Vienna he had spent much of his time with
his Czech and other Slav friends; here in Prague he was at the
centre of Czech life and culture. It did not much matter to Masaryk
then that the horizons of that life were limited, the extent of its
culture provincial and narrow, and its politics aimless or stagnant,
or both. As the years went by, Masaryk made his mark on many
an aspect of Czech life: he did much to contribute to the liveliness
of the nation.

The Masaryks and their two small children moved into a very
pleasant, small flat. It was in a house in Karlova ulice, in Smíchov,
in the north-east of Prague, next to a large garden on the hill called
Petřín, not very far from the castle, and a short walk from the
river. And the constant worry about money was at last over for
Masaryk: there was no longer any need for his family to live from
hand to mouth, and for Masaryk to earn small amounts by tuition,
or to borrow money from his friends.

Though Masaryk was not nominated full professor until January
1897, his salary in 1882 as a civil servant was at the eighth grade
of the Austrian civil service scale, quite a high grade, sometimes
reached by schoolmasters (also civil servants) towards the end of

their careers. For the sake of comparison, the head of district administration was then paid a salary of the seventh grade. This meant that Masaryk's starting salary was 1,600 gulden a year, and added to it were the so-called college fees, about 200 gulden, and a fee for running a seminar, 300 gulden; in May 1883 Masaryk was allowed expenses of 200 gulden for his move from Vienna to Prague. It was not a large salary by middle-class standards of the time but contrasted with the wages of, say, a miner (180–360 gulden a year, for a twelve-hour working day) it was quite generous. In any case, for the first time in his life, Masaryk could devote himself fully to his interests.

His inaugural lecture, on 16 October 1882, was entitled 'The Count of Probability and the Scepsis of David Hume'. Masaryk argued that Hume was wrong, on a number of counts, in his religious scepticism; that human reason was not as weak as Hume would have it, and the possibilities of knowing not as limited. Nevertheless in discussing Hume's philosophy, Masaryk showed how powerful it could be, at its best. 'Though I stand in opposition to Hume, I have retained enough of his scepticism in me that I do not trust academic philosophy at all,' Masaryk concluded.

It is not known how many listeners had heard of Hume and it is likely that, for many of them, a large part of Masaryk's lecture was impossible to follow. Apart from other things, Masaryk was saying that the established philosophical school, or schools, in Prague would, from now on, come under attack from him. In this respect, Prague was more German than the faculty of philosophy in Vienna. Its philosophical thinking flowed placidly in the channels established by Kant and Hegel, Herbart and Schopenhauer. And now Masaryk introduced to his audience an Englishman, with his strange habits of mind.

Masaryk's critical attitude to established authority as well as to apparently incontrovertible fact surprised the listeners to his first and subsequent lectures. It was not always a quality which pleased. On a number of occasions in the past, before he came to Prague, Masaryk had noticed certain Czech authoritarian attitudes. He now challenged them, perhaps without fully realizing the implications of his challenge.

On many occasions in the future. Masaryk was to earn the disapproval of some of the older professors at the university, and popularity with the students. For Prague, his conception of the university and of its functions was unusual. Whereas the university was designed to educate the elite, he wanted to make it accessible to a wider audience, and his approach to teaching was quite different from the approach of his older colleagues. For the students, the university teacher was, and was meant to be, a remote figure; patriarchal and therefore authoritarian, learned and therefore infallible. They listened to their professor in the lecture theatre, saw him go in and out of the theatre, taking no notice of anybody. No contact with the students was intended, and little was made.

Only in the Philosophy Club at the university, did students and the younger teachers meet from time to time to discuss their interests. Masaryk made his mark in the club, soon after his arrival in Prague. The club's members were amazed at the incident. It took place at an especially important meeting, on 28 October 1882. Professor Durdík, the senior philosopher, a follower of Herbart, addressed the club. Herbart was well known for his discovery of the five principles of ethics; his pupils then followed with the five principles of aesthetics; and Durdík completed the circle with his lecture to the club, entitled 'The five most significant names in the literature of the nineteenth century'. It was meant to be a humorous lecture (one of the professors at Prague later remarked that it was a curious thing to have wanted to do, if not downright ridiculous) and the professor's first choice was Byron, whose translator he was; then he put the philologist, Bopp, into the second place; Herbart, the philosopher, into third, adding that: 'Others might prefer better known writers, such as Schopenhauer or Hartmann, but their pessimism is no addition to our knowledge, leading, as it does, to confusions in connection with morality.' He also referred to Comte, remarking that: 'He proposes in substance exactly the same as what Kant has already put into practice.' The fourth place was allocated to Darwin. In the way of a joke, Durdík left the fifth place empty, so that: 'The admirer of another name, which is not given in the first four, can place his leader there. But we shall not abandon our four nominations, and the vacant last place will help us not to quarrel.'

A serious discussion followed. Masaryk spoke warmly of Comte, and said that his teaching differed from that of Kant. Durdík in the end conceded that Comte and Kant were two quite different

philosophers, but he did so without good grace. Durdík, the leading philosopher in the faculty, had been challenged by a much
younger colleague. He was reported to shake at such daring, and
never again came to a meeting of the Philosophy Club. He never
forgave Masaryk who, for his own part, was puzzled by the professor's violent reaction. Masaryk had wanted to make the discussion more lively.

It soon became apparent that Masaryk was not an academic, as
the term was currently used. His philosophy was closely linked
with his own life, and with the problems he himself had to come
to terms with. He was therefore not interested in philosophy as
a purely academic discipline. His approach was direct, popular
and personal; for this reason he attracted students, and antagonized
his colleagues. He had put, we have seen, a lot of himself into
his book on suicide, and he used the same technique in his teaching. He had a warm, soft Slovak voice, which he used in an abrupt
way; he used his hands a lot when he talked. He 'moulded his
ideas with his gestures'; he preferred seminars, with their more
direct personal contact with the students, to formal lectures.

Masaryk's style of teaching the young appeared especially
extraordinary when it was contrasted with the usual methods of
instruction in philosophy which contained many formulae and
definitions, as if meant to keep the students in their place: they
were expected to learn rather than to understand; to accept rather
than to question or criticize. Both Masaryk's subject matter and
his approach were different. His proper subject was man, and
man's nature; his capabilities and flaws; his attitude – and this was
unusual – to women, sex, love, family. Masaryk retained the socio-
logical slant in his philosophy: Comte, Spencer and Mill remained
his guides.

Masaryk was still a young man, and close to his pupils. On
many occasions his pupils accompanied him on the way home, still
arguing about the subject their teacher had brought to their attention. He even asked them to his own home. He set aside Friday
evenings for them; they were surprised at being invited. One of
his students later wrote: 'Nothing like that had happened to us
before. We could not wait for the evening. It was extraordinary
to visit a professor, talk to him in his own house, and in the end
stay there for dinner!'[2] Many of the students came from the country,

they were not used to social life, and did not have much of it in Prague. When they visited Masaryk's house, they were first asked to his study; they discussed politics, literature, any matters of common interest. From time to time, on those Friday evenings, other university teachers and Masaryk's friends were also invited, but they only provided the background for the students. Then Mrs Masaryk came in, and asked them to go to the dining room. She took part in the conversation. Her Czech was not very good yet, but she made her points, and the young men were as pleased as they were surprised to have a woman – and a foreigner at that – in their company.

Nevertheless the university was for Masaryk a point of departure. It was an important, but a small part in the life of the nation. And it was to the Czech national life that Masaryk began addressing himself with growing urgency. It was here, at the point where learning merged into politics, that Masaryk made his lasting mark. He was convinced that, if it were to prosper, the national movement had to be put on a 'scientific' basis. The scientists – people like Masaryk – were to provide for the Czechs what their nobility provided for the Hungarians, or the Poles: a compact and experienced group of political leaders. Without a scientific basis, politics, and even the arts and social life, relapsed into confusion. This was what Masaryk was saying to the Czechs in the early years of his life in Prague; and he had the personality and the energy to rally around him the people, most of them young and connected with the university, who were thinking on the same lines.

Masaryk and his friends at first opted for a magazine as the best vehicle for their plans. It was to be a comprehensive publication, and cover many academic disciplines as well as literary criticism. There was to be an editor for each discipline; Masaryk described himself as *redaktor-en-chef*. He found members of the editorial board in the various departments of the university. The faculty of theology had not been divided into Czech and German parts, and Masaryk won over for his plan Klement Borový, professor of Church law; from the faculty of law, Albín Bráf joined the editorial board. Bráf was a year younger than Masaryk, an economist with an interest in socialism. His personality was similar to Masaryk's in one respect: he was an impetuous person. At the early meetings of the editorial board at the Prague Hotel de Saxe,

Bráf took Masaryk's side more often than anyone else. Emerich Maixner became the editor responsible for medicine; three years older than Masaryk, he was the youngest professor at the faculty. In the faculty of philosophy, Masaryk chose August Seydler, from the department of natural science. The other sciences were represented by two members of the board: Karel Preis, the professor of analytical chemistry, and Josef Šolín, at forty-two the oldest member of the board, an expert on geometry.

Jan Otto became the magazine's publisher. It was called *Athenaeum*, after the London periodical, and was to appear in the middle of each month; the first number came out a year after Masaryk's inaugural lecture, on 15 October 1883. It was received well in Prague, where there was a shortage of lively, quality magazines. As in the case of Masaryk's university career, there were hints of controversies to come. One of Masaryk's innovations – notices written by authors of their own books – caused a few laughs in learned circles, but the first issue contained adverse criticism of books written in Czech, and they set off chain reactions of anger in the nervous, Czech-speaking intelligentsia. For instance, there was an extremely sharp criticism of a book on architecture in the first number of the *Athenaeum*, which had been written by a group of students and handed in to Masaryk. The book was by a colleague of Šolín, a member of the editorial board, who had never seen the review and, had he seen it, would not have agreed to having it published in the original form. Šolín thus became the first casualty of the new magazine, and resigned immediately after the appearance of its first number.

Nevertheless a new member of the editorial board was appointed, and the circle of the magazine's contributors and readers grew. At the university, a division between the older and the younger generation of teachers emerged: the younger generation tended to group itself around the *Athenaeum*, the older generation around the National Museum and its house magazine. It took almost four years before the storm around the *Athenaeum* broke, after the appearance of the February number in 1886.

The row revolved around the authenticity of two historical manuscripts. In 1817 a manuscript containing a number of epic and lyrical poems was found at Kralův Dvůr. The following year another manuscript was discovered at Zelená Hora, with a fragment of a poem about Libuše, the legendary founder of the first Czech dynasty. The first discovery was made by Václav Hanka, the librarian of the newly founded National Museum; there was some uncertainty about precisely how the other manuscript was found. In any case, it safely reached Hanka at his museum library. From the time of their appearance, the documents were faintly suspect. Josef Dobrovský, a Jesuit who had established Slav studies as a respectable academic subject, never regarded the manuscripts as a serious historical source, but as they gathered dust at the museum, they also acquired a certain respectable antiquity.

Dobrovský's successors, Jungmann and especially Palacký, found no difficulty in incorporating these documents into their historical studies, thereby presenting the Czechs with a history which was considerably longer than they could hope for. Hanka, encouraged by the success of his earlier finds, went on manufacturing historical documents. The *Song of Vyšehrad* was discovered (Vyšehrad had been the seat of the early Czech rulers, before they moved to the other side of the river; since the nineteenth century, eminent Czech patriots have been buried at the local cemetery, though not Hanka), and followed by the *Love Song of King Wenceslas*. Hanka had overreached himself and, in 1857, became unstuck.

The museum set up a commission to inquire into the historical fragments: the two later 'songs' were dismissed as forgeries; the two earlier documents were, however, passed as genuine by the commission. Two years later, following some high-quality detective work, a series of anonymous articles appeared in the *Tagesbote aus Böhmen*, proving the two documents to be forgeries, perpetrated by the librarian at the National Museum. The editor of the *Tagesbote* was convicted of libel against Hanka, but he was pardoned at once by the emperor, who had taken independent historical advice.

The two documents became the Czechs' legendary skeleton in the cupboard. It was half-opened again at the end of 1885, when Jan Gebauer, a leading philologist, wrote an article in an encyclopaedia, which expressed serious doubt about the manuscripts. Martin Hattala, a Slovak priest who was the senior professor of philology at the university, attacked Gebauer in a newspaper on 16 January 1886. A month later, Gebauer replied in the *Athenaeum*, where Masaryk supported him with an editorial. Though references

to the manuscripts as serious historical documents disappeared
from Czech history textbooks a few years later, in 1886 the fight
drew in every Czech patriot of any standing.

Gebauer fell ill during the row. A fight to the death was declared
on the two traitors by various patriotic societies. Masaryk had to
bear the brunt of the struggle, which went on for some three years.
The fact that Palacký had been dead for only ten years was introduced to prove that Gebauer's and Masaryk's action was tactless.
The full weight of a young and excitable nationalism was brought
to bear on those who were thought to have betrayed it. The
founder of the Czech Academy, Josef Hlávka, left a trust which
was to go to the person who would prove the manuscripts (and
their main message: that the Czechs were running their own state
when the Germans were still rootling around for acorns) genuine.
No payment was ever made from the trust. Masaryk, for the first
time in his life, was exposed to the full blast of Czech patriotic fury.

Some time before the outbreak of the manuscript controversy,
Masaryk had inherited a considerable amount of money, and the
Athenaeum, as well as the expenses connected with the controversy,
was financed by the inheritance. When Masaryk had moved from
Vienna to Prague, one of his students moved with him; his name
was Flesch, the son of a rich family from Brno. As a German,
Flesch entered the German University in Prague, but he continued
to regard Masaryk as his teacher. A melancholy youth, he shot
himself during a visit to Berlin in 1883, leaving all his money to
Masaryk. After a settlement with his family, Masaryk received the
sum of 62,000 gulden.

It did not last long. Neither Masaryk nor his wife were careful
managers: they had soon found out that a university salary alone
was not enough to run even an unostentatious household. They
entertained more than was usual for a young couple in Prague,
and Charlotte Masaryk was not used to running the same kind of
tight-fisted budget as were many of her Czech contemporaries.
Anyway, after the Masaryks had received the inheritance, in 1884,
they moved to a new flat in Vinohrady, a solid, middle-class, inner
suburb. Masaryk bought a cottage for his brother Ludvík at
Hustopeče, and helped him set up a printing shop; their father
gave up his work, and moved with his wife to Hustopeče as well.
Then there were Masaryk's old debts to be paid, and subsidies to

the magazine, and small loans to poor students. Ten years later nothing of the inheritance was left.

The *Athenaeum* was a learned magazine, and it survived until the year 1890. Its editor, however, was moving then more and more towards politics. He became connected with another magazine which was outspokenly political. This was *Čas* (Time), which had started as a fortnightly in 1886, became a weekly in 1889, and a daily in 1900. Its editor was Jan Herben, Masaryk's former pupil, who later became his admiring biographer. In 1889 three men guaranteed the finance necessary for *Čas*, made it into a weekly, and confirmed Jan Herben as its editor. He was to be paid 70 gulden a month, and run the editorial and administrative office in his own flat.

The three men who came to control *Čas* were Josef Kaizl, an academic economist who became a Reichsrat deputy in 1885 and who died, still a young man (he was four years younger than Masaryk) in 1901; Thomas Masaryk; and Karel Kramář, born in 1860, a lawyer and one of the first Czech students at the Paris Ecole des sciences politiques. Kramář became a deputy in 1891, at the same time as Masaryk, and was later one of Masaryk's rivals, with sharply opposed views on foreign policy. In 1918 the two men became the first president and the first prime minister of the new state of Czechoslovakia; their success did not make them ·better friends.

But for the time being their differences were not yet formed, and their politics and ambitions were similar. The three men and their friends were then described as 'realists'. Their political alignment was uncertain until, a few months after they had acquired *Čas*, they joined the Young Czech Party. This was in 1890, before the beginning of the election campaign. In March in the following year, Masaryk was elected deputy for a south Bohemian district, in the Young Czech interest, starting on this new career three days before his forty-first birthday.

The Parliament convened in Vienna on 9 April 1891. The Young Czechs were the majority in the Czech delegation, which refused to take the parliamentary oath in German. Masaryk spoke on a variety of subjects – school reform, public security, the need for a second Czech university. He was not a born orator, and he chose the muted, thoughtful ways of a university lecturer. By Viennese parliamentary standards, all went well until the budget debate in November 1892.

The Czechs, though they no longer boycotted the Parliament, often reminded it that they were not entirely happy with their position in the empire. It was not an easy subject for the deputies to tackle. It was elusive – they had regained their nationhood under Habsburg auspices, and they had as yet no plans for an independent state, the ultimate proof of their existence as a nation – and they easily became emotional. In November 1892 Masaryk himself tackled the delicate subject. Why were the Austrian peoples at loggerheads, why were the Slavs being oppressed in Austria, why was there no peace? Masaryk had a simple answer to this, and he outlined it to his colleagues in the Parliament.

It was because neither the Germans nor the government had any idea of the importance of the Czech question. The Czechs were not a small nation, Masaryk argued, and then proceeded to relate his nation to its European and global background. The Austrian Germans – the German state was then some twenty years old, and its rise had made a deep impression on the Germans in Austria – Masaryk said, were not prepared to give the Czechs and other Slavs of the monarchy a thought, and continued claiming privileges only for themselves. Masaryk said that the Czechs wanted their rights and their self-determination, and that the future of the Habsburg state depended on the solution of the Czech question. A German deputy, Menger, got up after Masaryk's speech, and accused Masaryk and his colleagues of being traitors. The Czechs did not let Menger continue his speech, and the chairman closed the session.

In 1892 Masaryk had also been elected a deputy to the Czech Diet; in the same year, he joined the delegations at the Reichsrat, the common meetings of the deputies from the Austrian as well as the Hungarian parts of the monarchy. He enjoyed political life, but his first excursion into it was brief. He resigned his mandates in September 1883. He was not comfortable in the Young Czech Party, and the fact that the party ran its own newspaper, *Národní Listy*, and Masaryk had his *Čas*, did not improve their relations. The party also tended to be radical in Prague, and moderate in Vienna; and there were too many men in the party who disapproved of Masaryk even more than he did of them.

He returned to the university, and his friends waited to see what Professor Masaryk would do next. Straightaway, in October 1893, Masaryk became the editor of *Naše Doba* (Our Time); only two of the contributors of the late *Athenaeum* joined him on the editorial board. Then five books, some of them pamphlets rather than books, followed each other in quick succession: *The Czech Question, Our Present Crisis* and *Jan Hus* came out first; *Karel Havlíček* followed in 1896, and *The Social Question* in 1898. They were all the results of Masaryk's lectures, and of articles in *Naše Doba*. Every time one of these studies appeared, there followed a more or less acrimonious controversy, especially in the case of Masaryk's historical studies. Here Masaryk encountered learning of high calibre, usually in the person of Professor Josef Pekař. Masaryk's view, for instance, of the importance of the 'humanitarian ideal' for Czech national revival, and his examination of the various sources of that idea, was severely criticized. He did not bother to define what he really meant by that concept; he was also told that he applied his critical apparatus too selectively, only to certain subjects; when it suited his argument, Masaryk suspended disbelief only too readily.

They were often controversies with scholars who still believed that the nation would best be served by dedicated intellectual work; they looked askance at Masaryk, who should have been one of them, but who liked politics too much. But like the politicians, the academics detected a certain sectarian quality in Masaryk's thinking and actions, and they did not on the whole like Herben, the editor of *Čas*, whom they suspected of snapping at them at Masaryk's bidding.

Then public life claimed Masaryk again. On 29 March 1899 the body of a girl who had been missing for several days was discovered in a birch copse near Polná. The girl's name was Anežka Hrůzová, and she had been murdered, but probably not on the spot where she was found. No traces of blood were found, and rumours soon spread that the girl had been murdered by the Jews, who had drained her blood, and used it for ritual purposes. A Jewish vagrant, Leopold Hilsner, was arrested; he was about twenty years old, stunted and feeble-minded. Damning witnesses came forward, and Hilsner was sentenced to death by hanging on 16 September 1899.

A week later *Čas* came out as the only newspaper in Bohemia against the sentence. It argued that no one, at the end of the nineteenth century, should believe superstitions about ritual murder. Masaryk was away on vacation at the time and, when he returned, he received many inquiries about his views on the Polná affair. One of his replies, to a former pupil in Vienna, was printed in the *Neue Freie Presse*, Vienna's leading newspaper. Masaryk became drawn into another public controversy.

He later remarked:

I was unhappy that such a dark superstition – I admit, a superstition based on the views expressed by doctors and other authorities – was possible. I am convinced that I acted correctly, and if I have ever been satisfied in my life, and my motives were quite clear to me, then it was about this case. The legal science, Liszt himself in Berlin, has already recognized the fact that the conduct of the trial was a classical case of how a biased view can affect not only people's heart and reason, but even their senses. ... I did not defend Hilsner, that is a matter for the police, for justice – to find out who was guilty and who was not; I took my stand, on purely ethical grounds, against blood superstition.[3]

There were student demonstrations against Masaryk; the clericals, the 'national workers' (they became better known under the name national socialists) who had been organized by the Young Czechs to oppose the advance of Marxist social democracy among the Czech workers, everyone with antisemitic bias united against Masaryk. One of his students summed up the case against Masaryk, on a blackboard in the lecture theatre, in this way: 'We hold against Masaryk that, in such difficult times, when it is essential that the nation should stand united as one man against the government which is our enemy, he wants to divide the whole nation for the sake of a Jew and, by dividing it, weaken it. He plays into the hands of the aggressive Germans! ... even Hilsner could not get a drop of Czech blood out of him.'[4]

After the demonstrations against him at the university, the faculty board asked Masaryk not to lecture for eight days; only two of his colleagues had condemned the demonstrations. Masaryk returned to teach on 27 November, and occasional attacks on him by the students continued. The appeal against the sentence on

Hilsner succeeded. Masaryk nevertheless became, at the end of the century, the most isolated figure in Czech public life. Even some of his friends from the small 'realist' circle turned away from him. Antisemitism was used to stimulate the animosity which had accumulated against Masaryk during his seventeen years' stay in Prague. In comparison with the Hilsner affair, the earlier manuscript controversy had been gentle discourse between civilized men.

Masaryk and his family were forced to lead an isolated, inward-looking life. Since 1892, they had been living in Malá Strana, the ancient quarter of the town, on the slope between the castle and the river. Charlotte Masaryk liked it there, because of Malá Strana's brooding, out-of-time charm; she gladly sacrificed modern comforts for ancient atmosphere. Their longest stay (fifteen years, between 1895 and 1910) was in Thunovská ulice, at the foot of the steps leading up to the castle. When the Masaryks moved from their flat and a group of nuns moved in, rumour in Prague had it that the nuns had the flat fumigated. The last flat the Masaryks ever had was further up the hill, at number 238, Kounicova. Masaryk's family spent the war years there, after he had gone abroad. They were reunited at the end of the year 1918, in the Hradčany castle, the former royal residence, which was not very far from the house where the Masaryks lived before, and during, the war.

When they moved to Malá Strana in 1892, their friends noticed a considerable change in the life of the family. The Masaryks had always run a simple household: it then became stark. There was soft-wood furniture only, and no curtains in the flat. Mrs Masaryk sold all her jewelry and other luxuries. Masaryk became very thin. He bought a bicycle and became very concerned about his health: he thought that he was suffering from a recurrence of his kidney complaint, and kept on looking up medical books.

This was in the middle of his first stint as a parliamentary deputy: the financial rewards of being a full-time politician were even smaller than those of a university teacher. Until the elections of 1891 Masaryk had been an assistant professor. By then the Flesch inheritance had been spent, and the Masaryks had four children: Alice, Herbert, Olga and Jan. The younger boy, Jan, was born on 14 September 1886. After many difficulties and delays Masaryk became full professor in January 1897. His basic salary was fixed at 2,480 gulden a year. The minister of education, having seen

Masaryk's papers, encouraged him to apply for an increase in his salary, because he had had to wait for a chair so long. He was awarded 1,000 gulden a year on top of his basic salary. This happened in September 1899, just before the Hilsner affair. It became publicly known in November, and Masaryk was accused of being paid by the government to defend the Jews.

After his three years in the Parliament, Masaryk again started running an open house for his students and former students; workers also came in from time to time, or anyone in need of advice. Charlotte Masaryk then joined the Social Democrat Party, taking a different political path from her husband. Masaryk, for his part, having once tasted political life, could not keep away from it for long. In the 1890s all his writing was political. While the Hilsner affair was raging in 1899, Masaryk was busy making plans for setting up a new political party and for transforming *Čas* into a daily. The party was established at meetings on 21 March and 2 April 1900; it was first called the Czech People's Party (realist); it was usually referred to as the 'Realist Party'. For a long time, it lived on the fringes of politics, outside the Parliament; only after the introduction of universal suffrage in Austria, at the elections in May 1907, did Masaryk manage to slip back into the Reichsrat. He was joined by another Progressive colleague, and their party had the smallest representation in the Parliament of all the Czech political organizations.

They had developed at the turn of the century. The Czech delegation to Vienna in 1907 was entirely different from the delegation Masaryk had joined at the time of his first excursion into politics, in 1891. The parties had become more diversified, and the introduction of general suffrage was followed by a large-scale redistribution of power between them. The Agrarians and the Social Democrats emerged as the strongest single parties: of the 108 deputies the Czechs sent to Vienna, the Agrarians accounted, in 1907, for twenty-eight and the Social Democrats for twenty-four. The clericals, divided into two groups, were represented by seventeen deputies, and the 'state-right democrats' by nine. The loosely linked group of the Young and the Old Czechs, as well as the National Socialists (the group was dominated by the Young Czechs, whose representation was drastically cut in the elections) sent twenty-six deputies to Vienna.

Masaryk was elected with the assistance of the Social Democrats, who did not put forward a candidate in his Moravian constituency, as one of the two deputies of the smallest Czech party represented in the Reichsrat. He was re-elected in 1911, and remained a member of the Parliament, in his rather unique and isolated position, until the outbreak of the war. In 1911 Masaryk gave his last lectures at the university; the year before he had celebrated his sixtieth birthday. Many of his contemporaries had died by then, or were about to retire from public life.

While he lived in Prague Masaryk provided his friends and critics with a few clues about his character and opinions. His politics were of the liberal kind, and he preferred representative, parliamentary democracy to the darker side of the Habsburg system: absolutism and rule by the civil service. Though he regarded Marxist socialism as one of the most important moving forces of modern times, he was not a socialist. He was highly critical of Marx in his lectures (one of the few points in his favour when he was being considered for a full professorship) and he published those lectures, in two volumes, under the title *The Social Question* in 1898. He had himself advanced the claim to a 'scientific' approach to politics; he disapproved of Marx's science mainly because, in Masaryk's view, it tended to disregard the individual and his conscience. Masaryk had left the Catholic Church and became a Protestant.

He preferred the empiricism of the English thinkers to anything the Germans had to offer, including Marx. He was a ruthless opponent of academic or any other cant, and of any form of untruth or distortion. But his 'critical' approach could sometimes be too insistent, an end in itself, rather than the means. In some of his writings Masaryk criticized so much that it was impossible to follow the various stages of his argument. Sometimes his prose can be quite difficult to follow; he became a master of the qualifying clause.

He also constantly crossed the borderline between academic and public life. Perhaps the position which was acceptable, or which passed unnoticed, in the time of Palacký, had become more difficult to sustain thirty or forty years later. As Czech political and social life became more diversified, so did the functions of people who took part in it become more specialized. There was perhaps no place any longer for a patriotic polymath in the national move-ment. Nevertheless Masaryk was too energetic for the groves of academe: even in the few periods when their calm broke, Masaryk had some energy to spare.

He was still changing and evolving as he approached his sixtieth birthday. His character had probably set by then, but certainly not his views. In 1908, for instance, in the second edition of *The Czech Question*, Masaryk stated that he had changed his views on the matter of revolution. He was no longer opposed to it on principle, and he accepted what he described as 'revolution of reform'. His view of the Habsburg Empire was quite flexible: until the out-break of the war, he regarded the state as an institution in which the Czechs would have to find their place. At the celebration of his sixtieth birthday, however, when he was asked by an old friend about what he thought of Austria, now that he had a close-up view of it, Masaryk replied, crossly: 'We should put a stick of dynamite under Austria, and blow it up. It deserves nothing else.'[5] There were other instances of flexibility. And of anger.

The key to Masaryk's character before the war was his relations with his Czech friends and enemies: after the war they contributed to the shaping of the new state. There is no doubt that a number of Masaryk's pupils remained devoted to him: Jan Herben, the editor of *Čas*, was perhaps the most faithful of them. Masaryk got on well with young people. In his old age he created a cult of youth: his friends and assistants were all much younger and Masaryk rather insisted on his youthful fitness. But soon after his arrival in Prague Masaryk had antagonized much of the older generation of university teachers and after that many of his con-temporaries who could have remained his allies in political life.

Of the prime movers behind *Čas*, both Kaizl and Kramář remained with the Young Czechs, the party which Masaryk had left in 1893, and which became one of the main targets of his attacks. Kaizl had died in 1901, and Kramář went on to become the leader of the party. They both had had sharp differences with Masaryk in their time. We have also seen that, soon after the first number of the *Athenaeum* had appeared in 1883, a member of the editorial board resigned straightaway because Masaryk did not consult him about a matter which came under his editorial com-petence. But it was Masaryk's relationship with another member of the editorial board, Albín Bráf, which throws a sharp light on Masaryk's position in Czech political life.

Bráf was a year younger than Masaryk; he read law at Prague University, and was appointed to the law faculty at the same time as Masaryk. Bráf taught political economy, and was responsible for that subject on the editorial board of the *Athenaeum*. In their early years at the Czech University, Masaryk and Bráf were on such friendly terms that Bráf could complain to Masaryk about his ill-luck in love, before his proposal to Libuše Riegrovà, Palacký's grand-daughter, had been accepted.

But Bráf's and Masaryk's paths parted. Bráf was never interested in standing for the Reichsrat, but became a member of the Czech Diet instead. He moved to the Upper House in Vienna in 1905, and in 1909 and then in 1911 became the minister of agriculture in the Austrian government. Bráf died in 1912, and he had started writing his memoirs four years before his death, at a most difficult time of his life, when his only son was dying.

A part of Bráf's memoirs described his relations with Masaryk. After the war their editor sent them to Masaryk, quite prepared to cut out any offending passages. Masaryk was then in the first year of presidency of the Czechoslovak republic. After reading the manuscript, on 6 June 1919, he wrote to the editor, remarking:

As far as I am concerned, I should like to see it published, because it is a part of the whole: Bráf did not understand me, that is true, but others did not understand me either, and I did not understand myself. At that time, I should say, I was chasing an ideal, which was not as clear to me then as it became during the war, and I then made – I know this best myself – many mistakes. Especially, I antagonized people.[6]

Masaryk had talent and courage, Bráf had written, but he was impatient, moody, and his manners were rather rough, in the 'Yankee way'. He never, for instance, 'learned to take his hat off properly'. Returning to the manuscript controversy, Bráf pointed out that the article by Gebauer, in the *Athenaeum*, was well argued; on the other hand, the editor's letter – Masaryk had told no one on the editorial board that it would be printed – was quite unnecessary and tactless.

There were two incidents which many years later stood out in

c

Bráf's memory as quite unforgivable. One involved Masaryk's view of the Czech national movement, the other his desire – and the way he went about it – to enter politics. After a party on a Saturday night, sometime in 1886, Masaryk, Bráf and a friend of theirs were walking home through quiet, deserted streets. They made them reverberate with a most unusual argument. As it turned into a quarrel, the three men kept on retracing their steps, unable to part company and go to their respective homes.

Masaryk was wondering whether the sacrifices which the Czechs were making in order to preserve their nationality were not too high: he asked whether it would not be better for the Czechs to join a great and civilized nation, and in that way release the energies which were being spent on the struggle for the preservation of Czech nationality for positive cultural and political work. Bráf argued that the denationalization of the broad mass of the people had not been successful before, and that it simply could not be done. He used rational arguments, though he knew that Masaryk was questioning the very existence of a movement which the Czechs had cherished over the decades.

Masaryk, however, went on with his argument, and pointed out that the development of denationalization would take a different course in the future. There was no point in arguing against Masaryk's rank heresy, and the three men parted company. Sometime after that incident, the first issue of *Čas*, in December 1886 carried an article by one of Masaryk's pupils, which posed a similar question and which was followed by a vitriolic public controversy. When the article appeared, Masaryk realized that his pupils – the author as well as the editor of *Čas*, Jan Herben – had gone too far, and in public. He was highly critical of the article, and of others printed in the first issue of the newspaper, but there can be little doubt that the question of wasted political energies had been very much on his mind at the time.

A few years later Masaryk began to look for ways of entering politics. He approached Bráf, and asked him whether his father-in-law, Rieger, the distinguished Czech politician, would recommend him for a parliamentary mandate. 'I could hardly become a minister, being a Protestant,' Masaryk said, and added, 'I can't therefore be suspected of being ambitious, and my academic and cultural work might prove useful for the parliamentary club.'[7] Bráf

agreed to help Masaryk, though not very readily. A certain coolness had developed between the two men; Bráf knew that Masaryk
did not hold Rieger in very high regard and may well have felt
that Masaryk was prepared to take Bráf's useful relationship with
the establishment too much for granted, without being properly
impressed by the company he found himself in. Bráf was probably
right.

At the time when Masaryk was still trying to gain admission
into the Old Czech party organization, in the spring of 1889,
Masaryk called on his friend one Sunday morning. Bráf inquired
what he could do for him, and Masaryk replied cheerfully, 'I have
come to see you about the mandates of course.' Bráf then explained
to Masaryk, solemnly and at length, the rules about admitting new
members and parliamentary candidates into the Old Czech Party.
He also said that Rieger and the party leadership would probably
not hesitate to recommend Masaryk for a mandate, though there
might be difficulties about Masaryk's friend, Kaizl, who had recently
sharply criticized the party's policy. Bráf did not feel that Masaryk's
dismissive comment on his friend – 'I do beg of you, leave Kaizl
out of this, he only cares about his ties, and not about politics'[8] –
struck at all the right note at such an important moment.

The negotiations with the Old Czechs failed, and Masaryk and
his friends emerged as Young Czech candidates in the elections of
1891. Bráf and other Czech politicians held against the 'realist'
group, and especially against Masaryk, that they had put themselves up for auction. Bráf went on to recount, in his memoirs, other
incidents of Masaryk's impatience and lack of tact. Many years
later, Masaryk did not dispute them. He simply pointed out that
Bráf, and many others, did not understand him; and that he,
Masaryk, certainly antagonized many people at that time.

Masaryk and Russia

IT seemed at that time, in the last years before the outbreak of
the war, that there were two Masaryks. There was the Masaryk
in Prague, an outsider, who had come from a remote part of the
country, was educated in Vienna, married a foreigner and upset
his compatriots many times, by often disregarding the rules which
they had evolved for the furtherance of their national cause.

The other Masaryk made his mark abroad. He was less occupied
than other Czech politicians with the affairs of their own parish.
When he celebrated his sixtieth birthday on 7 March 1910, and
a *Festschrift* was published for the occasion, the tributes to him
by Russian, Ukrainian and other Slav academics were very warm
indeed. Masaryk had been doing more travelling than was usual
for either an academic or politician; with the exception of two
visits to the University of Chicago, in 1902 and 1907, and to
England in 1901, his travels and his interests took him mainly
to Slav Europe.

As a student in Vienna, Masaryk had come under the influence
of Panslavism, which was then a part of the national movement
of the Czechs; there were traces of his interest in Russia on the
pages of the *Athenaeum*. He visited Russia in 1887 and again in
1890; he wanted to get leave of absence for the second trip, but
the faculty board, which did not like its members applying to the
Austrian authorities for leave to travel to Russia, recommended
him to wait for the summer vacation, when he could go where he
wanted, and do what he liked.

Masaryk and his wife were attracted by Tolstoy's exploration
of religion, though, on several occasions at Yasnaya Polyana,
Tolstoy's house, Masaryk disputed with him his pacifism as well

as his aristocratic choice of the simple life. Masaryk's travels in the Balkans had, on the other hand, a much more political purpose. He visited Bosnia-Herzegovina in 1892, a few months before his speech in the Reichsrat budget debate. In 1896 a group of Croat students who had run into political difficulties in their own country arrived in Prague, at the university. Many of them attended Masaryk's lectures, and held him in high regard.

While he was observing the political developments in the South Slav provinces of the Habsburg Empire – Croatia, a part of Hungary, and Slovenia and Dalmatia in Austria – Masaryk was evolving his ideas on South Slav unity, a complex subject, which was opened up by the political trials in the years 1909 and 1910. In those two years (they followed the annexation in 1908 of Bosnia-Herzegovina, the provinces which had been occupied by the Habsburg armies in 1878) Masaryk spent a lot of time in the Balkans: he was in Belgrade in the spring of 1909; in Zagreb, the capital of Croatia, in May that year, for the trial; after returning to Belgrade in June, he left in August on a trip to Dalmatia, Bosnia-Herzegovina, and Montenegro. He was back in Belgrade in October 1910.

The Balkan crisis was caused by the relations between Vienna and its former client state, the kingdom of Serbia, by Serbia moving closer to Russia, and by the fact that the Serbs had their own state, as well as being scattered throughout the South Slav provinces of the Habsburg Empire. The Serbs who were on trial in Zagreb in 1909 were accused of treason, that is of connections with Serbia, and with the anti-Habsburg movement directed from there. Masaryk observed the trial for a few days, and then returned to Vienna and put an urgent inquiry to the Reichsrat.

On 14 and 15 May 1909 Masaryk explained to his colleagues in the Parliament that the whole Zagreb case for the prosecution had been based on a clutch of forged documents. Though the defendants were sentenced, their sentences were later repealed. And before the end of the year another case involving forged documents was heard. This was in December in Vienna, against Dr Friedjung who had published an article in the *Neue Freie Presse* which accused a number of Serbs of running a conspiracy against the Habsburg state.

Friedjung maintained that he had documents to prove his case.

Masaryk, who appeared as a witness at the trial, was again able to prove that the documents at Friedjung's disposal were forged. The case was stopped, and Friedjung apologized. The documents had been forged at the Austrian embassy in Belgrade. Masaryk's contest with the diplomats, and with the foreign minister, Freiherr von Aehrenthal, was observed with great interest abroad.

Though the trials produced an adverse effect abroad, because the Habsburg authorities had resorted to forging documents to prove treason in their South Slav provinces, this does not mean that treason from the point of view of Vienna was not committed. Since the change of dynasty in Belgrade, following an unpleasantly bloody *coup* in 1903, Serbia's foreign policy had been gradually changing from dependence on Vienna to alignment with St Petersburg. The politicians and the military who had put the new dynasty into power in Belgrade were willing to use the Serbs in the Habsburg monarchy for terrorist purposes. An attempt on the life of the governor of Bosnia-Herzegovina was made in 1910; the terrorist movement culminated in the assassination of the heir to the throne, Franz Ferdinand, in June 1914.

It was a matter of opinion whether the Serb students were terrorists or dedicated patriots. There can be no question that, in the four or five years before the war numerous signals were reaching Vienna from the Balkans, as well as from the Ukrainian districts of Galicia and Bukovina, that the Habsburg Slavs were becoming increasingly hostile to the Habsburg monarchy, and that in some cases they were being encouraged by the Russians.

At the same time animosity between the Slavs and the Germans in the Habsburg monarchy was becoming more acute, largely for two paradoxical reasons. While the power of united Germany had grown since 1870, the political influence of the Germans in Austria diminished: after the introduction of universal suffrage in Austria in 1906, for instance, the Slavs disposed of the majority of votes in the Parliament. The Germans of Austria were therefore fighting a defensive action against the growth of Slav political influence. They succeeded in winning over the dynasty in Vienna, as well as the German Empire, for this policy, to the misfortune of everyone concerned: here were the first elements for the European chain reaction of August 1914.

Masaryk took, of course, the Slav side in the dispute, but he could not go all the way in his support for it. Tsarist Russia, the kingpin of Panslavism, was the reason for Masaryk's reluctance. He knew it quite well from his several visits there: he disliked its political regime, and he did not believe that a violent revolution could solve its problems. And when, after the failed revolution of 1905, interest in the Tsarist Empire increased in Western Europe, Masaryk decided to write a book on it.

It was his most important work, and it was interrupted by the outbreak of the war. The original two volumes of *Zur russischen Geschichte und Religionsphilosophie* were published in Jena in 1913; the first English edition of the book appeared, in 1919, under the enigmatic title, *The Spirit of Russia*. Masaryk had intended to illustrate the nature of the Russian revolutionary movement by writing the study around Dostoyevsky; he failed in doing that, though he gave Dostoyevsky a good deal of attention. By the standards of the time and of scholarship concerned with Slav matters, Masaryk's book rated high. It dealt with Russian philosophy, religion and literature, mainly of the nineteenth century; its political and historical contents were slighter in comparison.

The introductory part of the book covered the development of Russia until after the revolution of 1905 and expressed, on the whole, the kind of views which have become common currency. 'Russia has preserved the childhood of Europe; in the overwhelming mass of its peasant population it represents Christian medievalism and, in particular, Byzantine medievalism. It was but a question of time when this medievalism would awaken to modernity, and the awakening was in large part due to Peter and his successors.' Or, writing of the late eighteenth century: 'The bulk of the aristocracy was half-educated, while the court was immoral, a compost of unbridled sexuality, boorishness and cruelty, and its example was contagious.' Approaching his own times, Masaryk remarked that reaction bred revolution.

Of the events in 1905, Masaryk wrote: 'The October strike was a magnificent protest of united Russia against Tsarism.... The seriousness of the revolutionary aims was proved by the organization of the council of workers' deputies [Soviet].... The council did not consist solely of workers and socialists, but was an attempt of a deliberate fusion of all oppositional and revolutionary energies.' Nevertheless the Tsarist government gave away a little of its power grudgingly, drop by drop. The few weeks of freedom were, according to Masaryk, replaced by 'white terror'. Pogroms against the Jews, tolerated by the police; executions and prison sentences on the revolutionaries: 'It may be said without exaggeration that during the white terror fear of death ceased to exist.'

In describing the years after the revolution, Masaryk was highly critical of the Tsarist regime, though he did not point to the main reason for the failure of the revolution. Russia had lost the war against Japan but the Russian army and bureaucracy remained intact, and their power gradually reasserted itself. Nor did Masaryk analyse the revolutionary movements and their activities in any detail. When he was writing his Russia book, the Russian Social Democrats met in Prague in January 1912: they did not seek out Masaryk, nor did he them. From the few references made to them Lenin and Trotsky emerge as writers and philosophers, rather than as revolutionary leaders in Masaryk's book.

Masaryk's view of Tsarist Russia was critical, and he was unable therefore to join the ranks of the enthusiastic, pro-Russian politicians in Prague. There were many of them, in different parties: only the Social Democrats, and Masaryk, we have seen, was very close to them, were solidly opposed to the Tsarist establishment. The Young Czechs and their working-class off-shoot, the National Socialists, were committed to the Russian side, their leaders perhaps more than the rank-and-file of the party.

Karel Kramář, Masaryk's former ally, led the Young Czechs. Before the war, his ambition was to become the foreign minister of the Habsburgs: he wanted their state, dominated by the Slavs, to abandon its alliance with Berlin and opt for an alliance with Russia instead. Kramář's wife was Russian, and they spent the summers at their magnificent villa on the Crimea. Many of their friends were Russian, and for one of them, Svatkovski, the St Petersburg Telegraph Agency representative in Vienna, Kramář drafted his plan for a Slav confederation, which was to be ruled by the tsar, from St Petersburg. This was in May 1914. A month later, Kramář's plan reached the Russian foreign ministry from Vienna. The ambassador thought that the plan was 'of a fantastic nature, and because of the serious consequences it might have for its authors, should it become known, I regard it as my duty to request most humbly that it be kept in strict confidence'.[1]

There were other Czech politicians who were making contingency plans, in case of war. A few months before the conversation between Kramář and Svatkovski, in January 1914, the leader of the National Socialist Party, together with the director of one of the largest Czech banks, arrived in St Petersburg. Václav Klofáč, the politician, wanted to consult the Russian authorities on the organization of underground resistance in the Czech lands to the Habsburg Empire. Klofáč met Sazanov, the foreign minister, as well as the chief of the general staff; he came back to Prague with the impression that war was not imminent.

Soon after his return to Prague, Klofáč drafted a memorandum for the Russian authorities in which he explained how his party organization could be used to further the interests of the Tsarist Empire, and how much it would cost, in round rouble figures. Had Masaryk known of the plans then being made by Kramář and Klofáč he would have been highly critical of them. He had little faith in the ability of the Tsarist Empire to wage another war.

On the outbreak of the war, Kramář's pro-Russian position had a larger following than anything Masaryk could offer the nation. Resistance to Habsburg rule, such as it was after August 1914 (the majority of Czech politicians, even after the outbreak of the war, could not envisage a world without the Habsburg Empire), was therefore divided. On the one hand, there was the pro-Russian group, which believed that the Tsarist steamroller, the sheer weight of its man-power, would push the armies of the Central Powers (Germany, Austria-Hungary and, as of 1 November 1914, Turkey) westward, with ease. This was why Kramář and Klofáč as well as other pro-Russian politicians stayed in Prague after the outbreak of the war. They were getting ready to welcome their Slav brothers. Instead both Kramář and Klofáč were arrested, sentenced to death and reprieved only in the amnesty of July 1917.

Masaryk came to represent the other, 'Western' part of the resistance to the Habsburgs, but this happened gradually, as the Western (the British and French) side of the alliance against the centre of Europe proved to be more durable than its Eastern aspect. Nor did Masaryk leave Prague straightaway after the outbreak of the war. He tested the temperature of the war carefully, before he took the plunge: there was the possibility, however small and unwelcome from his point of view, that the Tsarist armies might reach Prague.

After the war, when Masaryk recollected his reasons for going into exile to take up arms against the Habsburg state, he wrote that 'talks with the politicians at home convinced me that the vast majority of the members of Parliament was anti-Habsburg'.[2] Masaryk underestimated the visionary aspect of his decision; we shall have an occasion to take a closer look at Masaryk's view of the political situation in Prague later.

There is no doubt that, before as well as after the outbreak of the war, those Czech politicians and industrialists whom the Habsburg monarchy suited were in the majority. Masaryk decided to break a habit which it had taken almost four centuries to establish. In addition, the Germans, the Italians, Romanians and the Serbs who lived in the Habsburg state had Germany, Italy, Romania and Serbia, their own nation states, to look to if there was to be no Austria-Hungary; the Poles and the Ukrainians had their compatriots living on the other side of the border. The Czechs, on the other hand, were not so advantaged: they would have to start at the beginning, and carve out their own state. Indeed, two weeks after the outbreak of the war, Masaryk argued that the war did not have a national or racial character, and that: 'The change of the map of Europe after the war may not be very considerable, but the war is certain to bring about far-reaching changes in social organism.'[3]

In that article published on 20 August 1914 Masaryk reacted to Kramář's view of the war as a gigantic clash between the Germans and the Slavs, a view based on the hope that the Slavs, led by Tsarist Russia, would emerge victorious from the contest. The outbreak of the war did not make Kramář's policy acceptable to Masaryk, nor did Masaryk care for the thought of the tsar dealing with the democratic and national aspirations of the small Slav peoples in Central and East Europe.

Masaryk's decision to go abroad for the duration of the war built up gradually, out of diverse considerations. In Austria he felt cut off from the outside world: he had been used to travel and contact with foreigners, and now he needed to test their attitudes to the war and to Austria-Hungary. According to a Czech-American friend of Masaryk, he said at the end of August

that: 'I should probably have to leave later, but I don't yet know
when. Here, I cannot be active politically, and I find it impossible
to remain inactive. The situation is bad. It's impossible to go
with Vienna, and here, it's impossible to go against it.'[4]

The Parliament in Vienna had not been meeting since March
1914, and the war had interrupted negotiations of a Czech-German
settlement in Bohemia: there was the danger that, in wartime,
the issue could be settled in favour of the Germans by an imperial
edict. Masaryk was also concerned that the army, as well as the
Austrian civil service, would welcome a tough policy with regard
to the Czechs. His fears were only partly justified. In the first two
years of the war, an acrimonious controversy developed between
the civil administration and the military, on the treatment of the
Czech and other Slavs of the monarchy. Though the military
extended their jurisdiction into many spheres of civilian life, they
failed to secure for themselves complete control of the Slav
territories.

By the end of August 1914 Masaryk had started corresponding
by messenger with Wickham Steed in London. Steed had been
The Times correspondent in Vienna and had returned to England
on the outbreak of the war; he had known Masaryk since the
Zagreb and Friedjung trials. Masaryk told Steed of disaffection
among the Czech troops, and suggested that as the Austrian army
was deployed on the Russian and Serbian fronts only the Russian
supreme command should facilitate the desertion of his countrymen from the Austro-Hungarian armies.

By the standards established later in the century, the Austrian
authorities were rather negligent about the possibilities of subversion: Masaryk was able to cross the Austro-Hungarian frontiers
in 1914 whenever he felt the need to do so. He spent the second
half of September in Rotterdam, and he wrote from there to Steed,
to Robert Seton-Watson and to Professor Denis at the Sorbonne.
Denis was a distinguished French scholar who specialized in Slav
studies; Seton-Watson, a young Scot, had travelled extensively
in Austria-Hungary and the Balkans before the war, concerning
himself with such matters as electoral practices in Hungary.
Masaryk wanted to meet at least one of these men on his visit to
the Netherlands, but this proved impossible and he had to write

letters instead. He promised his British and French acquaintances
that he would return to the Netherlands soon.

Between his two trips there, Masaryk got together a few of his
friends, all of them members of his own party, who were prepared to join him in the campaign against the Habsburgs: Jan
Herben, Cyril Dušek, who had taken over the editorship of *Čas*
from Herben, Přemysl Šámal, a lawyer who was to run Masaryk's
presidential chancellery after the war, and Eduard Beneš, who had
also been taught by Masaryk and was less than half Masaryk's age.
Since the entry of Britain into the war, Masaryk was convinced
that the Entente side (Britain, France and Russia, joined by Italy
in May 1915, and by the United States two years later, at a time
when Russia was on her way out of the war) was stronger; and
from Steed's messages he knew that Britain did not expect a sharp,
short campaign to win the war, but was ready for a long haul.

In the company of his party colleagues Masaryk therefore argued
that the Czechs should have their own representation abroad,
even if the Entente lost the war. His friends agreed with him, and
gave him financial support: Masaryk received 2,000 crowns from
Šámal, and Beneš also offered his savings for Masaryk's work
abroad; Charles R. Crane, an American industrialist who had
helped to fund the department of Slav studies at Chicago University, where Masaryk had held visiting appointments, contributed
£200, and Czech societies in America sent Mrs Masaryk $1,000.

At the end of September and early in October Masaryk discussed his plans for action against Austria-Hungary with a number
of Czech politicians, members of other small parties: the National
Socialist Party, the People's Party in Moravia, and the State-Rights
Party, which had already sent a representative to Switzerland. He
wanted to hear their views and, most of all, to get credentials for
his work abroad. He probably had not raised the question of
credentials with the National Socialists, though he did so with
Stránský, of the Moravian party, who agreed with him, as did
the leaders of the State-Rights Party.

Masaryk then left on his second visit to Rotterdam, where he
stayed between 13 and 29 October. He spent two days in his hotel
room with Seton-Watson, discussing the present and the future of
Austria-Hungary. Masaryk was in possession of some interesting
pieces of information about official Viennese policy: the brother

of one of the members of the Realist Party was the butler with the minister of the interior, and provided Masaryk with copies of official papers. On the basis of their conversations, Seton-Watson drafted a memorandum for the Entente governments.[5]

Masaryk maintained that he was 'speaking for' the Young Czechs, the State-Rights Party (called 'Constitutionals' in the memorandum), the National Socialists and the Socialists. He added that he had secured, 'in broad outline', the consent for his plans of 'all the middle-class parties of the nation at large and of the entire young generation'. Opposition was to be expected, according to Masaryk, only from the clericals and the aristocracy. Masaryk also told Seton-Watson about a conversation he had had with the governor of Bohemia, whom Masaryk had apparently told that: 'All Czech parties without exception have the Slav programme, and Slav sentiments. The nation is Russophil and Serbophil, and this fact cannot be changed.'

Masaryk's conversation with Seton-Watson occasionally broke the limits of poetic licence. There may have been language difficulties; the names of Czech political parties, and even more their alignments, were not easy to decipher. But even a casual acquaintance with Czech politics should have elicited an inquiry about the 'Socialists'; and if indeed Social Democrats were meant, an expression of surprise would have been in place at the dramatic change in their policies. The other large party, the Agrarians, were nowhere mentioned in Seton-Watson's report of his conversations with Masaryk; though the Young Czech and National Socialist leaders were anti-Habsburg, those leaders who had decided that Czech interests would be better served by Tsarist Russia than by the Habsburg monarchy, would not have regarded Masaryk as their suitable representative.

Masaryk went on to outline the shape of the future, independent Czech state. He was entering here a territory which the Czechs had left unexplored for some three centuries, and his plans changed several times during the war. He told Seton-Watson that unless Germany was decisively defeated in the war there would be no independent Bohemia; but if Germany was so beaten, the new state could be created on 'maximum lines'. This meant, for Masaryk, that the Slovak districts of Hungary would join the new state, a plan with far-reaching implications which neither Masaryk

nor Seton-Watson explored in their conversation. The idea fitted
easily into Masaryk's mind: those districts in Hungary were
familiar to him; he was, after all, half Slovak himself.

In this, the earliest stage in the making of the state, Masaryk
maintained that it could only become a kingdom, and not a
republic; and that, as Seton-Watson put it: 'In the interest of the
future Russo-Bohemian relations, this he [Masaryk] strongly
emphasized, it would be wiser not to put a Russian Grand Duke
on the throne, but rather a western prince, preferably a Dane or
a Belgian.' This important and imaginative memorandum had a
limited distribution in London: George Clerk, who was to become
the first minister to post-war Czechoslovakia, was given a copy at
the Foreign Office; so was Frederick Whyte, the Liberal MP for
Perth City, who became one of the founders, a year later, of *New
Europe,* a magazine which advocated drastic revisions of the map
of Europe, and especially of its central and eastern parts. Professor
Vinogradov, of Oxford University, promised to take the memorandum to Petrograd, and show it to the foreign minister there. For
the time being, none of the belligerent governments had an interest
in establishing an independent Czech state, and still less any plans
for doing so.

In his conversations with Seton-Watson, Masaryk quite freely
enlarged the scope of support in Prague for his plans, as well as
the strength of the pro-Russian movement among the Czechs. It
is true that there had been a certain drawing together between
Czech politicians after the outbreak of the war, but not enough to
justify Masaryk's remarks to Seton-Watson. Masaryk was determined that there should be no Austria-Hungary after the end of
the war. When he returned to Prague after his second journey to
Holland, his plans for the new state went through their first
metamorphosis.

The Czechs had run since 1861 their own gymnastic society
called *Sokol,* which linked physical fitness with their national
cause. It was a powerful, non-party organization; it was also rich
(it was run by Dr Josef Scheiner, a director of the bank of Bohemia)
and its members could become if necessary the nucleus of a
national militia. Masaryk valued his friendship with Scheiner,
and it was he who told Masaryk of a new idea, which had probably
originated in the Young Czech leadership. The idea concerned

the establishment of a corridor, cutting across Hungarian territory, which would link up the South Slav areas of the Habsburg monarchy with the new Czech and Slovak state in the north. Masaryk incorporated the corridor into his plans and it appeared in the first map of Czechoslovakia which he drew in March 1915.

Masaryk once more tried to meet Bohumír Šmeral, the Social Democrat leader; he had warned Masaryk, early in November, not to rely on Russia, and that there existed the possibility of a separate peace between Russia and Germany. When Šmeral saw Beneš later, and was told of Masaryk's plans, he described them as fantastic, and certain to lead the nation into another disaster. But Masaryk did not confine himself to conferring with Czech politicians in the Habsburg monarchy only: he talked to the Austrians (Joseph Redlich was one of the politicians he saw in Vienna) and they were pessimistic about Austria's military prospects. On his return journey from Holland, Masaryk had stopped in Berlin, where Karl Kautsky, the venerated leader of the German Social Democrat Party (he was known as the 'Pope of Marxism'), told Masaryk that, even if the Central Powers won the war, Austria-Hungary would probably fall apart.

In the weeks after Masaryk's return from Holland, the situation in Prague was getting more and more dangerous for him: the military authorities had started taking steps to suppress treason. On 26 November 1914, for instance, Cyril Dušek, the editor of *Čas,* was arrested; since the outbreak of the war, the newspaper had been confiscated on no fewer than seventy-nine occasions. When Masaryk left for another trip abroad, in the second half of December, there were doubts in his mind as to his return to Prague. He arrived in Venice on 19 December 1914, and told the Vienna correspondent of *Čas,* who met him in Venice, that 'this time nobody will be able to keep me quiet'. The following day Masaryk wrote to a Czech banker in Chicago, asking him to forward at least $10,000. When Masaryk arrived in Rome a few days later, he met Kramář's Russian friend, Svatkovski, who told Masaryk of the plans for the confederation of the Slav peoples. Masaryk, who was surprised to hear of these plans for the first time, remarked that: 'This is a question which would depend on the

political and military strength of Russia at the time of the conclusion of hostilities.'

Masaryk told the Russian correspondent about the memorandum
which he had worked out with Seton-Watson and which had been
forwarded to Petrograd. He also informed Svatkovski that whereas
on his earlier trips abroad he had acted only in the role of an
observer, he now represented three Czech political parties: his
own, the State-Rights Party and the National Socialists. (Again,
there is no evidence that Klofáč, the National Socialist leader, had
given Masaryk any kind of a mandate, or that Masaryk knew of
the offers Klofáč had been making to the Russian authorities
before the outbreak of the war.) The two men got on quite well
together; Svatkovski had probably by then started doubting the
feasibility of any plans based on the belief in Russia's military
strength.

Masaryk had an introduction to Prince von Bülow, the new
German ambassador to Rome, who however refused to see him;
nor did Masaryk manage to see the Russian ambassador. He talked
instead to Giers, the Russian minister to Montenegro, who was
then visiting Rome. Early in January 1915 the minister reported
to Petrograd that Masaryk seemed to be holding back a lot, and
that he had 'certain doubts about the realization of Czech independence within the framework of Russia'. The minister regarded
some of Masaryk's remarks as unsuitable 'for a representative of
the Czech nation, especially at a time when this nation desires
to enter the womb of the Russian Empire'.[6]

According to the report of the Russian diplomat, Masaryk told
him that the Czechs would wish to have a Russian king, and
that they would most definitely refuse to be ruled by a member
of a German dynasty. Another report on Masaryk's visit to Rome
gave a different picture of his thinking on the subject: 'If Bohemia
became an independent state, it would be a monarchy with a
dynasty from the English reigning family.' This was an entry in
the diary of Ante Trumbić, a Croat politician from the Dalmatian
coast (a Habsburg territory) who had left the country soon after
the outbreak of the war; he later became the chairman of the
South Slav (Yugoslav) national committee in exile. Masaryk also
told Trumbić of the plan for the Czech-South Slav corridor, saying

that: 'Bohemia and Yugoslavia must most certainly be linked together, territorially.'[7]

A few days before Masaryk left Rome, he sent a message through the British diplomatic bag to Wickham Steed that he was on his way to Geneva. He arrived in Switzerland on 16 January 1915. Masaryk's previous trips had been of an exploratory nature. Italy, for instance, had not yet decided which side to join, and the whole nature of the European war had been, for Masaryk, with his tentative plans, too open and difficult to evaluate. But after the first six months of hostilities it had become clear that victory would not be easy for any country to come by, and that there was a lot of long-term, organizational work to be done by those few men who had taken up arms in exile against the Habsburg Empire.

In Geneva Masaryk set about this work in an unhurried way. He made friends in the Czech colony in Switzerland, and got in touch with Lev Sychrava, a young journalist who had been sent abroad by the leaders of the State-Rights Party. He was glad to have access again to books and newspapers from Austria-Hungary and soon he had collected a 'respectable war library'. Though he went to the Austrian consulate to get a visa against the possibility of a trip to Prague, he was warned that it would be unsafe for him to return. Early in 1915 the long period of Masaryk's wartime exile began.

He had taken with him on his trip to Rome only his younger daughter, Olga, who acted as his secretary throughout the war, based most of the time in London. The rest of his family stayed behind in Prague, and the four wartime years of Masaryk's absence were not easy ones for them. Some two months after his arrival in Geneva, Masaryk heard about the death of his eldest child, Herbert. He was a painter, who had died of typhus while working for Polish refugees; he was then thirty-five, and had two young daughters, Anna and Herberta.

Masaryk hated receiving anonymous letters from Prague, pointing to the finger of God, or to the fate of all traitors. His wife Charlotte was placed under police surveillance. Her nerves, never very strong – she had suffered a mental breakdown after the birth of her first daughter, Alice – were worn down during the war. Charlie, the woman whom Masaryk had admired more than anyone else, spent the rest of her life in and out of mental homes. Alice, the elder daughter, was eventually arrested in October 1915 and released in July the following year. Jan Masaryk, who had returned to Prague some months before the outbreak of the war, after living in the United States, was conscripted into the Austrian army and for the first time found that he was the member of the family to whom the others looked for comfort.

In Geneva Masaryk took up the threads of the underground connections with Prague. He believed such links to be essential for his political work and, in spite of the relative inexperience of the Czechs in underground revolutionary operations, the links of the Czechs with their home country could not be matched by any other of the anti-Habsburg exiles. There were of course to be misunderstandings between the Czech politicians at home and abroad, and they were working under different pressures. Fear of Austrian police measures in Prague and disappointment with the slow progress of the anti-Habsburg action abroad were often reflected in the early communications with Prague. From time to time these underground links broke down, but never for good.

Masaryk had started making arrangements for these under-ground connections during his last weeks in Prague in December 1914. The reason he wanted to return to Prague from Geneva was that he had left the secret organization half made. He needed an organization at home to which he could refer for two purposes: to raise support from other Czech politicians for his action against the Habsburgs, and to receive swift intelligence of any movement that they might make towards publicly dissociating themselves from his aims.

This was the beginning of his long and close association with Eduard Beneš: it was to lead to Beneš's becoming the first foreign minister of Czechoslovakia, and the second president. It was an association rather than a friendship; the two men remained on formal terms. Beneš was neither a politician nor a scholar, and Masaryk used, and probably regarded, the younger man as a high-quality secretary. But Beneš was efficient, hard-working, discreet and completely loyal. Masaryk therefore entrusted him with maintaining links between himself and the politicians in Prague, and he also left Beneš with precise instructions, in case the tsar's armies ever reached the Czech lands.

Masaryk recommended that, in such an eventuality, a national committee should be established which would guarantee the customary civil freedoms and, Masaryk added, there should be 'no welcoming and non-welcoming of the Russians'. He also gave Beneš the names of all his important contacts abroad: apart from Steed and Seton-Watson, Ernest Brain, *The Times* correspondent in Holland, Professor Denis in France, and Professor Milyukov, who became foreign minister in the Russian revolutionary government after March 1917. Of the American Czechs, Emil Voska, who had taken Masaryk's first messages out of Prague to London, was the person he trusted most. In Prague Scheiner, with his financial and manpower resources, was the key person from Masaryk's point of view.

When Masaryk did not return to Prague, Beneš travelled to Switzerland. He met Masaryk, as well as Svatkovski, in Zurich on 1 and 2 February 1915. Beneš was empowered to convey Masaryk's plans to those Czech politicians with whom Masaryk had talked in Prague in December and who were not yet aware of the plans; to ask other politicians and journalists to join him abroad; to look for additional financial means; and, finally, 'after the manner of Russian revolutionary practices', to set up a secret organization in Prague, with the twofold task of influencing politics at home and keeping in touch with politicians abroad. Beneš was to consult Dr Scheiner about the composition of the secret committee: Masaryk stipulated that his own party should be represented by Přemysl Šámal, a young lawyer who had taken over the leadership of the party in December 1914, that Beneš should become the secretary to the committee, and that the clerical parties should be excluded from it. Beneš also took back with him a message to Kramář: it was both from Masaryk and from Svatkovski, and asked Kramář to come abroad. But he was still convinced that the Russian armies would soon arrive in Prague, and he wanted to be there to welcome them.

Early in March 1915, in Přemysl Šámal's flat, the first meeting of the secret committee took place. (It became known as *Mafie*, a name which had been associated with Masaryk and his friends on another occasion many years before, during the manuscript controversy.) Kramář and another Young Czech politician, Alois Rašín, as well as Scheiner, Beneš and Šámal took part. At this and the subsequent meetings the discussion centred on who, of the leading Czech politicians, should go abroad. Scheiner was refused a passport, and Kramář would not leave Prague.

In any case, as far as Kramář was concerned, taking an interest in *Mafie* was a small part of his secret work, of which the organizers of *Mafie* – Beneš, Šámal or Masaryk – knew nothing. Apart from Svatkovski, Kramář had been in touch, through a correspondent on his party's newspaper, with the Russian minister to Sofia, and with the military attaché; there were other sources of information abroad which Kramář kept secret from his fellow conspirators.

Through his Bulgarian connection Kramář got to know of the suspicions then existing between the Allies. They strengthened his resolution to work in the interest of Russia, and of his plan for the Slav confederation. Kramář's correspondent called on Sir Henry Bax-Ironside, the British minister to Sofia, and told him how very anti-Austrian and pro-Russian the Czechs were. Instead of welcoming this piece of good news, Sir Henry explained to his Czech visitor that the policy of HM government was to preserve Austria-Hungary, and that it opposed any extension of the influence of the empire of the tsars. Kramář therefore knew that little support would be forthcoming for the anti-Habsburg cause from the West, and that Masaryk was wasting his time.

Kramář was surprised when he received the joint invitation from Masaryk and Svatkovski. Early in March, he wrote to Svatkovski, in case his Russian friend had come under Masaryk's influence: 'Insist with all your strength on the Slav Empire.... The Slav question must be solved as a whole, by Russia. Masaryk has his own special views, but seems to be prepared to cooperate at present. You must assure Petrograd that there exists complete agreement in all our leading circles.'[8] Kramář also sent a message to Masaryk urging that he should do nothing to prejudice the form of the future Czech state, that he should work for the establishment of a Slav Empire, and that there would be a considerable amount of money transferred abroad.

Kramář was right to fear that Svatkovski would come under Masaryk's influence: Svatkovski had collected a lot of material on the Czech question by then, and most of it had come from Masaryk. He wrote a comprehensive memorandum, entitled 'The Czech Question, Kramář, Masaryk, the Parties and Emigration', for Sazanov, the Russian foreign minister. Svatkovski pointed out that Kramář was unable to act decisively, 'because Czech politicians look with more sympathy to Masaryk's activity, who is working abroad and who is getting ready to publish a newspaper in Paris, in support of the Czech interest'. Svatkovski reported that Kramář had been discussing the transfer of his property abroad with his lawyers in Prague, while maintaining, on the other hand, that 'everything had been arranged in Russia'. And this was indeed the weakness in Kramář's position: if the Russians had any plans for the Czechs, it was time, as Masaryk maintained, that they told somebody about them. In any case, the alignment between Kramář and Masaryk through the *Mafie* was one of expediency: their positions were far apart, and the nature of the war made their differences sharper.

After much deliberation on whom to send abroad, the *Mafie* made a really bad choice. Josef Dürich, a parliamentary deputy of the Agrarians, formerly a member of the Old Czech Party, and a partisan of Kramář's pro-Russian policy, was going abroad anyway. He had been issued a passport in February 1915; his two daughters and son-in-law had moved from Paris to Spain, and Dürich wanted to visit them. He had talked to Švehla, the leader of his party, and to Kramář; he was prepared to stay on abroad. He did not expect his absence from Prague to be too long: like Kramář and many other Czech politicians, he expected the war to last a few months, at most.

He did not really enjoy his prolonged stay in foreign countries. Dürich was a provincial kind of politician, and not eminent in his own province; Masaryk was to have many difficulties with him. Before his departure Kramář gave Dürich 30,000 crowns, and simple advice: he was to work 'for the great Slav Empire'. Dürich boarded the Vienna-Zurich express in the evening of 8 May 1915.

Beneš had been warned, when he discussed Masaryk's plans in Prague, that there was little interest in the Czech problem in the Allied countries, and especially in the West. Once Masaryk had decided to make a public appearance and set out the case for an independent Bohemia – he made this decision early in the spring of 1915 – his work was designed to remedy that lack of interest. In May 1915 Professor Denis began to publish a magazine called

La Nation Tchèque, which was financed from the resources put at Masaryk's disposal by the Czechs in America; other magazines publicizing the cause of Czech independence started appearing soon. Their impact on official thinking in Paris or in London remained negligible for the time being.

In April messages were arriving in Geneva for Masaryk from Prague; early in May Dürich was on his way to Switzerland. But Masaryk was no longer available there. Seton-Watson had been asking him urgently to come to London since the beginning of May; on 20 April 1915 Masaryk kept his appointment with George Clerk in the Foreign Office. Masaryk explained to Clerk the way he saw the war situation, and his plans for the Czechs. Clerk pointed to the difficulties a Czech state, surrounded by the Germans, would experience. He asked whether Masaryk knew what intentions the Russians had for the Poles and the Czechs, and whether Masaryk could draft a brief memorandum for Sir Edward Grey on the Czech question.

It was entitled *Independent Bohemia*, and reached the Foreign Office early in May 1915. It was calculated to appeal to the Western Allies, and centred on the argument that Europe should be rearranged on the basis of the 'modern principle of nationality'. Turning his attention to the global situation, Masaryk pointed out that there were only three great states in Europe – Germany, Britain and Russia; he indicated that the German plans for eastward expansion – the *Drang nach Osten* and the Berlin-Baghdad strategy – must be taken seriously, and that an understanding between England and Russia was possible and necessary. One was a sea power and the other a continental power: 'Czech politicians believe that Constantinople and the Straits can only belong to Russia.' (Masaryk did not know that, in the course of the bidding for the adherence of Italy to the Entente, such a promise had recently been made by London to the Russians.) There was no conflict of interest between Russia and England, in Masaryk's view, and the war had drawn them closer together.

There was no place for Austria-Hungary in Masaryk's Europe of the future. It had failed to protect and administer the peoples in its care, and it was now merely an appendage of Germany. The creation of new states, of Poland (Masaryk said nothing about the acceptability of a united Poland to Tsarist diplomacy) as well as of the Czech and Serbo-Croat states would become an essential part of a new Europe; and such a policy would have the added attraction, especially for England and Russia, of cutting across the plans of Germany.

As in the case of the 'modern principle of nationality' Masaryk made a shrewd estimate of the appeal, in London, of his arguments. He played down the role of Austria-Hungary in the war: Germany was England's principal enemy. He said nothing about the ethnically mixed nature of East Europe, implying that there would be no problems in setting up nation states in that area. He may have overdone his description of the level of and the necessity for amity between England and Russia, but this was a way of solving a dilemma which was then uppermost in his mind. It concerned the position of the Czechs between the East and the West of Europe.

Personally, Masaryk was at home in the West. He did not appear, even to those Englishmen, Frenchmen and, later, Americans who were not familiar with the ways of East Europe and the Balkans, as eccentric and foreign as many other exiles from the Habsburg Empire did. His life-long preference for English and American writing and attitudes of mind, his fluency in English, which he had spoken frequently with his wife, assisted him in his wartime work. He could think in terms acceptable to the English and the Americans and he never made the mistake of complicating political issues by adding unnecessary academic detail. He changed his linen frequently and kept his appointments.

The situation in Russia, on the other hand, caused Masaryk many difficulties which were exacerbated by the arrival of Dürich in Switzerland, and by his claim to have special responsibility for Russia. Masaryk and George Clerk may well have wondered what the intentions of the tsar were with regard to the Czechs. In clearcut, Western terms, there was no way of knowing. Certainly the hopes of the pro-Russian Czechs, and their ambitious pre-war plans, had been nourished by the Czechs' own isolation rather than by any official encouragement from the Russian side. Nevertheless once the war broke out, while Masaryk was still uncertain about what kind of action to take against the Habsburgs, or when he was still operating largely on the level of publicity in the West, things started happening to the Czechs in Russia.

There was a large colony in Russia before the war of between

60,000 and 100,000 people. There were the Czech farmers in Volhynia, and teachers, industrialists, technicians, managers and staff of branches of Czech firms were to be found in almost every large town in European Russia. There were some 20,000 Czechs living in or near Kiev. In Moscow, Petrograd, Warsaw, as well as in Kiev, they ran their own societies. The vast majority of them supported Russia after the outbreak of the war, and were gratified that the tsar's manifesto on 2 August 1914 proclaimed that: 'Russia, united with the Slav peoples by faith and blood, following her historical mission, cannot be indifferent to their fate.'

But on the same day a tsar's edict ordered the deportation of enemy aliens, and the confiscation of their property. Most of the Czech residents in Russia applied for Russian citizenship, or tried to enlist in the Russian army. Some of them even joined the Orthodox Church in their Slav enthusiasm. The Czechs organized 'Committees for the Relief of the Victims of War' on the Russian pattern, and offered to get together a unit of Czech volunteers.

The tsar received their representatives on 20 August and then again on 24 September: at their first audience, the Czechs delivered an address to the tsar which concluded with the sentence: 'Let the free and independent Crown of St Wenceslas reflect the rays of the Crown of the Romanovs.' During the second audience, the tsar showed a considerable interest in Slovakia, and asked the delegation to explain the problem to him on a map. Permission to form a Czech unit had been granted in August; by the end of October 1914 the Czech *Družina*, about 800 men, left for the front line. They were all Russian subjects, and at least a third of their officers had to be Russian-born.

Grand Duke Nikolai Nikolaevich, the supreme commander of the army, had also issued his manifesto to the Slav subjects of the Habsburgs in August: the Czech unit was to be regarded, in the view of the army command, not as a fighting unit, but as a unit of 'propagandists, working in the interest of the Russian army'. The *Družina* was divided when it arrived at the front into half-platoons which were attached to different regiments of the third army on the south-eastern front. The troops knew Czech, and many of them German, as well as the order of command in the Austro-Hungarian army; they soon proved their usefulness in reconnaissance work. The idea, however, of using the *Družina* as the nucleus of the future Czech army was dissipated in the process; the plan for recruiting Czech prisoners-of-war into the Russian army took a long time to materialize.

Between 7 and 11 March 1915 the first meeting of representatives of the Czech societies in Russia (a Slovak also attended) took place in Moscow. There had been differences between the various societies and their members on their attitudes to Russia: should she be asked to help to establish an independent state of the Czechs and the Slovaks, or of the Czechs only, or should there be a Slav Empire?

The decision went in favour of an independent state, but it was added that such a state could 'maintain itself only in complete agreement with the whole Slav world, and especially with its great protector, Russia'. There had also been some doubts, on the official Russian side, whether Slovakia could become a part of that state; there existed no such differences between the Czechs at the meeting, which decided that Slovakia should be an autonomous part of the Czechoslovak state. The Czechs did not have a newspaper of their own at that time, and it was agreed that a weekly should be published. The first number of *Čechoslovák* appeared in Petrograd on 17 June 1915.

Though the Czechoslovak cause made good progress in Russia early in the war, no leading figure had emerged there, capable of organizing the Czech colony properly and speaking with authority on its behalf. Meanwhile Beneš left Prague, on a forged passport in September 1915, and soon an overall organization of anti-Habsburg Czechs began to emerge in Paris. On 14 November 1915, a 'Czech Committee Abroad', led by Masaryk, published a manifesto which declared war on Austria-Hungary. But many exiles of different nationalities and political convictions were then publishing manifestos, and it created little impression.

It was important for Masaryk and the Czech cause. It was signed by representatives of Czech immigrants in America, England, France and Russia; and by Masaryk and Dürich. Beneš knew that his name was too unknown and that he represented no one; his signature did not appear. The war had been going very badly for the Russians since May, and the German and Austro-Hungarian offensives had pushed the front line far to the east; nevertheless the reason for the publication of the manifesto was given: 'We are forced to take this step by an acute feeling of Slav reciprocity; we should like to express deep sympathy with our brothers the Serbs and the Russians, and with the Poles.'

Masaryk and Dürich never signed another manifesto together. Dürich took up Kramář's Slav cause, and wrought havoc with it among the exiles. Masaryk tried to ignore the differences between him and Dürich for a long time; his patience broke in the end. Dürich at first settled in Berne, where he led a quiet life, punctuated by frequent visits to the Russian embassy; he offered no help to Masaryk with his publicity work. He regarded himself as a more important exile than Masaryk: after all, he represented both the Young Czechs and the Agrarians, one a distinguished and the other a very large party. He moved to Paris in February 1916, and made difficulties there in the Czech colony; with Dürich in mind Masaryk later wrote that: 'In Paris the ambitions of the sundry bibulous aspirants to the future Russian Satrapy of Bohemia gave a little trouble.'

Dürich was waiting for an invitation to go to Russia, and had to wait for a long time; but once there, in July 1916, Russian officials started treating him with respect, and as 'a counterbalance to Professor Masaryk'. Though he was glad to be rid of Dürich, Beneš in Paris did not trust him to carry out the mission to Russia, especially when he found out, in the spring of 1916, about Dürich's private initiatives. Dürich had been in touch with Briand, the prime minister, and had been negotiating with the French foreign ministry, as well as the Russian embassy. The French authorities dealt with Dürich, and with the Czech question, as if they were a subdivision of their Russian policy, and they had a very specific task for Dürich to carry out in Russia.

France was then desperately short of manpower; nobody had envisaged the destruction and stalemate which modern armaments were capable of producing. In April 1916 the first Russian troops had started arriving in France, under General Lochvicky's command. Dürich had promised the French a recruitment drive among the Czech prisoners-of-war in Russia for the Russian units which were to be shipped to France, a promise cutting across the endeavours of the Czechs to form their own units. Early in 1916 Masaryk had maintained that the 'formation of the legions', as the Czech volunteer units came to be known, was the 'first requirement for the whole Czechoslovak nation', and that it was to be the basis for any diplomatic work in the future. For the time being Masaryk was unaware that Dürich had given away the chance of building such an army.

The Tsarist authorities had been following carefully the differences, groupings and regroupings in the Czech colony; shortly before Dürich arrived in Russia a foreign ministry official drafted a detailed memorandum on the subject. Priklonski, in a memorandum dated 1 June 1916, argued that the Czechs were following a twofold aim in Russia: the committee in Kiev was busy getting under its control all the Czechs resident in Russia, and intended to hand over that control to Masaryk's committee; they wanted to do the same with the Slovaks in Russia who, according to Priklonski, were 'nearest to us in language and in spirit'. He was concerned that the 'Czech committee in London' could not be controlled by the Russian government, and suggested that two committees, one Czech and the other Slovak, should be organized in Russia and run by men who were sympathetic to Russia and the Tsarist government. He added that the 'liberation of the Slavs should be cancelled forthwith', meaning that the various committees and their activities should come under the control of the foreign ministry. Dürich was to be invited to Russia straightaway, and given sufficient financial means to work in the interest of the Tsar's Empire.

Though Beneš kept Masaryk fully informed about Dürich's activities, Masaryk did not behave as if he shared the fears of his young friend, that Dürich was quite unsuited for the mission to Russia. Dürich was the only other senior politician in exile, and he represented, so to speak, the other aspect of Czech anti-Habsburg politics. In any case Masaryk was showing a reluctance at that time to get involved in the Russian tangle. He had refused a number of invitations from the Czech societies in Russia; instead, he gave Dürich 6,000 francs for his mission. Dürich left for Russia on 23 June 1916. A few days later two representatives of the Czech societies in Russia came to see Masaryk in London.

He went far to accommodate them and make concessions to pro-Russian policies. He agreed that the main task of the Czech troops would be to support, in co-operation with the Russian armies, the occupation of the Czech lands. He even said that he would be very happy if the heir apparent to the Russian throne took over the command of the Czech troops personally, and that he had always believed that the Romanov dynasty would be most popular in Bohemia. He added that: 'Russian wishes will always be decisive for us.'

Though Masaryk later amended the remarks he made to his visitors (the minutes of their meeting were revised) he appeared rather impatient with the ways in which Russia, and the Czechs in Russia, kept on impinging on his time and patience. But there was nothing he could do about that. Just as Dürich was the only other Czech parliamentary deputy abroad, and Masaryk therefore took trouble to avoid conflict with him as long as he could, so Russia was the only power, on the Allied side, with a strategic interest in East Europe. Masaryk may have wished that these problems, Dürich as well as Russia, would go away; and he had to take into account the opinions of his younger colleagues in Paris.

They were more impatient with Dürich than Masaryk was, and they were also placing their political stakes on the Western side of the alliance, in a more decisive way than Masaryk. Beneš of course was dedicated to Masaryk, and careful of his interests. Before Dürich left for Russia, Beneš had made certain that *La Nation Tchèque* published on 1 June 1916 the division of roles in the Czechoslovak Committee Abroad (it was referred to as *Le Conseil National Tchéco-slovaque* in the original text; here, it will be referred to as the Czechoslovak Council), which had started taking shape a few months before. Masaryk was to be its chairman, Dürich vice-chairman, and Beneš general secretary. Beneš had had to work hard to make Dürich agree to take the second place.

By this time, Masaryk and Beneš had won over another recruit for their cause, who was to play a key role in the anti-Habsburg movement. This was Milan Rastislav Štefánik, a thirty-six-year-old Slovak, an astronomer who had worked in France for many years before the war and who then became a French citizen. The Czech and Slovak *trojk*a – the heroic trinity of the Czechoslovak Republic, which after the war replaced the traditional crucifixes in schools with photographs of Masaryk, Beneš and Štefánik – was thus complete: Štefánik had the essential qualification in his Slovak origin. The three men worked together very well, and their qualities were complementary. There was no doubt of Masaryk's seniority: he formulated the broad policies of the Czechoslovak movement, and kept an eye on the purse strings of the Czech societies in America.

The two younger men were so different from each other that it is surprising that they could work together at all; it is all too easy to describe their characters in terms of the contrast between the sober Czechs and the romantic Slovaks. In any case, they worked together well because Beneš could be relied on to remain unemotional, and because he knew his limitations. Beneš's voice sounded curious even in Czech, because he tended to speak through his nose. His command of foreign languages, with the exception of French, was shamelessly atrocious. Beneš had to make up by dedicated work for his personality and his utter lack of charm. He knew that his usefulness was not immediately apparent. But he was infinitely patient, efficient and could bide his time before important benefits started coming his way.

Štefánik, on the other hand, saw himself as a figure of high romance. Masaryk had known him as a poor student in Prague. In France Štefánik's preferences and habits became increasingly aristocratic. He had joined the French air force after the outbreak of the war as a lieutenant; later he was made a temporary general. He was very proud of his rank and very fond of the external show of the military. He was certainly a good-looking man, rather short of stature, decisive in his actions, politically and socially very active, and not above using his popularity with women for political ends. His good-humoured, full Slav face was somewhat tense and watchful. He was extremely ambitious; his politics were of the authoritarian kind and, in comparison with those of Masaryk, rather reactionary.

Štefánik maintained that the differences between the Czechs and the Slovaks were insignificant, and that the Slovaks were, or could easily become, Czechs who lived in the East. He had started to work for the Czechoslovak cause in September 1915, when he went to Serbia to organize Czech volunteers there. On his way back he met in Rome Mme de Jouvenel (she supervised a political *salon* in Paris) who subsequently introduced Štefánik to leading French politicians and soldiers. In Paris therefore Štefánik moved on a high political level. This suited his personal predilections, and complemented Masaryk's and Beneš's everyday organizational and publicity work; in February 1916, Štefánik had arranged for Masaryk a meeting in Paris with the prime minister, Briand.

Beneš, we have seen, had agreed with Dürich that he should take the second place to Masaryk on the Czechoslovak Council. Štefánik got very cross when he heard that Dürich was to go to Russia. He wanted to go there himself, and asked Masaryk to arrange this with Briand and with the Russian missions to Western Europe. When Masaryk refused, Štefánik began to negotiate with the French and the Russian authorities himself. Štefánik finally gave way, and agreed to Dürich's departure after a quarrel in which no holds were barred, and after Dürich had promised to do nothing in Russia which would harm the unity of Czechoslovak leadership in Allied countries.

Nevertheless the younger men in Paris, and especially Štefánik, were less careful than Masaryk not to exacerbate the differences between the Czech exiles. Masaryk was away in London most of the time, and in any case he had tried to keep Dürich, and the Czech colony in Russia, within the fold of the anti-Habsburg movement led by himself. Štefánik, on the other hand, saw in Paris the growing distrust of Russian military strength (after the disastrous setbacks on the Russian front in 1915, the Russian troops sent to France proved less than useful), and of Russian ambitions in East Europe. He was in no doubt whose side he wanted the Czechoslovaks to take.

On the day Dürich left for Russia – 23 June 1916 – Štefánik called on the Russian ambassador to Paris; a week later, Beneš visited the French foreign ministry. Early in July Briand sent a note to the minister of war, recommending that Štefánik should be sent to Russia. Two weeks later the French supreme command agreed. General Joffre then wrote to Briand that Štefánik's journey had political motives. For the benefit of the French, Štefánik had given Masaryk's plans a French slant. He proposed that the Germans in Central and East Europe should be encircled by a number of independent kingdoms, of which the *'royaume tchèque de Bohême'* would be one; that this kingdom should be free from Russian influence; and that an 'autonomous Czech army' should fight on the French, and not the Russian, front, so that 'the independence of the future Czech kingdom from Russia would become apparent straightaway'.[9]

Štefánik then left for Russia a few weeks after Dürich, on 28 July; the minutes of Masaryk's meeting with the representatives of the Czech societies in Russia, early in July, were being revised. On 5 August Masaryk wrote to Štefánik, promising him that he would soon receive the revised minutes, and enclosing a letter for Dürich. Masaryk's former conciliatory attitude to Dürich gave way to a new and more aggressive tone: he wrote that he had been surprised by the haste with which Dürich departed for Russia (Dürich had in fact waited for many months for the invitation), and that he disapproved of Dürich's choice of companions on the journey.

Masaryk also referred to the differences between his friends – Beneš and Štefánik – and Dürich, and to the fact that Dürich had accepted a loan of 2,000 francs from a source of which Masaryk disapproved. If this knowledge became public, Masaryk wrote, 'You would have to resign your position on the committee.' He went on: 'I beg of you, give your time to the prisoners-of-war, so that they join the army, as soon as the army is established; the political and military action will be led by Mr Štefánik, who was sent by the French government.'[10]

In spite of the fact that Masaryk went on stressing, in his letter to Dürich, that Štefánik was sent to Russia by the French government, Dürich refused to become Štefánik's second-in-command. The day after his arrival in Petrograd, Štefánik had another stormy meeting with Dürich, who refused Štefánik's offer to accompany him on his visit to the *Stavka,* the Russian headquarters. The following day, Dürich was received by General Alexeev and, on 18 August 1916, by the tsar himself. Alexeev refused to consider sending any Czech troops to France, but he was glad to see Dürich, and expressed the hope that the confusions in the Czech colony would at last be sorted out. Dürich then travelled from Mogilev, the seat of the *Stavka,* to Kiev. He was received there by the Czech societies, with much pomp and ceremony, though it was made clear that he was welcomed as the man who, 'together with Masaryk, stands at the head of the Czech movement abroad'.

Štefánik followed Dürich on his travels in the Ukraine, and arrived in Kiev at the end of August. By then Dürich had explained to his friends that Štefánik was not a member of the Czechoslovak Council at all; he nevertheless signed another agreement, together with Štefánik and on behalf of the Council in Paris, with the Czech societies in Russia. The Slovak issue was one of the main points of the agreement, which stated that the Czechs and the Slovaks wished to create a 'unitary, politically indivisible and free nation under the protection of the Entente'. In contrast to the earlier declaration of the representatives of the Czech colonies in Russia, the agreement contained no reference to an autonomous Slovakia.

Though Beneš reported to Masaryk on the latest developments in Russia, saying that Štefánik was in a weak position there, Masaryk seemed to be standing aside from these developments throughout the year 1916. He let the younger men in Paris make the running, living quietly and apart from the main stream of events, in the British Isles. Even the Austrian authorities followed, with some concern, the activities of the Czechs in Russia; they were naturally suspicious of Russian intentions with regard to the Habsburg Slavs, and they gave more time to investigating those suspicions than to Masaryk's activities in London and in Paris.

In London, Masaryk lived in Hampstead, which was then still on the edge of the countryside. He and Olga first lived in lodgings in 4 Holford Road and then moved to a furnished house at 21 Platts Lane. From time to time, when the weather was good, he went to the centre of town on top of a bus. He spent nearly two years in London; it was the quietest period of his exile. He started teaching at King's College in the University of London; he read a lot, and sometimes went to the cinema. He heard of the arrest of his daughter Alice while he was living in London. He became seriously ill, suffering from blood poisoning. London doctors, Masaryk wrote later, were unable to work out what was the matter with him; he was provided with a Welsh nurse and sent to Bournemouth to be operated on. He even had enough time to develop a mild case of persecution mania: the surgeon who operated on him (a case of boils, a small benign tumour?) said that the complaint had been caused by the 'laundry'. Masaryk thought that 'my enemies were in this way trying to get at me', and started practising target shooting, to let 'the sleuths know that I was getting ready for them'.

He had time to reflect on the fashions of the day in literature, and on national characteristics:

Watching those films I realized that in modern English literature there was a good deal of cinematographic element in their fiction, in the case of Hardy, Meredith etc, a preference for puzzles and detective plots; the Germans and, in a similar way, we [the Czechs], instructed and corrupted by the Russians, analyse the soul and cultivate its secrets and sicknesses; the Englishman and the American remain more naïve preferring more mechanical puzzles. But he can be equally corrupted by modern theories, by problems and super-problems, and even by the ridiculous psychology of Freud; see for instance Mr Lawrence, sometimes almost like Barbusse or Jaeger![11]

Masaryk saw Beneš frequently, usually in London and sometimes in Paris; he kept in touch with George Clerk in the Foreign Office, and of course with his friends Seton-Watson, who was then editing *New Europe,* and Wickham Steed, in charge of the foreign columns of *The Times.* But the war was going on too long even for Masaryk, who had prepared himself for a long war. On the other hand, had the war ended at the turn of the years 1916 and 1917 (there were some signs that it might) the anti-Habsburg exiles would not have achieved any of their objectives.

For more than a year the Germans had been trying to knock Russia out of the war; they had failed to do this by an outright military victory, but there existed the possibility of a separate peace in the East. The Austrians also joined the separate peace stakes early in 1917; before that, there had been the peace offer by the Central Powers on 12 December 1916, which conflicted with, and became confused with, President Wilson's offer a week later. Talk of peace was very much in the air then; when the war got going again in the spring of 1917, it was a different kind of war.

The Allies' reply reached Washington on 11 January 1917; it made a reference to the 'liberation of Italians, of Slavs, of Romanians and the Czecho-Slovaks from foreign domination'. The reference to the Czecho-Slovaks was the first major achievement of the exiles. It was included after Beneš's concentrated pressure on the French foreign ministry. But Beneš had been told at the Quai d'Orsay that the final attitude of the Allies to Austria-

D

Hungary would depend on their success in the war. They had by no means committed themselves to a total break-up of the Habsburg Empire; their reply was consistent with, say, its federalization.

The exiles were jubilant about the reference, but it led to a breach between them and the politicians in Prague. Masaryk later wrote that: 'I did not and could not expect that our success in the Allied reply to President Wilson, a success won by an intense effort on our part, would bring about what I so greatly feared: that our members of parliament at home would disavow us.'[12] This is precisely what happened. The committee of the Union of Czech deputies considered the Allied reply on 21 January; they wrote to Czernin, the foreign minister, declaring that: 'The Czech nation will, as it has done in the past, continue to look for the proper conditions for its development only under the rule of the House of Habsburg in the future.'[13]

This was a serious blow to Masaryk. In spite of all his efforts to keep in touch and in step with Prague, he had been disowned by the Czech politicians. They were reacting predictably to a Western initiative, unsupported by any evidence of military success. The fighting on the western front was as inconclusive as ever.

There was little chance that the Russian armies would reach Prague; leading pro-Russian politicians there had been in prison for almost two years, since May 1915. Masaryk and his companions in exile tried to publicize instances of persecution in Austria-Hungary, but they soon found that the names of Kramář and Rašín, well-known in Prague, meant nothing to Western readers. Masaryk's hope that, by keeping lines of communication open, he would have access to information useful for publicity purposes, seems to have been misplaced.

In other respects as well, Masaryk's action in the West had made little headway. Even his thinking about the future Czecho-slovak state was very fluid. He was still unable to conceive of a Central Europe without dynasties; his various proposals for a Belgian, or Danish, or English, or Russian king for the yet un-formed state were probably ways for Masaryk of attracting inter-national attention to the Czech problem, rather than real political solutions.

Since early in 1916 Masaryk had insisted on the importance of a Czechoslovak army, which would fight on the Allied side, and underpin his diplomatic efforts. But not much progress had been made here either, and, in any case, the key to the establishment of such an army was in Russia.

On the positive side, Masaryk had established the leading position of the exiles and their National Council based on Paris in relation to the Czech and Slovak immigrants in the Allied countries and in America. After his experience with the colony in Russia, he would give little political leverage to the pre-war immigrants. They were to be the source of money and, possibly, of manpower; but that was all.

Inside the National Council, although Masaryk delegated a lot of authority to the younger men, and especially to Beneš and Štefánik, it was accepted that he alone was responsible for the broad outlines of the policy of the anti-Habsburg movement. He was its elder statesman.

At the end of 1916 he told Beneš that he would go on working in exile should the war be concluded soon. Early in 1917 Masaryk's hopes were still far from realization. He knew that it was his task to discipline himself to patience: that he would have to wait for the resolution of the conflict in Europe. He was prepared to wait for an unpredictable length of time until an as yet undefined situation should arise. Sooner or later, Masaryk knew, the finely poised balance of the European war would be disrupted.

The World Crisis

In the early hours of 6 April 1917 the United States Congress, after a debate lasting seventeen hours, accepted President Wilson's offer to take America into the war. The revolution in Russia was then less than a month old: the tsar had abdicated on 15 March. On 9 April, three days after America's declaration of war on Germany, Lenin and other Russian exiles boarded a train in Zurich, a journey which took Lenin to Petrograd and, seven months later, to supreme political power in Russia.

The second stage of the war acquired a political dynamism which had been absent in the first two years and more of European hostilities. It was also an incomparably more active time for Masaryk, who knew that it was a make or break period for all his plans. In the first months of the war he had written that the war was certain to bring about far-reaching changes in social organisms (see p. 66). It did that and more. The war did away with three powerful continental dynasties – the Romanovs, the Habsburgs and the Hohenzollerns – and removed Europe from its position of supremacy in world affairs. It undermined conventional diplomacy, as well as the social cohesion – more in the East than in the West – of the whole continent. While soldiers and civilians were becoming interchangeable, and vast conscript armies were fighting over small pieces of ground ravaged by war, the wisdom of rulers, and their right to rule, was difficult to uphold. The war also destroyed, temporarily, the military power of both Russia and Germany, and created a power vacuum, equally temporary, in the centre of Europe. It was in this vacuum that, for better or worse, Masaryk established his new state.

The March revolution in Russia opened up new possibilities for

Masaryk and his anti-Habsburg policy. Professor Milyukov, the eminent historian whom Masaryk had known before the war and met again in London during the war, became the foreign minister in the revolutionary government. Masaryk sent telegrams to the president of the Duma, the parliament, and to Milyukov, congratulating them on the success of the revolution. In his message to the foreign minister Masaryk said that: 'Free Russia has every right to liberate the Slavs from German-Magyar-Turkish domination. . . . Free Russia is the greatest blow to Prussianism and Pan-Germanism, free Russia means the death of Jesuit Austria . . . and consolidation of the Entente.'[1] Masaryk then shared the view prevalent in London and Paris that the revolution would consolidate Russia's war effort and that Russia was a great country, which could manage war and revolution at the same time, a very optimistic view, given Russian performance on the eastern front during the previous two years.

Nevertheless in his war memoirs Masaryk wrote that he had feared revolution in Russia from the very beginning, 'and when it actually came, I was surprised, and unpleasantly at that'.[2] Masaryk had been badly shaken by the dissociation from his plans of the Czech deputies in Prague only two months earlier; now, in March 1917, he had in mind the possibility of concessions by the Habsburg authorities to the Slavs of Austria-Hungary. His reading of the situation was correct: the foreign minister wrote to Emperor Karl (Franz Josef had died in November 1916, and with him an era of Habsburg history and its policies) at that time about 'the facility with which the strongest monarchy in the world was overthrown', saying that the revolution in Russia would affect the Habsburg Slavs more than the Germans. Preparations were immediately started for the convening of the Reichsrat and for the amnesty of political prisoners, and the emperor made promises of constitutional rule.

Masaryk's concern with these new developments in Austria-Hungary was clearly expressed in a message he sent to Prague in April 1917. It drew the attention of Czech politicians to 'the success we have achieved here', ie the reference to the Czecho-Slovaks in the Allied reply to President Wilson, and went on: 'The present situation urgently requires the settling of the question of who should negotiate in the name of the Austrian nationalities, whether the dynasty and the diplomats or the nationalities themselves.'[3] Masaryk asked the Czech deputies not to say anything which would facilitate Austria's conduct of the war; and also 'to prevent the disavowal of our action at any price', and demand the historical rights of the Czechs, without in any way jeopardizing the annexation of Slovakia, or the break-up of Austria-Hungary. One sentence stood out towards the end of the message: 'Remember that there is a revolution in Russia and that they will have a republic there.'

The communications with Prague continued, but Masaryk's actions were no longer limited by them. The constraint imposed on him by considerations of the effect of his actions in Prague fell away. The situation in the Czech movement in Russia also started turning in his favour. In January 1917 Dürich had established a committee independent of Masaryk's Czechoslovak Council, which received subsidies from the Tsarist government; but after the revolution the importance of the societies of Czech immigrants in Russia declined, as did the significance of their quarrels. The revolution activated the prisoners-of-war – there were still some 20,000 of them in the camps, and many tens of thousands of Czechs and Slovaks were working in the Russian armaments industry – and they began to take on the role the immigrants had played before the revolution. The first issue of *Čechoslovák* after the revolution, published on 27 March, carried a report on the expulsion of Dürich from the Czechoslovak National Council. Poor uncomprehending Dürich disappeared from the scenes of political action, to return to Prague after the war, forgotten and welcomed by nobody.

The prisoners-of-war soon found a leader in Masaryk. He had no longer any reason to postpone his trip to Russia. His friend Milyukov declared on 4 April that the 'liberation of Slav peoples living in Austria-Hungary, the unification of Italian and Romanian territories, the creation of Czechoslovak and Serbo-Croat states, the unification of the Ukrainian territories of Austria-Hungary with Russia – such are the tasks before the future peace conference. The question of the domination over Constantinople and the question of European Turkey must also be regarded as the gravest problems of the war.' It was a programme not much different from the declared intentions of the Tsarist government, and it was in sharp contrast to the slogan of the socialist Soviet in Petrograd, 'peace

without annexations and indemnities'. The Czechs might be prepared to fight for at least some of Milyukov's objectives; the
question was whether the Russians were.[4]

As far as the Czechs in Russia were concerned, the situation was
therefore ready for Masaryk's arrival; but there was some uncertainty about how the Czechs would fit into the Russian revolutionary
background. Masaryk meant to leave London early in April; again
there was a delay, perhaps momentary hesitation on his part. It
arose out of meetings with Russian exiles in London, one of them
Boris Savinkov, a member of the Social Revolutionary Party, a
novelist, and an organizer of assassinations against Tsarist officials.
Savinkov told Masaryk that Russia wanted to be out of the war
and that it could not manage both war and revolution. But Štefánik,
who had just returned from Russia, put Masaryk's mind at rest
again by telling him that the 'campaign of the Russian army against
the Germans will be more active and effective' now, after the
disappearance of the Tsarist regime; he also recommended the
expulsion of Dürich from the National Czechoslovak Council, to
which Masaryk agreed. Masaryk finally left for Russia on 6 May
1917, travelling via Aberdeen on a British passport in the name
of Thomas George Marsden.

He arrived in Petrograd on the night of 15 May; in an interview
for *Epocha*, published on Monday 21 May 1917, he stated:

> We want to be free and independent, we are asking for self-
> determination, like every other nation. The achievement of these
> aims is the basis of my activity.... But the concept of self-deter-
> mination cannot be expressed under the constraining influence
> of Austria-Hungary.... Self-determination means the possibility
> of free organization of the nation and of its representatives.

In another interview a few days later Masaryk questioned the idea
of peace without annexations, adding that he was surprised by the
'simplicity of its authors'.[5]

By the time Masaryk reached Petrograd, Milyukov had left the
government. Guchkov, the minister of war, and after him Kerenski,
were not enthusiastic about Masaryk's plans. Guchkov was convinced that Czech and Slovak prisoners-of-war were more useful
in factories than at the front, and that any further recruitment for
the Czechoslovak brigade should stop.

As a Social Revolutionary and a member of the Soviet, Kerenski, who succeeded Guchkov in May, held against the Czechs their 'national chauvinism'; the new commander of the Kiev military district, Colonel Oberuchov, was afraid that the Czech example might make the non-Russian nationalities, especially the Ukrainians, want to establish their own units. The Russian high command nevertheless saw the situation differently from the politicians or from Oberuchov. At a time when their own troops had started voting with their feet, and their front line was melting away, they were looking for troops who wanted to go on fighting. Soon, during the ill-starred Kerenski offensive in July, they were to be proved right in their view of the fighting capacities of the Czechs and the Slovaks.

In the meantime Albert Thomas, the French socialist minister of munitions, had arrived in Russia, and Masaryk put to him a proposal on the transfer of the Czechoslovak troops to France. In Petrograd, in late May and early June 1917, Masaryk reported on the talks with Thomas to the Russian branch of his Czechoslovak National Council, and the meeting resolved that new recruitment of the prisoners-of-war should be carried out for the French front in the first place, and for the Russian front in the second. Thomas got in touch with the Russian provisional government; on 13 June Masaryk made an agreement with him on the transfer of 30,000 prisoners-of-war to France, concerning those prisoners-of-war who were to be employed in the armaments industry. The ground had been prepared for this agreement not only by Štefánik but by Dürich as well: but Masaryk's agreement with Thomas did not concern troops. It was nevertheless welcome to Masaryk: the Russian conundrum had again started to affect him.

The main task of Albert Thomas, and of many other visiting Western politicians and soldiers at that time, was to convince Russia to remain in the war, and to make the country pursue her war effort with more vigour. Kerenski gave in, and an offensive was launched. The platoons of the Czechoslovak brigade had for the first time in the war been concentrated in one place: near Zborov, a little town in the Ukraine, north-west of Tarnapol. The attack was launched on 2 July 1917, the Czechs fighting alongside the Finns. In Petrograd Masaryk was unable to sleep the night before the battle; the Czechs, however, won a convincing victory, the only one of the whole Kerenski offensive. Kerenski at once visited that part of the front line, and made the brigade commander a general. In Kiev Colonel Oberuchov was beating his breast in abject contrition.

One part of the Czech brigade did refuse to fight, consisting mainly of immigrant farmers from Volhynia who had done their share of fighting before Zborov; a small counter-revolutionary unit of volunteers placed itself at the disposal of General Kornilov. Local influences had started to take their toll before the Czechoslovak brigade's hour of triumph. But the offensive and Zborov were important for Masaryk, and removed official resistance to the recruitment of prisoners-of-war. At the time of Masaryk's arrival in Russia the original *Družina* consisted of some 8,000 officers and troops; by the end of September an additional 21,760 men had been recruited, and another 9,780 by the end of 1917.[6]

Masaryk visited the *Stavka*, the supreme headquarters, soon after the battle at Zborov, and negotiated with General Brusilov, whom he asked for permission to transfer the greater part of the Czechoslovak army corps to the French front. Masaryk also told Brusilov that once the army corps was established it should come under the control of the Russian branch of the Czechoslovak National Council; and that it could be used against Austria-Hungary and Germany, but not in Russian civil hostilities.

After his visit to the *Stavka* with Jiří Klecanda, the secretary of the Czechoslovak National Council, Masaryk toured Czech units and prisoner-of-war camps: from the *Stavka* to Bobrinsk, then to Kiev on 29 July, and from there to Borispol, where the second division was stationed. He also called on the original brigade at Polonne. The Czech and Slovak troops had waited for him for a long time. Masaryk made speeches, explaining his policies to the troops, persuading men to join the future army corps. The troops and their officers, for their part, treated Masaryk with the ceremony and circumstance due to the head of a state: guards of honour, regimental bands, carriages and regimental flags carried by horsemen.

On the morning of 19 August Masaryk came to Novosielice to visit the third division. He stayed with Count Dunina-Karwicki at the castle. The count gave a lunch in Masaryk's honour, and invited all the division's officers as well; after lunch Masaryk walked about in the park chatting to the men. Novosielice was his last stop but one before returning to Moscow. On 21 August he visited the high command of the south-western front in order to discuss the formation of a full army corps. This was at the height of the summer of 1917; Masaryk's wide-brimmed hat, his heavy overcoat loosely draped over his shoulders, became a familiar sight in the Ukrainian villages near the front line.

Masaryk cherished the idea of an army: there was nothing he would not do for it. It was for the sake of that army that he made his first agreement, with Albert Thomas, in June 1917. At a meeting of some 5,000 prisoners-of-war in Kiev on 17 July Masaryk had said that 'our military action here [in Russia] . . . is the culmination of our defence against Austria'. But there were problems. The prisoners-of-war were not all that easy to win over to the idea of a revolutionary army: once again they were being asked to fight. Before the Bolshevik revolution in November 1917 less than fifteen per cent of the Czech and Slovak prisoners in Russia had joined the volunteers.

There were also the problems of officers and of discipline in the volunteer army, and Masaryk had to deal with them. Were the officers to retain their former Austro-Hungarian ranks? Masaryk insisted that all former Austro-Hungarian officers should go through a six-week training or re-education course; later, the French disciplinary code was introduced. The original brigade had developed its own representative organs – the beginnings of a dual command – at the platoon, regimental and brigade levels, and the question was whether these representative organs would be duplicated throughout the army corps. It was a volunteer army, and the answer was yes. On his visit to the army corps the following year, Štefánik did not get on at all well with the representative bodies.

At its meeting on 31 August in Moscow the National Council in Russia approved Masaryk's policy that 'the creation of an independent army, as large and well-armed as possible, is now our main task'. Masaryk had originally meant to spend a few weeks in Russia; he stayed there for nearly a year. By the time of the Bolshevik revolution, early in November 1917, there was a Czech army corps in the Russian army consisting of some 39,000 troops, concentrated in the Kiev area in the Ukraine. Masaryk had been promised the army's transfer to France, and it was committed to non-interference in Russian internal affairs.

Masaryk had to stay in Russia much longer than he had intended, and the longer he stayed, the more out of step he was with Russian developments. Masaryk disapproved of the growing unwillingness of the Russians to go on fighting. In the matter of peace Masaryk took the side of the Western Allies and of Kerenski. He later wrote of his surprise at how little the Tsarist regime had left behind it; this was perhaps true of the visible signs of Tsarism, but not of its policies. Successive revolutionary governments kept on postponing internal reforms, and concentrated on fighting the war and winning the same benefits abroad as the Tsarist government had hoped for.

Masaryk spent six months in Russia after the Bolshevik revolution in November 1917. He witnessed the revolutionary action of the Bolsheviks in Petrograd, Moscow and Kiev. In Petrograd he lived near the telephone and telegraph exchange, the object of some fighting; he walked to the office of the Czechoslovak National Council without taking much notice of the firing in the streets. This alarmed his colleagues in the office, and he was given a bodyguard. He then moved to Moscow, where the office of the Council was to follow him. He arrived at the Hotel Metropol, which was taken over by Kerenski's troops. Masaryk spent six days in the hotel during the Bolshevik siege. In Kiev he also lived through the siege of the town by the Bolsheviks. He wrote in his memoirs: 'Even now, after years of diverse experiences, I remember the Bolshevik occupation of the capitals of Russia, and it all seems to me an oppressive dream.'[7]

Masaryk strongly disapproved of Bolshevik policies. Though he had known a number of Russian revolutionaries, he never met Lenin; the nearest he ever got to meeting a Bolshevik was Maxim Gorky. He charged Lenin with using Russia for the realization of the ideals of communism in Europe, and with misunderstanding the situation in Russia as well as in Europe. Marx and Engels had waited for a 'definitive revolution'; 'Lenin and his adherents were not put off, and waited again for a social revolution. When? Where?' Masaryk asked in his memoirs.[8]

Nevertheless, Masaryk conceded, the way for Lenin's regime had been prepared by Kerenski and the revolutionary provisional government; Masaryk's opinion of Lenin as a person and politician was by no means low. Bolshevism had 'sparked off a desire for freedom', and demonstrated the necessity for work. Lenin was an industrious person, and a good example. In a reflective mood, writing of political practice, Masaryk emphasized the necessity for compromise; even the greatest radicals made them, and so did Lenin, the most eminent of radicals.[9]

This was Masaryk recollecting the war in tranquillity, in the mid 1920s. The war, and Lenin's policies, had aroused violent passions; Lenin took on, so to speak, the whole European establishment, dedicated to the pursuit of the war. In contrast to Lenin, Masaryk played along with established governments; he did so because he wanted to destroy one of them – Austria-Hungary – and also because he never could quite see the point of a revolution. 'In no discipline nowadays,' Masaryk wrote, 'in administration or in politics, does the ABC have to be invented again, and independently.' To his mind the Bolsheviks had erred in trying that invention, and relapsing into primitive ways in consequence.

Masaryk was prepared to fight for his policies during the war, and to persuade other people to fight for them as well. During his stay in Russia they came into ever sharper conflict with the policies of the Soviet, and even more with the policies of Lenin. We have seen what Masaryk had to say about peace without annexations or indemnities, the foreign policy of the Soviet. In his memoirs he referred to his suspicions of Lenin in an oblique way. Soon after his arrival in Russia, Masaryk wrote, the influence of Lenin and of the Bolsheviks was everywhere making itself felt; and with it 'pacifism and a certain Germanophilism'.

On 26 July 1917 *Čechoslovák*, the newspaper of the Czechoslovak Council, made the same point more bluntly: referring to the Bolshevik July uprising, and Kerenski's charges against Lenin and his comrades, it wrote that 'a band of paid agents of the German government succeeded in stirring up unrest in Petrograd'. Indeed, the groundless description of Lenin as a paid agent of the German government persisted in the publicity of the Czechoslovak republic. The first US mission to the newly established state brought with it to Prague copies of several political pamphlets, including Czech and German translations of the forged Sisson documents on the 'German-Bolshevik conspiracy'. They enjoyed a wide distribution, in schools as well as in political circles, with official encouragement.[10]

Bolshevism in the war was, Masaryk himself wrote, a military problem for him, a problem of the Soviet regime's attitude to the Czechoslovak army corps in Russia.[11] But it was more than that. The conflict of interests between Lenin and Russia's allies – England, France and America, with Masaryk resolutely supporting their position – concerned Russia's remaining in the war. In that conflict there could be no compromise. The Germans certainly had an interest in the Bolshevik regime and its peace policies prevailing in Russia – and a very short-sighted policy it proved to be; the Allies, on the other hand, wanted the Bolshevik regime to disappear, for exactly the same reasons. It is also certain that Masaryk and the Russian branch of the Czechoslovak National Council became involved in secret activities to unseat the Bolsheviks.

Boris Savinkov, the Social Revolutionary opponent of the Soviet regime, returned to Russia after the end of the civil war; he was arrested, tried in August 1924 and sentenced to death. During his trial Savinkov said that in 1918 he had received 200,000 roubles from Masaryk for the establishment of an anti-Bolshevik terrorist organization which was preparing an attempt on Lenin's life. The president's office in Prague officially denied the accusation that Masaryk had dealt with Savinkov in the matter, and stated that Masaryk's talks with Savinkov were confined to discussions of the 'moral value of terror'. The communiqué added that Masaryk knew that Savinkov was then living in poverty, and that he was thinking of emigrating. Masaryk offered him financial assistance. Though Savinkov received none, the Czechoslovak press agency stated: 'If the report is correct that he [Savinkov] received some assistance from the Czech side, he perhaps received it from secretary Klecanda, who was informed about the matter. Klecanda unfortunately died suddenly and therefore rendered no accounts.'[12]

The Czechoslovak News Agency (ČTK) report also pointed out that Masaryk had supported many Russian intellectuals after the war, which was of course true. But Savinkov was an unusual kind of intellectual. He had been a member of the 'combat section' of the Social Revolutionary Party, which specialized in political assassinations; he had taken part in the murder of the minister of the interior, Pleve, in July 1904, and then of Grand Duke Sergei in February 1905. Masaryk met Savinkov in Moscow on 2 and 5 March 1918, and made cryptic notes on their conversation.

The two men discussed the movement against the Soviets, and who was who in it; Masaryk suggested to Savinkov that corn should be bought up so that it would not fall into German hands. The question of a *coup d'état* against the Bolshevik regime was raised; and so was the technique in which Savinkov could claim some expertise – political assassination. The last part of Masaryk's notes on his conversation with Savinkov reads simply:

> Terror: the action against Grand Duke Sergei cost only 7,000 r[oubles]
>
> Plehwe 30,000.
>
> I can provide some financial means = to Šíp, so that Klecanda 200,000 r.

The last sentence of Masaryk's notes, 'I can provide some financial means', was written overleaf, along the left-hand edge of the paper, and at each end of the sentence there was the sign ≡ which Masaryk sometimes used to indicate the summary, or the conclusions, of his conversations. However the name of Lenin was nowhere mentioned in Masaryk's notes; the statement that the money was intended for the assassination of Lenin was made by Savinkov during his trial in 1924.

At the time of Masaryk's conversation with Savinkov, the outcome of the war hung in the balance: the Bolsheviks had just agreed to make peace with the Central Powers (the treaties of Brest-Litovsk were finally ratified on 29 March 1918), and the Germans were about to launch the biggest offensive ever, on the western front. Though the Americans had entered the war almost a year before, the full weight of their manpower and material resources had not yet made itself felt. The mood in military and political circles in London and Paris was pessimistic in the extreme, and there was still a hope there that somehow Russia could be manoeuvred back into the war. The interest in London and Paris was therefore in the re-establishment of the front in the east, and in stopping the German troops being transferred from there to the west, rather than in the internal situation in Russia. The two aspects of the war were however inextricably linked. It mattered whether the Allied representatives in Russia saw Lenin as an agent of Germany, because such a view would make it possible for them to take action against him and his regime; more important, Lenin was, before their very eyes, taking Russia out of the war.

Early in 1918 in Petrograd and Moscow there were Allied funds available for the twin purposes of keeping Russia in the war and disposing of the new Soviet regime. There were many eager, more or less useful recipients for these funds, and Savinkov was among them. Masaryk would have received the news that he was regarded by some as a potential political assassin with sorrow, but not with horror. The suggestion would have struck him, whether there was any truth in it or not, as irrelevant in a serious political situation, parallel in its nature to the glib description of Lenin as a paid and faithful agent of Germany. Masaryk knew that his objectives in the war were, as Lenin's were, clearcut and far from base. Nevertheless many years after the end of the war Masaryk told Čapek that: 'Revolutions and war are not waged without deceit and lies. It is stupid to try to see in them only heroism – Achilles would not have been possible without Odysseus.'

The future of the Czechoslovak army in Russia remained Masaryk's main concern. When Kiev fell to the Red Army on 8 February 1918, the Czech army corps found itself on Soviet territory. Following Masaryk's directives it had maintained strict neutrality in the course of the fighting. The Czechoslovak second division was stationed on the bank of the Dnieper, and when Soviet troops passed through its territory an agreement was made between the commanders on 'strict armed neutrality', the Czechs being assigned to guard duties. And on 3 February Masaryk's Council issued an address to the citizens of Kiev which stated that: 'In internal political conflicts in Russia the Czechoslovak army has maintained, maintains and will maintain the strictest neutrality.'[13]

Masaryk was anxious to get the Czechoslovak army corps out of Russia at the earliest opportunity; so far, only some 2,000 Czechs had left for France, under the agreement with Albert Thomas. The possibility of employing the Czechoslovak troops on the Romanian front was briefly considered, and dismissed; France remained their destination. Even Masaryk considered their travel plans 'fantastic': from Kiev across Siberia to Vladivostok, and to France via the Far East. But in the end not a single man of the Czechoslovak army corps in Russia saw active service in France.

It took some time to extricate the army from the Ukraine. In mid-February, after the peace negotiations in Brest-Litovsk had broken down, the Germans resumed their advance on the eastern front. For a short time there was the possibility of co-operation between the Allies and the Bolsheviks, in what was then described as 'revolutionary war' between the Soviets and the Germans. This was not really a welcome alternative for Masaryk. The socialists among the prisoners-of-war, as well as in the army corps, might again be tempted, as indeed some were, away from his and into the Red Army.

Masaryk jealously guarded the policy guidelines he had laid down for the army corps; in the fluid military situation in the Ukraine they made complete sense. He left for Moscow on 21 February, while the German advance was in full swing; he negotiated there with the French consul and the military attaché about the transfer of the troops to France. Six days after his arrival in Moscow, on 27 February, he made his last public speech in Russia; on 3 March he drafted a 'memorandum for the information of the Soviet government and Allied representative offices in Soviet Russia'; on 2 and 5 March he saw Savinkov. On 8 March Masaryk left Moscow for good, on his way to Washington.

In his speech on 27 February 1918 Masaryk again said that the whole army corps would be transferred to France 'in parties', and that recruitment for the corps would go on. In addition Masaryk wrote in the memorandum that the army corps comprised more than 40,000 men, that his Council had had applications from 50,000 prisoners-of-war and that: 'Such a good army must not be left inactive; the political significance of the action is also considerable, so that economic reservations cannot be decisive. Our army would not only be an addition to the armies of the Allies; it would also seal the political dissolution of Austria-Hungary.'

Nevertheless Masaryk also referred in the memorandum to the question of whether the Czechoslovaks could fight in Russia.

Even nowadays the formation of a volunteer army would be possible. . . . It is significant that the government in Petrograd has made a call for generals, staff and cadre officers, and that comrade

Lenin has said, jokingly, that Russia could make war if it had as many well-organized armies as there are resolutions for the war.... I conclude that a new Russian army could be built only after a few months.... Russia must form her own army and it is not out of the question that she could again attack the enemy who had forced her to accept such humiliating and thieving peace.... Our army is the only organized military force in Russia; in agreement with the Petrograd government the Allies might agree to our army fighting on the Russian front.... Neither in Austria nor in Germany do I expect an important revolution; if this really happened, a part of our army could take part in it. At least in Galicia.... Further than Galicia – to Moravia or even to Bohemia – we could penetrate only in the case of a more general uprising.[14]

Masaryk wrote the memorandum, it should be remembered, two days after Kiev had fallen to the advancing German and Austrian armies, and on the day the Russian delegation finally gave in at Brest-Litovsk and signed the peace treaty. Lenin had viewed the concept of 'revolutionary war' as a sham, and after much argument got his own way. At the time of writing his memorandum Masaryk was probably unaware of the fact that peace had been signed, and the possibility of the resumption of hostilities on the eastern front must have been very much on his mind. In addition Masaryk knew that no firm agreement existed between the Western Allies on the transfer of Czechoslovak troops to France.

The idea, we know, had been raised many times before; by Dürich, by Štefánik, and then by Masaryk himself. But Masaryk's agreement with Albert Thomas of 13 June 1917 had concerned the transfer of industrial workers only; the army did not lie within Thomas's competence. In any case, only a small fraction of Czech and Slovak workers (of the agreed total of 30,000 men) had found their way to France. And a few days after Masaryk had left Moscow, the foreign ministry in Paris wrote to 'the chairman of the Czech National Committee' (presumably Masaryk) that in view of his agreement with the Soviet government, 'the head of the French military mission to Russia gave the Czechs freedom of action and broke off negotiations on their transfer to France, which he had initiated on the order of the minister of war.'[15]

The message from Paris, which indicated that something was going seriously wrong with his plans, never reached Masaryk. On the other hand, the Soviet authorities had nothing against the Czechoslovak troops leaving Russia. Muraviev, the commander of the Red Army in the Ukraine, let Masaryk know that much on 16 February 1918; on 26 March Stalin, the commissar for nationalities, spelled out the conditions for their departure. By then the Czechoslovaks had withdrawn from the Ukraine to south Russia, waiting to embark on their long trek across Siberia to Vladivostok.

Masaryk took the same route to Washington, several weeks before the first party of troops boarded the trans-Siberian railway. When he left Moscow on 8 March he was satisfied that they would follow him soon. By then he had spent ten months in Russia, and his view of the war differed from that of his colleagues in Paris. Again, as in the case of Masaryk's prolonged stay in London early in the war, the pace of Czechoslovak political action was being forced in Paris by Beneš and Štefánik. They soon came to understand that the plans the Allies had for the Czechoslovak troops in Russia were different from those of Masaryk, and they were quick to use the leverage placed in their hands by the presence of a disciplined army corps in Russia.

Well before Masaryk reached Tokyo on his way to America, Beneš had received (on 1 April) a message from the French military attaché to London expressing some doubts about the Czechoslovak army ever reaching Europe by the proposed route. The War Office in London had told the military attaché that there was a severe shortage of shipping facilities, and that if the army was a military factor at all it could operate best within Russia. Beneš understood the hint at once, and began to use the presence of the army in Russia as an important counter for the recognition in London and Paris of an independent Czechoslovak state.

For the time being the withdrawal was proceeding smoothly; but soon, step by step, the Czechoslovak army was to be drawn into the conflict with the Bolsheviks. The first serious fight between them flared up near Chelyabinsk, on the trans-Siberian railway, in mid-May 1918. On 18 May Lord Robert Cecil wrote to Clemenceau that he had seen Beneš, who was certain that the Czechoslovak troops would carry out any orders by the National

Council, and that: 'He is prepared to get the necessary orders sent on condition that we make a declaration recognizing the Czechoslovaks as our allies and the justice of their claim to independence.'[16] The Czechoslovak army corps therefore stayed on in Russia for more than two years: long after the end of the war it fought in the Allied war of intervention against the Soviet regime.

A long time after the armistice, at their meeting in June 1919 at Tomsk, the representatives of the Czechoslovak fighting units in Russia sent a telegram to Masaryk begging him to help them. It said that the troops were physically and morally exhausted, homesick, and running the risk of political and class breakdown. The evacuation of the Czechoslovak army from Siberia was completed as late as November 1920. At a congress in Prague three years later the socialists who had fought in Russia resolved that: 'The conflict between the Czechoslovak revolutionary movement abroad and the revolution of the Russian people was an historical misunderstanding.'[17]

We left Masaryk on his long way across Siberia in March 1918. He reached Vladivostok, the last point on the trans-Siberian railway, on 1 April. He meant to sail to America direct, but there were some difficulties, so he travelled by the Manchurian railway across Korea to Pusan, and sailed from there to Japan. He arrived in Tokyo on 7 April, received a US visa on 13 April and left Yokohama for Vancouver on 29 April.

Masaryk's difficulties in Vladivostok may have been caused by the request from Lansing, the secretary of state in Washington, to the US ambassador to Tokyo to get in touch with Masaryk before his arrival in America. Masaryk met Roland Sletor Morris, the ambassador, soon after his arrival in the Japanese capital. He prepared a confidential memorandum for Sletor on 10 April, arguing strongly against intervention in Russia.

He recommended that the Allies recognize the Bolshevik government '*de facto*, it is not necessary to discuss a recognition *de iure*', and added that: 'If the Allies were on good terms with the Bolsheviks, they could influence them. The Germans have recognized them, having concluded peace with them.' Masaryk argued that the monarchist movement was weak, and that the Kadets (the Constitutional Democrat party) and the Social Revolutionaries had begun to organize themselves against the Bolsheviks, 'and do not expect any great success of these parties. The Allies expected that Alexeev and Kornilov will have a great success on the Don; I did not believe it and refused to enter an alliance with them, though I had been invited by the leaders. The same goes for Semenov and others.'

Masaryk was convinced that the Bolsheviks would retain power longer than their opponents supposed; the Bolsheviks had set about their task of running Russia in earnest, whereas the other parties suffered from political ineptitude, 'the curse of Tsarism'. Perhaps a coalition government of the Bolsheviks, Socialists and Kadets, Masaryk thought, could achieve consensus after some time. Masaryk pointed out that the Allies should be united in their policy towards Russia; that they must support her, 'at any cost and by every means'. All the small nations in the East – the Finns, Poles, Estonians, Lithuanians, Latvians, Czechs and Slovaks, Romanians, etc – needed a strong Russia, because otherwise they would be at the mercy of the Germans and the Austrians. Masaryk expressed the hope that the Japanese would take no action against Russia; and he wrote that he had seen no armed German or Austrian prisoners-of-war anywhere on his journey across Siberia. But, he added, the Allies must fight German and Austrian influence in Russia by every means.[18]

Masaryk once more described the Czechoslovak army in Russia, and assumed that it was to be transferred to France. His whole argument was based on his view of the Russian situation, and on the assumption that instead of hostility the Allies would choose the path of friendliness towards the Bolsheviks. But this was not to be. Masaryk's aims had not yet been recognized by the Allies; the recognition of the Czechoslovak state and the making of the decision to intervene against the Bolsheviks proceeded concurrently in the spring and summer months of 1918. Often these two developments crossed each other; instead of becoming an asset on the western front (its value was not agreed on in the Western capitals, and Masaryk and his friends in Paris had to argue it again and again) the Czechoslovak army corps assumed an importance out of proportion to its size in Russia itself. The more important it became in terms of the policy of intervention, the less Masaryk could control its future. Its control passed into the hands of the French and other Allied political and military leaders.

Having done all he could for his army, Masaryk turned away from the old seat of weakness of the wartime alliance to its new source of strength. American men and arms started pouring into France. Early in the summer of 1918, Allied resistance on the western front stiffened, and there was little doubt that the final military decision there would go against the Germans. The new world came to redress the balance of the old; Masaryk's arrival in America was well-timed.

He had a rest on the ship sailing to Vancouver; the weather was good, and the passage smooth. He could be well satisfied with political developments. The various peace efforts in 1917 and early in 1918, especially those initiated by Vienna and the Vatican, had come to nothing. In the process Austria-Hungary had become more and more dependent on Germany; Masaryk's old argument – that Austrian policy was totally subordinated to Berlin – became true. And the Czechs in Prague had also shown signs of life: there had been the writers' manifesto in May 1917, which spoke of 'a democratic Europe, consisting of free and autonomous states', and called on the Czech deputies to resign their mandates if they were not prepared to act according to the wishes of the nation. The Epiphany declaration in 1918 of the Czech deputies, without giving up the idea of a Habsburg state, also made a reference to 'the right to a free national life and self-determination, whatever their size and irrespective of whose rule they live under'. In the meantime Beneš and Štefánik in Paris had applied for the formation of a Czech unit in France in June 1917, and in September a similar application was made in Italy. On 10 April 1918 in Rome a congress of 'oppressed peoples of Austria-Hungary' published its resolution against the continued existence of the Habsburg Empire.

Masaryk arrived in Chicago on 5 May 1918. After Prague, Chicago was the second largest Czech town. The Czech and Slovak colonies in America had grown fast in the years before the war: in 1910 there were 500,000 Czechs and 280,000 Slovaks living in the United States and ten years later their number reached 1,200,000, with more Slovaks than Czechs. Chicago was the Czech centre, most Slovaks living in Pittsburgh. They were largely workers, miners and farmers; there were some lawyers and doctors and a few industrialists and bankers. The first generation of immigrants never lost interest in their home country, and they were organized in many societies which reflected their social, religious and national origins. The war drew them closer together. The Czech and Slovak umbrella organizations, the National Union and the Slovak League, had established a branch of the Czechoslovak National Council in America in March 1918. It was without a chairman, as was the Russian branch; the chairman was to be a member of the Paris Council, then present in the country.

Masaryk was welcomed at the Chicago railway station by a vast crowd of Czechs and Slovaks. The president of Chicago University, the university which many years ago had invited an obscure professor from Central Europe to lecture on Slav studies, was waiting for Masaryk at his hotel, the Blackstone on Michigan Boulevard. From there Masaryk left for Washington, Boston and New York. On 28 May he was back in Chicago, and then travelled to Pittsburgh, Cleveland and Philadelphia. He gave lectures and interviews, and everywhere received an enthusiastic welcome from the Czech colonies. He remembered the saying of Spurgeon, the preacher, that he would stand on his head for a good cause. This is what Masaryk did, and he had a consistently good press. On 14 July 1918, for instance, the New York *Sun* published a feature on Masaryk entitled 'The New Masters of Siberia'.

Indeed, on 20 July Masaryk wrote to the acting secretary of state:

> You will understand our wish that the great American Republic would join the French Republic in recognizing our National Council (in Paris) as the representative of the future Government of the Czechoslovak Free State. I think that this recognition has become practically necessary: I dispose of three armies (Russia, France and Italy), I am, as a wit has said, the master of Siberia and half Russia, and yet I am in the United States formally as a private man.[19]

Masaryk was then getting a litle impatient, as he expected official America to move faster in the fast-moving last months of the war.

Masaryk was very fond of America, and had many ties there. He had received a hero's welcome from his compatriots. On 30 June he concluded with them the so-called Pittsburgh convention on the foundation of a state of the Czechs and the Slovaks. The Slovak League was strongly represented, and the convention promised the Slovaks autonomy, with their own representative assembly. But the plan which the Czech and Slovak immigrants welcomed with enthusiasm had a less warm reception in official quarters.

Masaryk did not express it outright in his war memoirs, but they bear witness to his temporary disappointment. In the American chapter he recapitulated the course of the whole war, of the Czecho-slovak action during it, of the achievements and setbacks of the other Slav peoples. He even amended his view of America. He described for the first time the flawed side of the United States, as he saw it: the literary struggle against obsolete forms of puritanism; the literary origins and development of decadence; the increase in divorces and abortions. Masaryk sketched in his thoughts about the sources of decadence: in France the wars and constant blood-letting of the people was blamed for its decadence, in America the absence of such national pastimes. He concluded: 'And who knows what the effects are of the blending and mixture of peoples (the Americans call America "the great melting-pot") not only morally, but also biologically? Nervousness and psychosis are wide-spread and the number of suicides is increasing, as in Europe. The nervousness – or I should rather say nerviness – of the American woman is especially coming to the surface.'[20]

Masaryk's memoirs wandered in time and from place to place, without coming to grips with the matter which he came to settle in Washington. He had good introductions there. Charles Crane, the industrialist whom Masaryk had known since the turn of the century, and who had financed the department of Slav studies at Chicago University, was very helpful to Masaryk. They had last seen each other in Kiev a few months before. In Washington, David Houston, the former professor of political science, now the secretary for agriculture, was Crane's friend; Crane's son Richard, who became the first US ambassador to Prague, was Lansing's private secretary.

Masaryk had come to Washington on his first visit on 9 May. He was finally received by President Wilson on 18 June. Masaryk had prepared himself carefully before he came to see Wilson, and was familiar with the president's background and interests. The two old men (Wilson was six years younger than Masaryk), both of them former academics now applying their minds to other matters, could have been expected to have a lot in common. But Masaryk, who in his old age was habitually either magnanimous or non-committal about people, was unable to control his irritation with Wilson.

'My relations with President Wilson were always purely matter of fact,' Masaryk introduced the subject in his memoirs.[21] The flat statement was followed by a hint at their first disagreement: 'Perhaps the President was a greater pacifist than I was.' When Masaryk suggested that Republican politicians should be asked to attend the peace conference, Wilson told him that the parties would quarrel and that he himself had no talent for the compromises required by a coalition. It was Masaryk's impression that: 'For an American, Wilson is more of a theorist than a practical person, a deductive rather than an inductive thinker.' Masaryk was incredulous when he heard that Wilson preferred to correspond with members of his cabinet; it confirmed his view of Wilson as a solitary, perhaps isolated, person.

Talking to Karel Čapek, many years later, Masaryk had a mild, old man's revenge on the American president. 'My first impression of him was one of such perfect *neatness*; I said to myself, it's obvious he has a wife who loves him.' In 1918, however, Masaryk had come to Washington to instruct Wilson in matters European; the American president would have none of that, and it is not surprising that the two former professors did not get on at all well.

At one point, Wilson thought it necessary to say to Masaryk: 'I shall tell you frankly, I come from a line of Scottish Presbyterians, and therefore I am a bit stubborn.'[22] Masaryk could not but agree with that statement, though he did not indicate at which point of their conversation the president used it. In any case, the conversation could not have been going very well.

He was disappointed in Washington, and Wilson was the main cause of his disappointment. For a long time Wilson would not be moved from the position on Austria-Hungary he had taken in the tenth of his Fourteen Points of January 1918: 'The peoples of Austria-Hungary, whose place among the nations we want to see safeguarded and assured, should be accorded the freest opportunity for autonomous development.' No mention of the break-up of Austria-Hungary. America was not, as Masaryk had hoped, to lead the world in officially recognizing the right of the Czechoslovak peoples to independence.

While Masaryk was still insisting on the transfer of the Czechoslovak troops from Russia to France (according to his own notes
he asked Wilson for his help with this on 19 June 1918), the matter
had been settled in Europe quite differently. Even Wilson himself
was then more interested in intervention than in helping Masaryk
with his plan. Masaryk's record of their first meeting read: 'The
main topic of discussion was the question of intervention in Russia,
the question whether the Japanese could intervene in Siberia and
administer Siberia, and whether our Czech units could be used for
that purpose. I expressed my view of the matter, that I am not an
advocate of the so-called intervention, because I cannot see what
its results would be.'[23]

The exiles themselves were deeply divided on the question. In
Paris we have noted Beneš's quick grasp of the benefits of inter-
vention for the Czechoslovak cause, and what he said to Allied
leaders. But it was not for him to commit the Czechoslovak army
in Russia one way or the other, and Beneš knew this. His colleague
Štefánik felt no such restraint. As early as February 1918, when
he was visiting Italy, Štefánik had criticized Masaryk's policies in
Russia, and threatened to take the army into his own hands. In
April, when Masaryk's Tokyo memorandum became known in the
Paris office of the National Council, Štefánik was again highly
critical. There were other dissenters among the exiles. Lev Borský,
one of the first advocates of the break-up of the Habsburg Empire
before the war, put the matter bluntly in a conversation with a
friend in March 1918. He said that: 'It is of course better to ally
ourselves with the bureaucracy, with the clergy, the way Dürich
did. Masaryk held on to another policy, which failed completely
and which led to the destruction of everything. Masaryk opted for
the whore democracy instead, and – as a Slav – he now perhaps sees
where it got him.'[24] The commanders of the Czech army corps were
also divided, and some of them were ready to fight the Bolsheviks.
They were doing so at several points along the trans-Siberian railway at the time of the meeting between President Wilson and
Masaryk.

Despite Masaryk's visit to Washington, the fate of the Habsburg
monarchy was settled first in Europe, and then in America. The
Allies could weaken the enemy either by detaching Austria-Hungary
from her alliance, or by destroying it. When Austria-Hungary proved

impossible to separate from Berlin, the other policy was used. The Allies came to appreciate the propaganda value of the exiles' movements with regard to Austria-Hungary's cohesion and willingness to fight; nevertheless they postponed the final decision on the break-up of the Habsburg Empire as long as they could.

Again France led the field: in a message to Prague on 8 July 1918 Beneš described 'our greatest political success, on 29 June, we have had so far'. The French government, Beneš wrote, had recognized 'our independence, all our historical rights, the Slovak situation, and binds France to support us at the peace negotiations, and to recognize that the National Council is a delegation of the provisional government'. France's recognition that the Czechs and the Slovaks had the right to independence and that Masaryk's National Council should play a leading role in the new state was the result of Beneš's negotiations with Balfour and Robert Cecil and, after his return from London, with Pichon and Clemenceau. He then wrote to Prague saying what Pichon had told him: 'We want you to be free. We want to destroy Austria. You have done what you could, and we are expecting still more help from your people at home.'[25] Beneš's messages to Prague were growing more and more optimistic; and in every one of them he stressed that 'unity and co-operation between us is essential'.

Following the French recognition, on 9 August 1917 Balfour declared the Czechoslovaks an allied nation, and the National Council a 'trustee' of the future Czechoslovak government. Finally, on 3 September, the US government recognized that a state of war existed between Czechoslovakia and Germany and Austria-Hungary, and that the National Council was a *de facto* government. It had at the time no territory to rule, but that small difficulty was soon taken care of.

With Masaryk's agreement, Beneš had been planning a meeting between Prague politicians and representatives of the National Council since early 1917. In July 1918 he insisted that such a meeting take place soon. It finally took place in Geneva at the end of October; the luckless government in Vienna made no difficulties. On 25 October 1918 two financial experts and five politicians left Vienna for Geneva, to come face-to-face the following day with Beneš, and his three secretaries. A week before, on 18 October,

Masaryk had turned down Emperor Karl's offer of federalization of Austria-Hungary in his Washington declaration.

Of the five politicians, we know Kramář and Klofáč already. Antonín Kalina was a deputy of the small Progressive Party, which had supported Masaryk's plans since he had gone into exile; Staněk and Habrman were Social Democrats. Habrman had met Masaryk in Geneva in the spring of 1915 and had listened to Masaryk's plans without committing his party. They were all older than Beneš, and vastly more experienced than he was in the political ways of Prague, but Beneš held the trump card. Masaryk's policy, which he had faithfully supported since the beginning of the war, had proved successful, and had the backing of the victorious powers. The men on the delegation from Prague had either vacillated, like Habrman, or backed the wrong horse, like Kramář, or stayed ineffectually in Prague, like Kalina.

Beneš and his three secretaries, a sight of utmost efficiency, faced the delegation with confidence. Beneš secured their agreement to do nothing without the approval of the National Council; he removed their doubts as to the establishment of a Czechoslovak state and its representation at the peace conference. Beneš also said that the National Council had made no commitments as to the form of the future state, though he reminded them that Masaryk had said in his Washington declaration of 18 October that the new state should become a republic. Kramář, who had admired the Tsarist regime, did not like what Beneš had to say on that point, but conceded that: 'If our state is to be a monarchy, it must be an extremely democratic one, like England.' Despite his misfortunes during the war – his arrest, sentence to death, the fall of the Russian monarchy – Kramář had not lost all his fighting spirit.

In the evening of 28 October, before the five politicians returned from Geneva, the National Committee in Prague, an organization of Czech political leaders which had been established in late 1916, passed a 'law on the establishment of an independent Czechoslovak state'. Neither Masaryk, Beneš, Štefánik, nor the senior politicians who represented the Committee in Geneva, were in Prague for the declaration of independence. The revolution in Prague was a bloodless, gentle takeover of power from officials and army officers who no longer wanted to be responsible for the administration of a Habsburg province; many people cheered, and the more daring of them took down the signs bearing the double-headed eagle, the Habsburg emblem.

Masaryk was still in the United States, sending memoranda to Wilson and Lansing, warning them of the duplicity of Vienna and Berlin, advising them not to negotiate with the German or Austrian rulers, but 'with the representatives of the German people in Germany, and with the representatives of the peoples of Austria-Hungary'.[26] He also started negotiating loans for the army in Siberia and for the new state, and revising his study *New Europe*, which he intended to put before the peace conference. He telegraphed instructions to Beneš on 29 October on how to conduct the demobilization of the Czech armies after armistice, not forgetting the German troops who would return to the new state, and asking: 'If possible, begin negotiations with Lenin about letting our army in Russia go home.'

He did not know what was happening in Prague; he was disturbed by news reports of Beneš's negotiations in Geneva. Early in November his mind was put at rest: he received a cable from Geneva dated 4 November, one from Paris dated 5 November. The seven delegates from Prague thanked him 'on behalf of the nation' for what he had done for it. In the second telegram Beneš explained that 'our cabinet' (meaning the National Council in Paris) would be completed in Prague. Beneš was to be the foreign minister and Štefánik the minister of war; for the time being, Kramář would 'have the right to sign for you' as the prime minister. 'You, as the President of the Republic, should return at once ... you have boundless authority, and are being expected.'[27]

5

The President

AT a meeting of the Czech deputies in Prague on 14 November 1918, Karel Kramář made public the Geneva agreement of the previous month, between Kramář and the other deputies, and Beneš. Kramář, speaking as the first prime minister of the new state, declared the Habsburg dynasty deposed; Czechoslovakia a republic; and Masaryk its first president.

In fact Emperor Karl had given up any claim to rule his dominions a week before; the Czechoslovak republic was yet to be established. Masaryk was still in America, and was informed of his election by a cable. He later spoke of his surprise at the news,[1] but he knew that Beneš had been working to secure the leading position for him in the new state, and that his work abroad and the victory of the Allies gave him a prestige which no other Czech politician could remotely match.

Straightaway Masaryk sent a message to the Czech troops in Italy, France and Russia about the establishment of the new state. The troops in Italy and France were soon to return to their home country; as for the legion in Russia, 'the dear boys will have to stay a while alongside their allies'.[2]

Masaryk visited President Wilson for the last time on 15 November. He thanked the president for what he had done for the Czechoslovak people, and left the White House with a feeling of relief. He then negotiated a loan for the new state of $10 million, and sailed from New York with his daughter Olga on 20 November. On board ship they celebrated Charlotte Masaryk's birthday with roses in their cabins. Masaryk thought of his previous journeys by sea, and especially of his first crossing to America in 1878. Now, forty years later, a few days after an armistice concluding the most devastating war in history, Masaryk sailed in the opposite direction. His compatriots had made him their president, and he was wondering what this meant, and what kind of a situation he would find at home.

He was old and tired. He had been away from Western Europe since leaving Aberdeen for Russia in May 1917. Those two and a half years had been the most active in his life. He had lost the habit of regular sleep. His brain had been 'always working like a wound-up watch, thinking, comparing, calculating, estimating what the following day would bring on the battlefields and in the ministries of various countries: that constant measuring of distance and deviations from our aim.'[3] On SS *Carmania* he was as happy as a philosopher turned politician could be: his wartime work had succeeded beyond his expectations; there was to be a Czechoslovak state, and Masaryk kept repeating to himself that the Czechs and the Slovaks were really free, and that they were to have their own republic. He did not talk much, and from time to time he thought about the forthcoming peace conference.

In Prague Masaryk was badly needed; Beneš kept on receiving inquiries from there about his arrival. He was needed because he had the authority of the victor behind him, and more. He had, as we know, been close to the Social Democrat Party before the war, and he was trusted by the leaders of the working-class movement much more than, say, Kramář, the prime minister. Though the revolution in Prague at the end of October had been a gentle and gradual takeover of power, there were two streams clearly visible in that movement. Both the socialists and the leaders of the middle-class parties had been agreed on the necessity of building an independent state, but in every other way they had grown apart during the war, and the victory of the Bolsheviks had encouraged the growth of a radical group within the Social Democrat Party.

Karel Kramář, who had admired and then lost the Tsarist regime, was subsequently driven to a position on the far right by the events in Russia. He was certain of Masaryk's influence over the socialists. On 15 November 1918 he wrote to Beneš in Paris:

Our situation is still quite unsettled – there is a lot of lunacy going on here ... our socialists are very afraid of opposition in their own ranks, of Bolshevism, and so the going is a bit hard. You and Masaryk must return soon, you have for the time being – this never happens for long in the Czech lands – unused popularity and authority, and you will certainly succeed in pacifying our partisans of Bolshevism. . . . Masaryk should return as soon as possible, it would have a good effect. Especially now, at a critical time, his influence on the socialists would be very useful. We have here in Prague Bolshevik agitators. . . . Everyone sends you many regards, and they look forward to seeing you. Your office will be up above, at the castle. With affectionate kisses, Yours, Kramář.[4]

The need in Prague, acutely felt by middle-class politicians, was for a *deus ex machina,* for some outside influence capable of integrating divisive political forces. The authority of the Habsburgs had only recently been withdrawn, and life had to be breathed into the instruments of government left behind, especially the Czech parts of the former Austro-Hungarian army and of the bureaucracy. Masaryk was therefore cast in the role of such a benign outside influence; the last sentence in Kramář's letter, 'Your office will be up above, at the castle,' summed up the expectations, as well as the supplication, of the Prague politicians.

The question was whether it was the right role for Masaryk to play, and whether he was not going to disappoint the hopes of both his former friends and his enemies. The war had been the making of Masaryk, and he came out of it a different man. Before the war he had not been conspicuous either for his tactical sense or for the ability to please people. There had been in his politics an uncompromising core, nourished by some religious zeal. This was not an unusual feature in the development of the Czech people, especially in that period just before they passed under the rule of the Habsburgs. Jan Hus had been burnt at the stake on the borderline where medieval religion merged with politics. Czech Protestants, the Union of Czech Brethren in particular, developed such stubbornness under persecution that their compatriots referred to them, with much affection and some incredulity, as 'rams'. When Masaryk was about to found his own party at the turn of the century he wanted to call it the Union of Czech Brethren. A friend of his who went to the foundation meetings of that party thought, looking at the people present, that the name would have been quite appropriate.

We know, on the other hand, that as a young man Masaryk wanted to be a diplomat, and the war provided him with an experience of diplomacy which no other Czech had had in many generations. It was an experience which had a profound effect on the Czechoslovak state and on its citizens. It showed them that major political problems could be solved outside the country, and that exile provided not only political solutions, but also glory for the exiles. The war had taught Masaryk patience and the necessity for compromise, and it changed his views on some important subjects.

The independent state of the Czechs and the Slovaks was his overriding objective, and all his personality and everything he did, was subordinated to that aim. Masaryk, with all his doubts about revolutions, became a revolutionary during the war. He had to learn how to use men in a war, and what their value was as soldiers. He had opposed the conclusion of the war before he achieved his aim; he could therefore appear unreasonable, even bloodthirsty. When the Czechs on the eastern front, who fought on the Russian side, were captured and sometimes executed, Masaryk told 'his boys': 'You will have the opportunity and power to revenge yourselves on those who will fall into your hands, and I hope that there will be many such Germans and Hungarians: an eye for an eye, a tooth for a tooth.'[5]

This was a different Masaryk from the moralizing politician and academic of before the war, and he now had the power to shape the new state. He spent a week in London (arriving there on 29 November), during which time he discussed the situation in Central and East Europe with Steed and Seton-Watson. Reaching Paris on 7 December, Masaryk then met Clemenceau for the first time, and talked to Venizelos and Take Ionescu, the Greek and Romanian politicians, about the organization of small nations in East Europe.

He met Beneš for the first time since his departure to Russia many months before, and they talked about the situation in Prague. Masaryk was pessimistic about it, and said that the beginning would be difficult; he talked to Beneš about the characters of the politicians involved and their histories (much of this was unknown

1 T. G. Masaryk and friends in Leipzig. Sitting, left to right: Masaryk, A. Schlesinger, Karl Göring, Justus Lockwood. Standing: Albert Rindskopf, Gustav Schirmer, Alexander Knopf.

2 T. G. Masaryk after his arrival in Prague, 1877.

3 Charlotte, at the time of her engagement to T. G. Masaryk, 1877.

4 Max Švabinský's drawing of Masaryk, 1902.

5 OPPOSITE TOP: Arrival of T. G. Masaryk in Prague, 1918.

6 BOTTOM: Masaryk with the Czechoslovakian troops in Russia, 1918.

7 Charlotte and Thomas Masaryk, at a *Sokol* festival, Prague 1920.

8 Ramsay Macdonald, President Masaryk, and Dr Beneš, 1925.

9 Thomas Masaryk and grandson, probably taken at Masaryk's Slovak.country house, Topolčianky, 1926.

10 TOP: Francis Crane (Leatherbee) Masaryk and Jan Masaryk.

11 BOTTOM: Thomas and Jan Masaryk, Lány, 1934.

12 OPPOSITE TOP: Thomas Masaryk receiving a doctorate at Oxford University.

13 BOTTOM: Jan Masaryk, Czechoslovakian minister, arriving in London in September 1938.

14 Jan Masaryk and Anthony Eden.

15 Jan Masaryk with a portrait of his father, in his Westminster flat, 1941.

to the younger man, and surprised him) without making the prospects look brighter. When Beneš reminded Masaryk of his newly gained popularity and authority, Masaryk waved the thought away, and said, 'We shall see.' From France, Masaryk went to Italy, where the king and a military parade were awaiting him. On 20 December the train taking Masaryk and a unit of Czechs who had fought in Italy to Prague crossed the border of Bohemia.

His son, Jan, was waiting for him at the border station of Dobříště, and told him that his wife, Charlotte, had been ill and was at that time in a mental home. The party spent the night on the way so as not to arrive in Prague late in the evening. On Saturday 21 December 1918 Masaryk returned to Prague. It was, as a newspaper put it, 'a royal welcome for our first President'. A cannon shot announced the arrival of his train, and it pulled up under the glass and iron arch of the station. Masaryk briefly embraced and kissed his daughter Alice, and the official part of the welcome started at once. Dr Šámal, the founding member of the *Mafie*, who was then the mayor of Prague, stood beside him and they were faced by the members of the government, lined up behind Kramář. Masaryk was wearing a frock-coat, and his friends thought how strange he looked; his face was rather red, his eyes blood-shot. He was excited, and had not been feeling well for some time.

Kramář delivered the welcoming address, and Masaryk listened carefully, with his head slightly tilted towards the speaker. He began his reply with the words: 'Forgive me, but I will not speak at length. In any case, I don't know what I should say to you.' But then his voice broke, and he had to fight back tears; after a few moments his voice steadied and he continued his speech, adding: 'It is the first time in four years that I have been so moved.' After the two speeches Masaryk and Kramář embraced and kissed, and then the ceremony continued. Kramář addressed himself, in a long speech, to the foreign representatives who had arrived with Masaryk, and who were standing on his left: Clement Simon, the first French minister to Prague; General Piccione; and Cunningham, the British military attaché. They replied, one after the other, after which everyone came to shake Masaryk's hand.

The procession then moved from the platform to a long waiting room in the building, which was full of friends of the Masaryk

E

family and people who had helped the cause of the anti-Habsburg revolution. At the end of the room, Šámal introduced Masaryk to the superintendent of the Prague police who had, as Šámal explained, been the 'biggest traitor of all of us'. Masaryk told him that he hoped he would now stop being a traitor. Those people who could get in waited for Masaryk in the big station hall. Singing began as he walked in, and then Jirásek, the distinguished author of historical novels, made another speech of welcome.

An old imperial coach was waiting in front of the station, drawn by four white horses and decorated with white and blue lilac. Masaryk refused to get into it, and got into one of the cars instead. The triumphal procession across Prague began. The car was surrounded by members of the gymnastic organization, *Sokol,* and by Czechs in French, Italian and Russian uniforms. There were more stops, and more speeches. In the square outside the town hall Masaryk looked at the massive statue of Jan Hus, which had been put there in 1915, and which he had not seen before. The procession broke up on the left bank of the river, outside the building of the Diet in the Little Quarter.

The chairman of the National Assembly, in whose car Masaryk had ridden, made a speech, followed by a speech by the Slovak representative in the Assembly. Then Masaryk took his presidential oath, and asked the deputies to come and see him at the castle at two o'clock on the following day. He left the Assembly to visit his wife at a nursing home on the outskirts of the town, and spent the evening at the castle with his friends. He dined with the foreign representatives and several members of his government, and retired to his provisional quarters in the castle at about eleven o'clock. Throughout the evening a choir was singing in one of the castle courtyards.

In the former palace of Czech kings and more recently of Habsburg administrators of the dominions of the crown of Bohemia, Masaryk's head rested uneasily. He hardly slept at all that night; there were many things on his mind. He had just taken his constitutional oath. But he knew that though his present authority was immense, the power basis of that authority was narrow; that his own party, and his circle of political adherents, had been the smallest in Czech politics before the war and that the organization of his party had not grown during the war. He knew well the people who had spent the war in Prague, and their political ambitions. They had at their disposal large organizations, their party newspapers and printing presses, their funds. There was Karel Kramář. In his welcoming speech to Masaryk at the railway station he had said that the Czechs had changed, and that they had a deep admiration for Masaryk's work abroad. He also referred to the suffering of the politicians at home at the hands of the Austro-Hungarian authorities. But he said nothing about his bitter disappointment at the outcome of the revolution in Russia. It is true that, in the distant past, Masaryk and Kramář had thought of each other as political allies. In 1918 Masaryk knew that there would be trouble with Kramář, and with many others more or less like him.

Kramář's political style (it allowed his political biases to become firmly held principles) was reflected in a conversation with Masaryk shortly after the latter's arrival in Prague. It concerned the powers of the president, the powers, in fact, of Masaryk himself. Kramář told Masaryk: 'Thank God we have you, but I beg of you and beseech you, remain above the clouds, because whoever immerses himself in political life here a bit more deeply will not be able to defend himself against mud-slinging, and will lose the authority which he needs so much.'[6] The president was thus to be a symbol, and real political authority would lie elsewhere.

But Masaryk knew the kind of state he wanted. Though he was concerned that it should have an operative central authority, and he himself was prepared to obey the decisions of the government, he would not sit symbolically in his presidential chair, above the clouds. The provisional constitution, as it had been worked out by the Assembly before Masaryk's return, had limited the president's power over the government, and entirely cut out the possibility of direct contact between him and the Parliament. His first address to the Assembly therefore found its way into the records of the Assembly in a roundabout manner, as late as March 1919.

The meeting with the deputies on 22 December 1918 at the castle, which Masaryk had asked for on the day of his arrival, was, technically, not a meeting of the Assembly. He had taken the trouble to send the text of his address to the cabinet by a special messenger from the border station on 20 December; the cabinet had deleted two passages. One of them concerned amnesty for everyone who had worked in the interest of Austria during the war; the other was a warning against antisemitism. Masaryk spoke of the work against the Habsburg Empire abroad, and then moved on quickly to the work of the Paris peace conference, and the question of security and defence of the new state. 'I am certain that the whole people will love our boys as much as I do. I used to be an antimilitarist, and did not like the Austrian army; but we did not organize this army of ours because we were militarists, but to fight for and maintain freedom and democracy. For that defence we have to have our army.'[7]

He referred to the Germans on the territory of the new state: they were to be its citizens, and Masaryk asked them to recognize the new situation. 'The American Republic went to war rather than allow the secession of its south. We shall never allow the secession of our ethnically mixed north.' The Germans of Bohemia and Moravia had hoped to become a part of the German state. After Masaryk's speech, their press conceded that their hopes had been false, and that the Allies at the peace conference would go far to please the Czechs. 'The Germans will have to be satisfied with self-determination of the second class.'

The central part of the speech was the final resolution of the East-West conflict, as it affected the Czechs and the Slovaks. They had nothing to learn from the East, from Russia. Masaryk first approached the question in an oblique way:

> We want to devote ourselves to peaceful work of administration. The basis of democracy lies in administration and autonomy. Democracy does not mean domination, but work for the securing of justice. And justice is the mathematics of humanism.... The Russian revolution has not been, and is not, creative enough, the Russians did not learn to administer, and without administration there can be no democracy. I doubt that Russia, without the assistance of the Allies, will soon be able to help herself.

Masaryk was therefore able to make the point quite bluntly: 'We, the Czechs and the Slovaks, could not stand aside in that fight ... the fate of our nation is quite logically linked with the West, and with its modern democracy.'

Masaryk knew that the chaos and poverty brought about by the war would have a nationally divisive effect in Central and Eastern Europe; he frequently warned the small, newly-created states against the extremes of nationalism and constantly advocated their unity. He was especially concerned with the Germans of Bohemia and Moravia: three days after his return, on 23 December 1918, he made a gesture of conciliation. In the evening of that day Masaryk, together with every member of the cabinet, attended a gala performance at the German theatre in Prague. But the Germans were slow to forgive Masaryk for bringing the Czechs out of the war on the side of the victors, and for describing the Germans in his address on 22 December with a lack of political tact, as 'immigrants and colonists'. When Masaryk was elected to his second term as president, in 1920, the leader of the German deputies in the Parliament shouted 'German immigrants and colonists are leaving!' and walked out, together with other Germans. But before such scenes could take place in the Parliament, the four German districts, as they had been constituted after the withdrawal of Habsburg power – Deutschböhmen, Sudetenland, Südmähren and Böhmerwald Gau – had to be occupied by Czech troops.

There was no reference to Slovakia in Masaryk's address, nor did Prague government exercise effective control over Slovak territory. The Slovaks were, after all, the other constituent nationality of the new state; the Germans, Hungarians and others were to be minority nationalities, protected by minority laws. Masaryk, partly a Slovak himself, found it hard to visualize the difficulties the Slovaks might encounter in the new state; Štefánik, we know, had envisaged a new nationality, the Czechoslovak, into which the Slovaks would gladly merge.

During the war the handful of patriots in Slovakia had been silent until the last possible moment; there were many fewer of them than in the Czech lands, and the Budapest government had no doubt as to its right to rule Slovakia. The Czechs therefore had been making the running with regard to the common state with the Slovaks. They had refused, in the Vienna Parliament, the government's offer of a federal state because the Slovaks were not affected by that offer; again and again, the Czechs said that they wanted no independence for themselves without the Slovaks. There existed in Slovakia a united National Party at the time, and it was up to its leaders to make a response to so much wooing from the Czechs. An extended committee of the party met at Turčanský Sväty Martin on 30 October 1918. Nobody present had heard of the proclamation, two days earlier, of the Czechoslovak state in Prague. Nevertheless the meeting was enthusiastic for freedom and a Czechoslovak state. No steps were taken to translate this enthusiasm into reality. Neither of the two leading Slovak politicians, Vavro Šrobár and Milan Hodža, were present at the main part of the meeting; one of them was in Prague, the other in Budapest. Andrej Hlinka was then among the most enthusiastic speakers for the unity of the Czechs and the Slovaks: 'We are one and one we shall remain. No one and nothing can ever tear us apart.' Such enthusiasm, at any rate on the part of Hlinka, was not to last. He was to lead Slovak opposition to the Prague government and then lay the foundations for the separate state of Slovakia under Hitler's protection.

The only concrete results of the meeting on 30 October were the election of a National Committee of twenty men and the resolution in favour of a Czechoslovak state. It was said again, by the Slovaks themselves, that the 'Slovak nation is a part, linguistically, culturally and historically, of a united Czecho-Slovak nation'. The original text of the resolution contained a demand for Slovak representation at the peace conference. When Milan Hodža, the most decisive and the best informed of the Slovak politicians, arrived from Budapest in the evening of 30 October he made his friends delete that demand. He said that a Czechoslovak government was already in existence abroad, and that it would represent the Slovaks at the peace conference. Hodža also told the delegates about the beginnings of a revolution in Hungary.

On the following day those delegates who stayed on at Turčanský Sväty Martin discussed, among many other matters, Slovak autonomy in the new state. But only a few people were left, and no minutes were kept of the meeting. Out of its ragged end, the rumour of a 'secret clause' in the declaration developed. The secret clause apparently was meant to limit the unitary state to ten years, after which the Slovaks would decide whether they wanted to go on with that arrangement, or opt for autonomy or for complete Slovak independence. Though no one ever saw the 'secret clause', it was to cause bitterness and controversy in the new state.

For the time being the declaration of 30 October 1918 was no more than a declaration of intent. The Slovaks started sending deputies to the National Assembly in Prague, and expected the Czechs to help them win the control of their country from the Hungarians. Scheiner was then the commander of the army, which consisted mainly of Czech volunteers. They were ill-equipped and undisciplined; of the regular troops of the former Austro-Hungarian army, not many wanted to go on fighting. The Czechs assumed that the wind of change would be on their side in Slovakia as well: they were surprised when they ran into stiff Hungarian opposition. By the time Masaryk arrived in Prague, the Czechs had withdrawn from Slovakia, and the country was in the possession of the Hungarian military.

Václav Klofáč, who was known in public for his sentiments against the military, became a minister of war in mid-November. (There was another minister of war in exile, Štefánik, but he was then visiting the Czechoslovak troops in Siberia, and was killed in an air crash on 19 May 1919, when attempting to land his plane outside Bratislava, in Slovakia.) The professional soldiers, who tried to help Klofáč build the new army, did not have an easy time. The prime minister, Kramář, kept on saying that the Czech troops would arrive within the next few days from the Allied countries, and that all would be well. But most of the troops from Russia were not to arrive for almost two years; by the end of January 1919, only three Czechoslovak divisions, one of them from France and two from Italy, had returned home. They were well armed and disciplined, and became the lynch-pin in the construction of the new army.

The operations in Slovakia were conducted under Italian command by General Piccione and then under General Pellé of the French army. But sharp differences between the French and Italian military missions to Slovakia developed, and hampered the conduct of the operations against the Hungarians. Early in the spring of 1919 thirty-two platoons of the former Czechoslovak legion in Italy and seventy platoons of the home Czech army were taking part in the operations in Slovakia. Once again the Czechs became involved in fighting a Communist regime: a

Soviet government, with Bela Kun as its foreign minister, came into power in Budapest in March 1919.

By the end of June, the fighting in Slovakia came to an end. The Czechoslovak republic had by then assumed most of its geographical shape; only the border disputes with the Poles dragged on until 1924. While the fight for Slovakia was going on, the peace conference in Paris dealt with the Czechoslovaks most generously. Their delegation was led by Kramář, and Beneš was also there; it contained experts on every imaginable border dispute. The Czechs retained the border districts inhabited largely by the Germans. The border fixed between Slovakia and Hungary also gave the Slovaks a large Hungarian minority to look after. Finally the Ukrainian territory of Carpathian Ruthenia was tagged on to the new state, giving it a common border with Romania.

The work of Masaryk during the war, and his loyalty to the Western Allies, was largely responsible for their magnanimity to the new Czechoslovak state during the peace conference. Czechoslovakia emerged on the side of the victors; the Germans of Bohemia and Moravia had clearly not been on the winning side, and they were now unable to exercise political choice. Nevertheless it was natural for the Czechs to want their lands to make a compact unit, with the natural defences and the important industries of the border areas; Masaryk supported those ambitions, and sought, at the same time, an understanding with the Germans.

Slovakia was a different matter. The Czechs had lived through an industrial evolution which had lasted a century; the Slovaks were predominantly an agricultural people. They had lived for centuries in a different civilization from the Czechs, under Hungarian rule. Nevertheless the Czechs and the Slovaks wanted to live in a common state; separately their numbers were too small, even at a time when the creation of small states was the order of the day. Masaryk understood and greatly encouraged that trend, though he could see no reason why the two peoples should not eventually grow into one. The founders of Czechoslovakia were therefore not very interested in Slovak autonomy; even Štefánik thought that the Slovaks would do well to merge with the Czechs. Nevertheless the argument concerning Slovak autonomy flared up intermittently before and after the Second World War, until 1969, when Czechoslovakia became a federal state.

There was another feature of the union between the Czechs and the Slovaks which went largely unnoticed at the time. There is no evidence that it was considered by Masaryk during the First World War, nor was there any trace of it in political writing in Czechoslovakia after the war. The matter can be put quite simply. By their union with the Slovaks, the Czechs acquired a direct link with the East: the centre of geographical – and political – gravity of the new state lay much further to the east than the centre of the Czech lands alone.

Anyone travelling east of Prague notices even nowadays (more than half a century ago the differences were even sharper) the differences between the Czech lands and Slovakia, and, going further, the similarities between Slovakia and the Ukraine. Despite their frequent historical conflicts with the Germans, the Czechs had always remained anchored, though sometimes insecurely, in the Western orbit. The Slovaks, on the other hand, were linked, by their habits, their economic and historical developments, with the East and the eastern plains rather than with Western Europe. Masaryk, with his pro-Western orientation, welcomed the Slovak connection, and more. The president and his government also gratefully acepted, from the hands of the victors, Carpathian Ruthenia, a gift of questionable value. It further undercut the claim of the government in Prague to run a national state; it complicated the administration of the state and extended its border. And this eastward extension of Czechoslovakia took place at a time when the Russians were fighting their own civil war, and were unable to pay much attention to the outside world, and under the presidency of Masaryk, whose policies and preferences lay elsewhere.

It is however time to turn away from Slovakia and look at the centre of political action in Prague. Here, Masaryk's influence was even greater than on the shaping of the frontiers of the new state. We remember the conversation between Masaryk and Kramář, and how Kramář wanted to keep the reality of political power, and how the president was to be merely its symbol. Masaryk had asked the deputies of the National Assembly to visit him at the castle the day after he arrived in Prague, but his address to them was treated as if it had never happened. A few weeks after his arrival Masaryk started growing visibly restless and unhappy

about the place where he was about to be put as the first president
of Czechoslovakia.

Political amity – almost a complete truce – was first broken
when Masaryk publicly attacked the politicians who had shaped
the provisional constitution. He said that their improvised constitutional handiwork bore every mark of the dilettante, and that
it would not last. It did not. The constitution had other critics
besides Masaryk, and other supporters besides Kramář. One of
the latter, for instance, warned that:

> If the matter concerned Masaryk alone, it would really be very
> simple. We perhaps would not hesitate to entrust him, for the
> time being, with the whole power of the state, because we have
> unlimited trust in him. But is it a matter only of this president?
> Have all the future possibilities been taken into consideration?
> A mediocre, even an incapable person could become the
> president; and should we put the greater part of the state power
> into the hands of this unknown person?[8]

Masaryk however persisted. He wanted to have the constitutional
right of direct contact with the cabinet, and with the Parliament as
well as its committees. One of the chief draftsmen of the constitution then explained that he had not realized the extent to which
the powers of the president would be limited in practice. Kramář
became isolated inside his own party (which was no longer called
Young Czech but National Democrat). Most of Kramář's colleagues
wanted the presidency to be a strong one. Limitations on the
powers of the president in fact became a left-wing cause, supported
mainly by the Social Democrats.

The debate was then transferred into the constitutional committee of the National Assembly, and this committee gave Masaryk
what he wanted, and more. The government was to have, according
to the provisional constitution, seventeen members: the amendment gave the president the right to decide himself the number
of cabinet ministers. The other amendment, passed by the National
Assembly on 23 May 1919, gave the president the right to nomin-
ate the government; to be in touch with it by writing or in person;
to chair the meetings of the cabinet, without having a vote; to
address the Parliament on the state of the republic; to recommend
certain measures to Parliament, and to return laws to Parliament

for reconsideration. An impressive list of presidential powers: Masaryk had won his first battle at home.

He won it against the opposition of his former allies, the Social Democrats, the largest, but also the most vulnerable party in the National Assembly. It had three members in Kramář's cabinet, a representation which did not reflect the real strength of the party. But the vulnerability of the Social Democrats derived from another source. A social revolution had taken place in Russia. In the territory of the former Habsburg monarchy, the two strongest peoples, the Germans and the Hungarians, also gave their own revolutions a socialist stamp: the Germans in Austria had opted for a moderate socialism, which proved more lasting; the Hungarians had their short-lived Soviet republic. The Germans and the Hungarians knew that, whatever happened, they would at least have their own state. Their revolutions were therefore concerned rather with social reform than with the creation of a state. The Czech revolution in October 1918 – if so peaceful an event deserves such a violent name – had a much more national character. The Czechs made certain of their own state first. In that way social reform had to take place after national revolution, and the Social Democrats after the middle-class parties.

A large party, therefore, torn between two loyalties: to the new state and to its own constituency, the hungry, war-weary masses. For a time it looked as if the stability of Czechoslovakia – and perhaps even Masaryk's own political future – would depend on the success of the Social Democrats in solving their political dilemma, and involving in the state-making process a popular movement which scorned every form of political authority.

Within the Social Democrat Party itself, there was much controversy. It is worth bearing in mind that until 1918 and the end of the Habsburg monarchy, the Social Democrats had never been admitted into any government and that they themselves refused any co-operation with the middle-class parties. But they joined Kramář's government, although the socialists' presence in the cabinet had not been approved by the party congress. It took place in December 1918, and had to establish whether the habits of the past no longer applied, and whether it was safe for socialists to co-operate with the middle classes.

Those Social Democrats who had favoured, early in the war

the survival of Austria-Hungary and who had later not taken much interest in the movement for national independence, formed the left wing of the party; they were joined by some of the younger comrades. Social reform remained their main concern. Their opponents, therefore, were the adherents of Masaryk and advocates of co-operation with the middle-class parties. They were the nationalists within Social Democracy.

A week after the arrival of Masaryk in Prague, those two groups set out to contest the adherence of the Czech workers. On the left there existed enthusiasm for Russian Bolshevism. Debating at the party congress was interrupted by 'The Bolsheviks are right!' and other cries; a delegate dismissed the Czechoslovak troops in Russia as 'executioners of the Russian revolution'. The proper row then began. A patriotic Social Democrat jumped on the platform and shouted 'Long live the Legion! Long live the Czechoslovak republic!' and scored a temporary emotional victory. One of the younger men, Antonín Zápotocký, who represented Kladno, the heavy industry district near Prague, and who was soon to become one of the founders of the Communist Party and, many years later, the second Communist president of Czechoslovakia, pointed out that: 'The comrades who had helped to break up the old Austrian state came into too close a contact with the bourgeoisie.... I think that the time has come to stop going in the national direction and start socialist, proletariat policy.'[9]

The Social Democrat left wing therefore opposed any co-operation with the middle-class parties and, by doing so, it spoke in terms to which party members had been accustomed. Far-reaching concessions were made, in the final resolution of the congress, to the left wing: it asked for the nationalization of the mines, water power, railways, armament factories, and of all monopolies. But all this was to be done gradually, using the 'instruments of democratic constitution of the republic'; only the expropriation of large estates was to go ahead straightaway.

Masaryk, who had decided to stand aside from the parties without making any one of them his own, did not renew his pre-war association with the Social Democrats. On the contrary. He came under constant pressure from them concerning his own powers as president and, especially, legislation for far-reaching social reform. The party had also been strongly pacifist before the war, and was not much help to Masaryk in the course of the construction of the new Czechoslovak army. But all these were domestic matters: the pressure from the right on Masaryk was of a different kind. It mainly concerned foreign policy, and arose out of the differences between himself and Kramář.

Here Beneš, the foreign minister, had to bear the main brunt of the onslaught. He returned to Prague from the peace conference on 24 September 1919. In his first speech to the National Assembly, addressing himself to the problem of Russia, he said:

> It is very likely that the question of the internal organization of Russia will go on tearing apart the whole Russian people and that its intervention in world politics cannot be expected, for a long time. In these circumstances it is necessary to maintain a certain reserve, because our relationship with Russia is one of the most vital problems of our existence, and any politician aware of his responsibilities must take serious account of these questions.

But reserve was the last thing Kramář could maintain with regard to Russia. He had been replaced as prime minister by Tusar, a Social Democrat, in July 1919, and he was rather at a loose end. In a speech on 4 October, he put forward an extreme view on the policy of intervention. It was not enough for him that the Czechoslovak troops in Russia had been drawn into internal Russian conflicts, and that they were fighting the Soviets. He was certain that a few thousand volunteers could be found in Czechoslovakia, who 'in agreement with the Allies, and together with brother Yugoslavs, and with Russian prisoners of war, would go and meet our boys in Siberia, so that they could come home as soon as possible, not via Vladivostok, but victoriously, through Moscow'.[10]

Kramář made the speech and left for Paris. His party newspaper announced that from Paris he would go on to Odessa, in order to 'lay the definitive foundations for a new Russia'. Kramář was then afraid that the Russians would get rid of the Bolsheviks on their own, without his help, and he very much wanted the Czechs to stake their claim to the gratitude of the Russians in the future. When it came to Russia, Kramář simply could not be trusted.

The invitation to Kramář came from Maklakov, the former

Tsarist ambassador to Paris. He had asked Kramář to go to Russia and visit Denikin, the most promising counter-revolutionary leader to date. It is very likely that when he attended the peace conference Kramář took the concern of Allied politicians with the turn of internal affairs in Russia too literally; he mentioned the idea to Beneš during the conference, who agreed with the plan. But when Beneš returned to Prague he realized that any such enterprise would become the subject of the fiercest domestic controversy. Masaryk was concerned with the opposition of the left Social Democrats; Tusar, the prime minister, disapproved of Kramář's journey and rebuked Beneš for having agreed to it in the first place. Masaryk then asked Beneš whether he could try and stop Kramář going; Beneš tried, and earned Kramář's wrath and lasting enmity. A tense meeting took place between the two men a few hours before Kramář's departure.

Nevertheless a few days later Kramář and his friend Maklakov were on board a French warship; they carried with them a French foreign ministry declaration on the Russian question for Denikin, and a draft constitution for Russia, which Kramář had worked out with Boris Savinkov's help. Kramář travelled hopefully to Russia and was glad to be away from Prague. Czechoslovakia was not the kind of state he had had in mind before the war. A young foreign minister daring to tell him what to do; Czechoslovak politics too disorderly for his liking, too unpredictable; and no strong ties developing with other Slav countries.

Kramář blamed Masaryk for this. Russia, Kramář thought, would redeem his failure in Czechoslovakia, and he saw the future of Czechoslovakia only within the context of his Slav policy. Most of all, he disapproved of Masaryk's remark that his, Masaryk's, most important achievement during the war had been that he 'did not give in to the Russian orientation'. But when he arrived in South Russia, Kramář was shattered by what he found there. 'People whom we used to know as rich and elegant are hard pressed, near poverty.' The Russia Kramář had known was no longer there; the magnificent villa in the Crimea was no longer his. He wanted to reconcile Denikin with the exiles and with the Ukrainians, and in this he failed as well. Kramář returned to Paris, a bitterly disappointed man, on 23 November 1919.

Meanwhile, in Prague, Tusar's coalition with the Agrarians,

the 'red-green' coalition, saw a number of social laws through the Parliament, and Masaryk did not object that they had to be partly funded by foreign loans. Civil servants' salaries were reviewed, and a law on war pensions was passed; there was a law on miners' participation in the running of their own industry and in its profits; the requirement that schoolmistresses should remain unmarried was scrapped.

Of the major acts of socialization, only one had been passed. This was the land reform act, which was published on 16 May 1919 in its draft, 'framework' form: many important details still remained to be written into the law. The main part of the act provided for estates over a certain size to be confiscated; they were not nationalized, but put under the temporary administration of the state. One of the deputies remarked that: 'These few paragraphs completely strike out landed aristocracy from the future history of the nation.' The reform was an act of revenge reaching back three centuries, when land passed under the control of those families which were prepared to be Catholic and loyal to the Habsburg dynasty. Very few Czechs expected the reform to bring about more efficient agriculture. It was seen rather as an act of national justice.

Land reform was an isolated act of the kind of legislation envisaged earlier, which included the nationalization of the mining and metallurgy industries. In these matters Masaryk and his early governments were unwilling to go too far; the president himself did a lot to soothe unrest among the workers. His travels in 1919 and 1920 took him largely to the industrial districts of Bohemia and Moravia. He visited Pilsen and its important Škoda plant in May 1919; in October he talked on the subject of revolution at the workers' centre in Hradec Králove; the first anniversary of the republic provided an occasion for a speech by Masaryk on socialism, Bolshevism, and intervention in Russia.

Masaryk was elected president for the second time on 25 May 1920. Tusar's government lasted till September, and after that Masaryk had to take out of the drawer a popular Habsburg device for dealing with political impasse: government by the civil servants. At the same time Masaryk visited other industrial and mining centres, in a situation much tenser than the year before. He was conciliatory: 'I was a worker myself, and I have always felt with you, and still feel with you.' He said that the Social Democrat Party was in the middle of a crisis – this was why its ministers had resigned – and added: 'You can be certain that in order to overcome the crisis, and you are now in the middle of it, you need brains and not fists. Remember it well!' Having said that, Masaryk turned straightaway to Russia: 'I know Bolshevik Russia well, I observed the Bolshevik revolution very carefully. I say here, according to my best knowledge and conscience that the Russian example is unsuitable for us, the Czechs ... in Bohemia we need a way, a method of work, a method of social changes, according to our own customs and according to our own needs.'[11]

It was however becoming increasingly difficult for Masaryk to reconcile the whole working-class movement to his policies. On the one hand, Beneš had written to Masaryk from the peace conference in Paris that it would be unwise for Czechoslovakia to have a Social Democrat prime minister, because he would frighten the other delegates; on the other hand, many socialists opposed any kind of participation in the government. As a journalist put it, 'Nobody then knew how to speak to the socialist left': the unity of the party, so much talked about and so much desired by many socialists, was no longer a tenable proposition.

The difficulties inside the Social Democrat Party culminated in the suppression of *Rudé Právo*, the newspaper of the socialist left. A general strike was declared in December 1920. Those Social Democrat members on the right wing of the party who had directed the action against *Rudé Právo* also kept in touch with the police who moved swiftly against the strikers. The strike was called off after three days of numerous clashes between the police and the strikers, and many arrests.

The bitterness and controversy after the general strike led to the final split within the working-class movement. The foundation congress of the Communist Party met in May 1921. Despite its deep differences with Masaryk and his governments, it took part in the parliamentary processes of the republic. In the elections of 1925 the Communist Party sent the second largest delegation to the Parliament. In contrast to all the other Czechoslovak parties, the Communist organization embraced members of all the nationalities of the state.

Nevertheless the Communists led an isolated political life. Adopting the attitude previously held by the Social Democrats, the Communists would not co-operate with the middle-class parties. They were potentially powerful and feared, but kept themselves outside the main stream of political life. After some hard fights party leadership came into the hands of those Communists who wanted to follow Lenin and his Russian experience. The struggle was finally concluded in 1929. Klement Gottwald was then appointed the general secretary of the party, and the emphasis in party work was shifted to the factories and trade unions.

But Masaryk's loyal friend, his biographer Herben, was of the opinion that the main threat to Masaryk did not come from the Communists. When he discussed these matters, he remarked that: 'The future must know how difficult it was to live in a nation which had been liberated, but not yet educated for liberty.'[12] The attacks on Masaryk repeated the pattern we have had occasion to note before the war. They came from people who played the political game according to the same rules as Masaryk.

These attacks again centred on Masaryk as an outsider; on the fact that, during the war, he had come into prominence abroad and not at home. One of his adversaries maintained that while Kramář had been living in the shadow of the gallows, Masaryk had been enjoying life under the peaceful skies of Switzerland.

The relationship between Masaryk and Beneš also came under close scrutiny. Masaryk was accused of designating Beneš as his successor as early as 1919 and it was hinted at a political dinner that the two men were so close that they must have something to hide. The rumours and accusations were fed especially by those Czechs who returned to Prague from abroad, and who had had differences with Masaryk or Beneš during the war; the atmosphere in the new state was shot through by suspicion and nerviness and every rumour gained credulous listeners. In the National Assembly, for instance, at a meeting of the chairmen of the party clubs, the leader of the Catholic People's Party, Dr Šrámek, said that it would be 'in the gentlemen's interest if they publicly rendered account of the collection [of monies] abroad, because many wild rumours are in circulation'. Tusar, the Social Democrat, came to the defence of Masaryk and Beneš: 'Sir, it is well known that revolutions are not made on the basis of double-entry book-keeping.'[13]

Beneš in particular became an easy target for many attacks. He had to defend himself in the Parliament in 1920, when he sued the authors of libellous pamphlets. At a court hearing in November 1920 a written submission by Masaryk was read out. Masaryk stated that, during the war, he had himself controlled the finances of the Czechoslovak movement abroad; that only when he left for Russia in May 1917 had financial control passed to Beneš. Masaryk pointed out that Beneš had his own money, and that he had given some to Masaryk for his own trip abroad. 'It is a great coarseness to talk of financial irregularities in connection with the work of Dr Beneš abroad. Whoever has given his life to a great idea, and worked in the shadow of death, as Dr Beneš has, would use money only as a means to his aim.'[14]

On his return to Prague in December 1918 Masaryk had not felt well; he suffered from recurrent colds and influenza. He returned to Prague castle from the country in January 1921 and came down with a severe angina, which was complicated by thrombosis in the leg. He stayed in bed for three months; his will to live and his physical toughness saw him through the ordeal. In May Masaryk was well enough to travel to Capri to recuperate; his friend and the chairman of Živnobanka, one of the largest of the Czech banks, Dr Preiss, provided two million crowns for the trip.

The trip to Capri reminded Masaryk of the pleasures of foreign travel. He returned to the island again in the following year, in June 1922, and started writing his war memoirs there. In 1923 he went on state visits to France, Belgium and England. Before the state visits Masaryk had spent a month in the Mediterranean, and on the North African coast. In 1924 he went south again, to Taormina in Sicily, for an extended family holiday. Alice and Jan came to Taormina with their father, as well as Herbert's widow and her two little girls. Masaryk's doctor and two secretaries travelled with the party which was later joined by Beneš, who had come to Italy to see Mussolini.

Masaryk was then seventy-four years old, and he had not yet discussed his retirement with anyone. He had become a public person, snatching privacy whenever he could. But he gladly made himself available for public functions, and no strain or dislike of those occasions were visible. The war had interrupted his family life, and it never returned to him. Masaryk, the most unsentimental of people, never complained. The holiday in Taormina was a rare interlude, which had had to be carefully planned. By then, the family itself had been severely depleted. Masaryk's eldest son, Herbert, had died during the war; a memorial exhibition of his painting was arranged in Prague soon after the war. Charlotte Masaryk had died at Lány, Masaryk's country house, on 13 May 1923; though she had lived with her husband since his return to Prague, there were frequent breaks for her treatment at a nursing home. Olga, who had been her father's companion during the war, was married to a Swiss doctor called Revilliod. Alice was busy with her Red Cross work, and a place had been found for Jan in the diplomatic service.

When his public functions were over, Masaryk was often a lonely man. He lived either at the castle in Prague, a magnificent complex of buildings with a number of grand and many rather poky rooms, or at Lány, a country house which was a short drive to the west of Prague. There was another country house at Topolčianky in Slovakia, which Masaryk used for longer stays during the summer. In the country he rode a lot and read novels in the evenings. His favourite dress consisted of riding breeches, a jacket which buttoned all the way up to the neck and bore a reasonable resemblance to the conventional Central European hunting jacket, and a cap decorated with a red and white ribbon, as a compliment to his legionaries. In the summer he preferred white or light-coloured clothes. All his hats were broad-brimmed. He was lean and fairly tall. His public image was carefully constructed and highly stylized: he was simply and elegantly dressed in a way country people would expect of a slightly idiosyncratic country gentleman. He was always presented as leading an active, ascetic and athletic life, underscored by deep reflection on matters concerning the intellect and politics. Not many jokes seem to have originated at the castle, though the figure, and the face especially, of President Masaryk lent itself to loving caricature.

It was then often said, and not always by Masaryk's enemies, that the Czechs had expected a president to return after the war and, instead, a professor came back. There is no doubt that the

Czechs expected too much of Masaryk – the 'father' or 'little father' or, for state occasions, the 'Liberator' of public currency – and that he was bound to disappoint them, at least occasionally. The politicians perhaps expected Masaryk to put behind him some of the former, pre-war animosities: to be, in fact, politically and personally more all-embracing, and help to heal the rifts produced by the war. Masaryk did not do badly in this regard, though his old habits asserted themselves from time to time.

Before the war he had narrowed his political base to the extent of running the smallest party in the country. He did not have the time and the taste for the personality conflicts and the com-promises usually required of members of a large party. He had warned Beneš, towards the end of the war, of the various person-ality conflicts built into Czech politics. After the war Masaryk preferred to run the most powerful office in Czechoslovakia on lines similar to those on which he had run the Realist Party before the war. We know that he felt at ease and even very happy with his students at the university, or with his followers in the party, or with the soldiers in his legion during the war, who were entirely dedicated to him. There was a whiff of the *Mafie*, of a secret organization, about Masaryk's activities; the name was applied to them, on two occasions, not entirely as a joke. Masaryk's personality attracted, and perhaps demanded, dedication.

In politics, however, there is a price to be paid for so much exclusiveness. Masaryk and Beneš had their offices at Prague castle; the two men were in constant and close touch, and other politicians resented that relationship. It seemed to leave too little of the president's time for them. Přemysl Šámal, another close friend of Masaryk, was the head of the president's chancery. Scheiner, the banker and the head of the *Sokol* organization, and Preiss, the chairman of Živnobanka, were also in constant and close touch with the castle. Alois Rašín, one of the founding members of the wartime *Mafie*, who successfully set up an independent Czecho-slovak currency as minister of finance after the war, also belonged to the president's inner circle.

The idea that there should be a new *Mafie*, some kind of a close-knit state council, was first expressed by Šámal late in 1921; by then, the six men – Masaryk, Beneš, Scheiner, Rašín, Preiss and Šámal – had been meeting regularly for some time. It was a powerful group, with far-reaching influence on the domestic, financial and foreign policies of the Czechoslovak state. The 'castle group' went on existing as long as Masaryk remained at the castle. Its composition changed from time to time. Alois Rašín, who was assassinated by a Communist student early in 1923, was the first casualty. Karel Čapek, the author, also became closely connected with the group; he was devoted to Masaryk, and did much to create the president's image, and put across his views on the policies of the new state.

Masaryk's *Mafie* at the castle was matched by a similar group of politicians, which was usually referred to as the 'Five'. It was to have a strong and lasting influence on the shaping of the state. After his return to Prague, Masaryk decided not to become associated with any political party: in an emergency, he could rely on the loyalty of the *Sokol* organization. Eventually, when Beneš joined the National Socialists, the party became a loyal supporter of Masaryk's and Beneš's policies. Nevertheless Masaryk's style of running Czechoslovakia was based on the interaction between the 'castle' group and the 'Five', representing the major political parties.

The civil servants' cabinet in 1920 could not rely on majority support in the Parliament; political governments, on the other hand, always consisted of heterogeneous coalitions, which fell apart because of internal fission rather than defeat in the elections. Political life moved from crisis to crisis, and parties tended to represent social and national pressure groups. The main task before the prime minister of a coalition government was therefore keeping the representatives of those pressure groups together. He had little time left for ruling the country.

Such was the situation in which the five-party consortium came into being, when the need for it was especially felt by the civil servants' government. The general strike and Masaryk's illness had provided a background of uncertainty; the 'Five' considered the question of Masaryk's successor. The people and parties involved were Rašín, representing the National Democrats and the only direct link with Masaryk's group; Švehla, the leader of the powerful Agrarian Party; Rudolf Bechyně, a Social Democrat of right-wing convictions; Jiří Stříbrný, the deputy chairman of the National Socialist Party, a journalist and owner of two popular dailies, who later joined the ranks of Czech fascists; and Jan Šrámek, representing the clericals.

Those men were the regular members of the Five. Their contacts with the castle group varied, with Stříbrný and Šrámek being less in touch with the castle than other members of the group. (The clericals held it against Masaryk that, as a resident of the castle, he had never set foot in the chapel of St Wenceslas, in the Catholic cathedral only a few steps from Masaryk's office and living quarters.) When one of the members of the Five was ill, or out of favour with his own party, or cross with the other members of the Five, a replacement for him was sent; Antonín Švehla was usually the chairman of the group.

At a time when German deputies amused themselves by throwing stink bombs in the Parliament, and when the Czech and Slovak parties found it easier to quarrel than to agree on constructive policies, the basic task of the Five was to organize the Parliament, and make it agree on essential legislation. Though the theory behind the institution of the Five was put down on paper only once, in an article by Rudolf Bechyně in 1922, there was never any doubt about its functions.

The Five was attacked again and again. There was no place for it, it was said, in the constitution; it usurped the powers of the Parliament. Bechyně pointed out that three hundred members did not constitute a parliament and that, without leadership, the Parliament could not legislate and, still less, lead the nation. 'The Five wants to be no more and no less than the leader of the Parliament', Bechyně argued, because otherwise the Parliament would become a divisive factor in the society.

We are a part of the most complex society in human history. The mechanics of capitalist production and market have torn the world into hostile peoples, have torn the people into classes and classes into groups. . . . Formal democracy knows of only one means to steer the state through these storms: an elected parliament. Every deputy brings to this common ground a part of the struggle which, outside, dissolves and decimates life. They bring it in order to continue the struggle, and regulate it by law.

Bechyně also remarked that the geographic position and ethnic composition of the state, and the political and social structure of its peoples were more complex than elsewhere, and that the conflicts were therefore bound to go deeper.

'Side by side within the Parliament,' Bechyně wrote, 'there sits a hungry stomach and dear flour; the mine owner's profit and the miner's wage; expensive fares and the necessities of life for the railwaymen; cheap flour from Romania and expensive rolls at a Prague baker's; the civil servant's power and the banker's interest; the official language of the state and the self-esteem of the Germans.'[15] The Five, Bechyně summed up, was therefore a necessity: the reverse side of chaos. The Czech parties, Bechyně could have added, had been used to being in opposition in Vienna for decades, and being in opposition became for them such a habit that it prevented them noticing the change in their political circumstances. Czech politicians therefore knew a lot about being in opposition and little about running the country; when they were faced with authority, their hackles rose instantly.

The Five therefore became a 'specialist workshop for compromise', which dampened down party conflict and laid down the ground rules for coalition government. As a by-product of their main work, the members of the Five also had to introduce discipline into their own parties, and set down the limits on the freedom of their actions. The Five became the real government behind the administration of the civil servants and in that way it became the target for much criticism. Masaryk, in his New Year's address in 1922, approved of the origins and the work of the Five. It did not contain any of Masaryk's rivals, and certainly not a single irreconcilable enemy. It made the running of the country much easier than it would have been otherwise.

The Five, with the castle group, introduced a particular style of government into Czechoslovakia. It was a government based on the consensus of the majority, and this meant the middle- and lower-middle-class Czech population, supported by as much of the Czech working class as the Social Democrats and the National Socialists could muster between them, and by the Agrarians. By October 1926, however, when the Agrarian leader Švehla formed another coalition government, the original Five had broken up. The National Democrats went into opposition, and their place in the government was taken by the Germans. There were two German ministers in the government: Dr Spina for the Agrarians, and

Mayer-Harting for the Christian Socialists. Both were professors at the German University in Prague. They joined the government after the treaty of Locarno, when Germany entered the League of Nations. For the time being it looked as if Masaryk's work for conciliation between the Czechs and the Germans would succeed.

German parties in the government also played a key role in the second presidential election in May 1927; without their help, Masaryk would not have remained in office. By 1926 his relationship with Kramář and the National Democrats had reached its lowest ebb and criticism of Masaryk and his style of government also became sharper. Many politicians – they were by no means all National Democrats – felt as if political life was going on elsewhere, not in the Parliament and the other usual places of business. But the Czechs and the Slovaks had no one whom they could put into Masaryk's place; Kramář, who had been his only serious rival, had proved his political uselessness on several occasions, usually in connection with Russia.

Despite his various idiosyncrasies and his old age, Masaryk stood head and shoulders above other politicians, and when criticism at home became too much for him, he had a number of ways in which he could frighten his compatriots. He could threaten resignation; or go abroad; or ask his friends to come to his aid. Before the presidential election in 1927 Masaryk tried them all. Support from his foreign friends was especially welcome, and received much publicity in Prague. The Czechs, with their xenophilia, enjoyed hearing about their failings from foreigners.

On the occasion of the anniversary of the foundation of the state, for instance, Masaryk's friend Seton-Watson (he then held the Masaryk Chair of Central and East European History at London University which was funded by the Czechoslovak government) said of the criticism of Masaryk: 'Fortunately not much of it has reached the English press. As an admirer of Czechoslovakia, I must express my disgust with the fact that such attacks can be made against the president and the foreign minister, whose prestige in Europe stands so high. The originators of these attacks must realize that they are stabbing the Czechoslovak state in the back.'[16]

In March 1927 Masaryk visited the League of Nations, unofficially attending one of its meetings. He left Geneva for Egypt,

Palestine and Greece, and he did not return to Prague until a few days before the election on 27 May. Kramář had been unable to summon enough courage to oppose Masaryk at the election, but his party and Hlinka's Slovak People's Party withdrew their support from Masaryk. The Communists put forward their own candidate, Václav Šturc, a little-known journalist who was expelled from the party three years later. For the second time Masaryk was elected president for seven years. He succeeded because of the support of the German votes. German Agrarians and Christian Socialists were joined by the Social Democrats, with their seventeen votes; together with his Czech supporters, they gave Masaryk just over the required three-fifths majority in the Parliament.

In 1928 the Czechoslovak republic celebrated its tenth anniversary; two years later, Masaryk his eightieth birthday. It still looked as if Masaryk would succeed in reconciling the contradiction between the desire of the Czechs to run their own state, and the necessity to concede full minority rights to the Germans and other peoples in Czechoslovakia. (At the time of her foundation, Czechoslovakia contained a 23·4 per cent German minority, 5·6 per cent Hungarian, 3·4 per cent Ukrainian, 0·6 per cent Polish and 1·3 per cent Jewish.) But the Germans never became reconciled to the Czech-run state: their historical memories and their economic strength made them regard conciliation as submission. Then the economic crisis came, and the rise of Hitler to power. Czechoslovak politics were becoming more and more fragmented. In the first twelve years of Czechoslovakia's existence, her peoples were ruled by ten governments; after 1930 the forming and reforming of governments and of political parties continued at a fast pace.

Some time before his own death in December 1938 Karel Čapek, the chronicler of Masaryk's life and his friend, said that the president had been clever in everything, including the choice of the time of his death in 1937. Masaryk, it is true, did not see the physical destruction of the state he had created, but he was not spared witnessing the first signs of mortal danger to that state. A special law was passed, by the National Assembly in 1930, that 'T. G. Masaryk deserved great merit of the state'. The Roman-style recognition of his services was a present for Masaryk's eightieth birthday. In the same year Masaryk spoke openly of 'those who are on principle against the republic and against democracy; there can be no agreement with them. Nor can there be any agreement with those, who are disappointed with the rewards of the revolution.'[17]

Masaryk was still optimistic, and said that he had every confidence in the future of the state. But the economic and political crisis pushed the men around him into new and unexpected positions. The civil war of Europe continued, despite Masaryk, who was convinced that it had stopped sometime around the day of the armistice. Jiří Stříbrný, a member of the original Five, was the first example of the way men could be changed by events, and of the direction which politics might take. In 1931 the Parliament set up a commission of inquiry into allegations of Stříbrný's corrupt practices; Stříbrný survived the inquiry to organize his fascist party.

He had left the National Socialist Party, of which he was the deputy chairman, in 1926. He had come into conflict with Beneš, who needed a political party to adopt him, and the National Socialists seemed the most suitable organization. In the same year, Stříbrný founded his own Slav National Socialist Party. He was joined by Karel Pergler, who had been Masaryk's dedicated secretary in America and who very much wanted to become the Czechoslovak minister to Washington after the war; Jan Masaryk went to Washington instead. The two men were supported by Gajda, a former general who had been stripped of his rank, and who had played a major role in leading the Czech troops in Russia into conflict with the Bolsheviks in the spring of 1918.

There was therefore to be no democratic Five for Stříbrný, but an association which was known as the 'three musketeers'. His party was renamed the National League in 1930; four years later the development of the fascist movement was completed when the National Union was born. In 1934 Kramář merged his National Democrats with the Union, and all the Czech fascists were concentrated in one organization. The point should be made here that, apart from the ways in which it fed on the successes of similar movements abroad, Czech fascism had its own local and very personal roots in the sources of men's past disappointments and envy.

The four fascist leaders had one thing in common: they were people who, in Masaryk's words, were 'disappointed with the rewards of the revolution'. They had had differences with Beneš, or with Masaryk, and they became bitterly hostile to the two men, and everything they stood for. In the case of Kramář there was no other way out of his political and personal disappointments. He blamed Masaryk for encouraging the Bolshevik trend in Czechoslovakia, and he did so against all visible evidence. In a letter to Masaryk written during the Paris peace conference, Kramář had referred to the 'Bolshevik-socialist policy' which was being pursued in Prague, and he never gave up that way of looking at the policies of Masaryk and Beneš. In Prague and in Russia the 'Bolsheviks' were Kramář's main enemies.

Nevertheless Stříbrný, Kramář and Pergler were all well known to Masaryk; Gajda had been one of the commanders of Masaryk's troops in Russia. The men who had founded the Communist Party, perhaps with the exception of Šmeral, and who came to run it towards the first decade after its foundation, had been educated in an entirely different political school. Nobody in the government, and very few people in the Parliament, knew much about them or how to talk to them. They fought the 'revisionists' – the Social Democrats who were prepared to co-operate with the middle-class parties – very hard. We know that in 1929 Klement Gottwald became the general secretary of the party, and a member of the National Assembly. Gottwald had been a member of the executive of the Communist International since 1928; he knew Masaryk slightly better than, many years ago, Masaryk had known, say, Emperor Franz Josef.

There had always existed a state of mutual incomprehension between the Communist Party and Masaryk's governments. From time to time incomprehension turned into bitter hostility. This happened again and again during the economic crisis in the early 1930s, and the hostility survived Masaryk and the first Czechoslovak republic. For instance, early in 1931 a clash took place between the gendarmerie and unemployed miners in the Duchcov coal district; four miners were killed and five seriously injured. They were by no means all socialists; one of them happened to be a member of Kramář's National Democrat Party.

Shortly after the demonstration, on 5 February 1931, Gottwald told the National Assembly:

Real peace and order, the kind of peace and order which we are fighting for, will be achieved only when you hang from the lampposts. Don't think that workers can be shot like rabbits, don't think that workers will forget the sacrifices which they are making in the fight for their existence, don't think that workers will forgive their murderers. The Communists and with them everyone, even your Social Democrat and National Socialist workers, will ask you to render accounts. Shame on you, shame, every drop of the workers' blood, every blow by the truncheon, every wound by the bayonet, every worker's life you will pay for on your own backs, in your own stomachs. And then, when you are swept away, there will be peace and order.[18]

Such oratory was not meant to promote civil peace. The Communists were accused of encouraging strikes and unrest, while they, in their turn, accused the police of brutality. From time to time they addressed Masaryk direct to inquire how the methods of the police fitted into his philosophy of humanism. The Communists never made their peace with Masaryk's republic. They saw Masaryk as a politician too closely aligned with the bourgeoisie for his own independence or their comfort. They came under almost constant harassment by the police.

On 11 July 1932 Prague police carried out searches at the offices of the Communist Trade Union Council; the Council and another Communist trade union organization were outlawed. On the same day the party headquarters were searched, and the pamphlet *Baťa is Bankrupt* was confiscated. The pamphlet was based on speeches to the Parliament and on the shoe company's own publicity material. The Communist leaders were convinced that the police action was carried out at the instigation of Thomas Baťa, whom Masaryk knew and liked as the leading Czech industrialist.

Gottwald himself was arrested for a short time; when another warrant was issued for his arrest in 1934, he left illegally for exile in the Soviet Union, and an office at the headquarters of the Comintern. Masaryk's relationship with the Communist Party, as well as the foreign policy of his state, ruled out any chance of exploring the possibility that the close political and personal links between members of the Czech and Russian Communist Parties might be used for the benefit of the Czechoslovak state.

Masaryk's foreign policy consisted of an attempt to link Czechoslovakia closely with the Western Powers, and to create a parallel system of alliances with the smaller states of Central and East Europe. Nevertheless in the years after the war differences between Britain and France on two key problems, the attitude to Germany and to the Soviet Union, divided the former allies. In each case Paris took a tougher foreign policy line than London; the French also pursued a more forward policy with regard to the small, new states of East Europe. Soon after the war the concept of the *cordon sanitaire* emerged: the zone of small East European states which could be turned against Germany but, with greater probability, against the Soviet Union.

Czechoslovakia therefore became closely linked to France. Her army had been under French command in the first two years of her existence. A formal treaty with France was concluded in 1924. By then, however, France had lost much of her influence and prestige in Europe to England. Alongside the French alliance Masaryk and Beneš built up a system of treaties with Romania and Yugoslavia, a system which became known as the Little Entente. All three countries had benefited from the peace treaties, and they all had an interest in preserving the post-war *status quo*. Hungarian revisionist claims or the restoration of the Habsburgs were the two subjects they could all agree on; but little else.

Indeed, despite the plans for a peaceful Central and Eastern Europe which had crowded the pages of *New Europe* and other magazines during the war, it may have occurred to Masaryk that, in reality, the situation was perilous for his new state, and that little remained of the grand wartime visions. But Masaryk was convinced, until the end of his life, that peace would prevail in Europe, that the armistice of 11 November 1918 would last. He had faith in the Western Powers and believed that, in spite of their differences, they would support the order they themselves had created. There was also the League of Nations to fall back on, and the hope that both Russia and Germany, the outcasts of post-war Europe, would be peacefully and gradually absorbed into the new European system.

A move towards the Soviet Union was made at the Genoa

conference between 10 and 19 April 1922. England, France, Italy, Japan and other capitalist states faced the Soviet representatives, for the first time since the end of the war, across the conference table. Germany had not been asked. Beneš represented Czechoslovakia. He gave the Soviets the impression that he did not expect them to stay in power for long, and that he would block their diplomatic recognition by every means. He had detailed instructions from Masaryk.

On 18 April Masaryk wrote to Beneš:

> The Russians must be told quite clearly that, because they accepted the invitation, they recognize the practical possibilities of capitalism, whereas capitalism does not recognize communism and Bolshevism; it cannot recognize them, because Russia and her achievements have proved the impossibility of Bolshevik communism. The Bolsheviks had expected a European revolution, they spent money on it, and they wanted to destroy capitalism. Now instead of revolution, communist revolutionaries go begging from the capitalists. This is the brutal fact which must be, though in a cautious form, clearly said.
>
> It is possible that the conference will strengthen communism in Europe and especially in our country; and therefore the approach in Genoa should be a careful one, stressing willingness and readiness to help Russia, offering a certain sum of money and merchandise, but doing it in such a way that the Russian people would see that Europe wants to help them, and not the Bolsheviks.

And Masaryk reminded Beneš: 'Don't forget, the Bolsheviks are Jesuits.'[19]

Though a trade agreement was concluded between Czechoslovakia and the Soviet Union a few weeks after the conference in Genoa, Masaryk and Beneš continued to rely on the French and Little Entente alliances for the security of their state. They also made approaches to Austria and Poland, but neither country appeared to be interested. Beneš staked a lot on the close integration of the Little Entente: the 'organizational pact', signed by Yugoslavia, Romania and Czechoslovakia on 16 February 1933 in Geneva was, in Beneš words, 'the first step towards integration, a synthesis, the creation of a new international community'. The pact provided for a common foreign policy of the three countries, for the existing bilateral treaties becoming trilateral, and for the creation of a permanent council. The Little Entente was all that remained of Masaryk's wartime plans for a new Europe which was to take the place of the rotten, feudal Habsburg Empire.

Such hopes had disappeared in the chaos of the post-war years, and in the scramble for pieces of territory on the borders of the new states. On the other hand Beneš's excessive caution, in no way discouraged by Masaryk, introduced unnecessary flaws into Czechoslovakia's structure of foreign relations. Though both Poland and Czechoslovakia were bound to France by treaties, Beneš would not consider offering Poland a military agreement because he did not want the country to be drawn into a conflict over the corridor or over Upper Silesia. The Polish treaty with France of 1921 contained a military obligation for both countries in the event of an attack by Germany; the Czechoslovak treaty of 1924, on the other hand, contained no such clause, because Beneš did not want Czechoslovakia to be drawn into a conflict between France and Germany.

In 1935, after the Soviet Union had joined the League of Nations, Beneš and the Soviet minister to Prague signed the Soviet-Czechoslovak Mutual Aid treaty on 16 May. The rise of Hitler had brought about realignments in Europe. Nevertheless Beneš made certain that any Soviet military assistance to Czechoslovakia would be hedged in by various provisions. Such assistance could be given, in the case of an unprovoked attack, only on the basis of a decision by the League of Nations; with the express consent of the transit states, that is Romania and Poland; and, it was added as an afterthought, 'obligations of mutual aid will become effective only in a situation foreseen in this treaty, and if the victim of the attack is assisted by France'. The treaty therefore hinged on a condition which was by no means firmly anchored in the Franco-Czechoslovak agreement.

The pact between the Soviet Union and Czechoslovakia was Beneš's first independent and major act of state. Masaryk's health was failing him at the time. The state he had created was by no means secure. There were brief times of respite for him from the day-to-day political problems. Sometimes his grandchildren came to visit him at Lány, at others the authors of books on his life and thoughts. There was Karel Čapek who, by 1934, had finished his *Conversations with Masaryk*; and Emil Ludwig, the German writer, had also seen a lot of Masaryk in connection with a similar book, designed for the export rather than the Czech market. More out of Masaryk's sight than Čapek or Ludwig, Zdeněk Nejedlý, the Communist intellectual and professor at the University of Prague, was about to complete his immensely detailed, four-volume work on Masaryk's youth, a book which Masaryk enjoyed having read to him at the end of his life.

The year 1933 had opened badly for Masaryk and his state. A week before Hitler came to power in Berlin at the end of January, Czech fascists had tried to force the issue in their country by a *putsch*. In the German border areas Konrad Henlein's Nazi Party, still disguised for the purposes of political convenience, was well on the way to becoming one of the most powerful organizations in the country. The economic crisis had been grinding on to its dreary climax; the ranks of the unemployed had been growing to reach almost a million men. The Europe Masaryk saw around him was not, he may have reflected, much of an improvement on the nineteenth century.

For the first time Masaryk's political touch was becoming uncertain. He considered the means by which democracy could be guided: emergency measures and enabling laws were rushed through Parliament. He also considered the ways in which the army could be improved. He wanted to make a gesture in reply to the arming of Germany: it caused his advisers many sleepless nights. He insisted that there should be a large military review to celebrate the fifteenth anniversary of the republic on 28 October 1933, and that he himself should review the troops on horseback. He was eighty-three years old and the cabinet and his friends were horrified by the idea. Masaryk would not give way. It was suggested that the horse should wear rubber shoes, so that he would not slip about on the cobblestones. 'I shall either do the review as a soldier would, or not at all,' Masaryk replied.

Troops of the Prague garrison, reinforced by country regiments, were lined up on both sides of Wenceslas Square. Masaryk mounted his horse at the lower end of the square, and rode alongside it, until he reached the statue of St Wenceslas, also on a horse, at the upper end of the square; then he rode down, taking a good look at the troops lined up on the opposite side. The crowds behind the ranks of the troops cheered; the organizers of the event gave a sigh of relief when Masaryk finally dismounted.

Masaryk was giving a lot of interviews to journalists at that time, and what he said contrasted with the political measures he was then taking. There would be no war, he insisted, because nobody could afford one; the League of Nations would survive, and establish itself as an important factor in international relations, despite indications to the contrary; so would democracy. 'I have no fear for democracy, anti-democratic movements are reactionary. Bolshevism is a more difficult problem.'[20] Speaking indirectly about Hitler, he said that 'strong men' could not bring health back to Europe; in a more direct way, he said: 'In any case, even Hitler and Mussolini must be seen as an expression of democracy, they became dictators because of the expression of the will of the majority. But it is not my kind of democracy.' There were references to 'democracy of authority' scattered throughout his interviews. Otherwise, he gave his interviewers an impression of optimism.

On 24 May 1934 Masaryk was elected president of Czechoslovakia for the third and last time. In 1920 he had been elected by 284 parliamentary votes; in 1927 by 274; in 1934 the number of votes cast for Masaryk reached 327. Again the Communists put forward their own candidate; one Slovak and two Hungarian parties abstained in the election. Again there was no other serious candidate. The election took place in the Hall of the Kings at the castle, in an atmosphere of barely controlled emotion. The king was very old; his young state was in grave danger.

When Masaryk walked into the hall to hear the results of the election his step was infirm; he groped a little on the way to his seat. For the first time the ceremony was broadcast. The listeners could clearly hear the clerk's insistent prompting when Masaryk took his constitutional oath. Masaryk had been ill since the beginning of the month, partially losing the sight of his right eye and he was partly paralysed by the end of the summer. When Beneš visited him at Lány in August 1934, Masaryk sometimes would not speak at all; at others he spoke only slurred English. There was some improvement at the end of August; the doctors were optimistic. He joked with his literary secretary, who had attended a philosophers' conference in Prague, 'I have packed up my little philosophy shop.' Political visitors again started calling on him at his country house.

But it was difficult for Masaryk to remain in office. He was unable to sign state papers; he knew that the country needed strong leadership. The combination of the Czech and German parties which had put Masaryk into office was being constantly eroded. In the parliamentary election in May 1935 1,249,530 votes were cast for Henlein's Nazi Party. Its election funds had been generously and secretly supplied from Berlin; it received the second highest number of votes, at the expense of the other German parties. In November 1935 a new government was formed, led by Milan Hodža, of the Agrarian Party. A strong party and a strong prime minister. All Masaryk had to do was to make certain that they would support his own candidate for the presidency: Eduard Beneš.

Masaryk asked Hodža to visit him at Lány, and told him of his intention to resign, but there were difficulties with other members of the party, who were opposed to Beneš, and wanted to name their own candidate. Hodža offered to resign, but Masaryk turned down the offer. Masaryk then abdicated on 14 December 1935, and Beneš was duly elected the second president four days later.

On the day of Masaryk's abdication, the prime minister, the speaker of the Parliament, and the chairman of the Senate came to Lány; also his daughters, Alice and Olga, and granddaughter Anna, Masaryk's personal doctor, together with various secretaries. Dr Šámal, the head of Masaryk's chancery, addressed the three holders of political office present, and then read out Masaryk's note of abdication:

The office of the president is difficult and responsible, and requires therefore his full faculties. I see that I can no longer manage the office, and I am therefore giving it up. I have been elected the president of our republic four times; perhaps this entitles me to beg you and the whole Czechoslovak nation, as well as our compatriots of other nationalities, to remember, when conducting the affairs of the state, that states live on those ideals which gave them birth. I have always been aware of that. We need a good foreign policy and justice to all citizens, of whatever nationality. I should also like to tell you that I recommend as my successor Dr Beneš; I have worked with him abroad and at home and I know him. I beg you, Mr Prime Minister, to acknowledge my abdication and take the necessary steps.[21]

There was a long pause when Šámal finished reading the note; the women cried. The three politicians made their replies, one after the other. When they left the house, the presidential flag was lowered and put away. Masaryk lived in retirement at Lány. Every Friday Beneš came to see him. Jan Masaryk, who was then the Czechoslovak minister to London, also spent some time at Lány, and other members of the family often came to see the old man. He planned to finish his book on Russia, the writing of which had been interrupted by the outbreak of the war in 1914. He continued to take an interest in political events at home and abroad, and his secretaries and relations came to read to him and make their reports. He asked the Senate to drop its plans for making 7 March, his birthday, a national holiday; he preferred, he said, people to remember him by their work.

On 13 May 1937, on the anniversary of the death of his wife Charlotte, Masaryk visited the cemetery at Lány, where she was buried – his last visit there. Occasional visits to Prague became a habit of his retirement; he was driven around the town, always taking different routes, and then back to Lány. Thomas Masaryk died on 14 September 1937. Jan returned to Prague from London straightaway. It was his fifty-first birthday.

The Patrimony

DAY and night queues miles long shuffled their way up the hill to the castle, where Masaryk was lying in state, among palms and torches, flanked by guards of honour. He was buried at Lány, next to his wife. Karel Čapek, walking behind Masaryk's surviving relatives, could not bear seeing the coffin being lowered into the raw earth, and left the procession. He went to the grave-digger's cottage to write a report on Masaryk's last journey.

Masaryk left a state behind him, and a way of running it; also a president, his own choice. He had founded an improbable dynasty. Masaryk had been very firm about Beneš's succession, and had his own way. He nominated the person to whom he had been tied by habit, and who was absolutely loyal to him. Eventually Jan Masaryk became foreign minister to Beneš, loyal to Beneš as Beneš had been to Thomas Masaryk: their names and policies marked out an era in the history of the country.

Nevertheless the relationship between Thomas Masaryk and Beneš had been curiously formal, at times even cold. There was no place for familiarity in that relationship, and Masaryk never used the relaxed 'thou' form of address when speaking to Beneš. He had treated and used Beneš as a very efficient secretary during the war; and when he left Beneš to work on his own, Beneš did not make mistakes, or pursue a policy in opposition to Masaryk's. After the war Beneš often bore the brunt of attacks intended for Masaryk, and that way, their relationship was made even closer. It may be that Masaryk made a mistake in his recommendation.

Beneš was efficient and hard working, and he was used to filling in details into Masaryk's grand design. There may have been times when his cautious plodding and lack of sparkle seemed very desirable qualities to Masaryk. Beneš was born on 28 May 1884; he was thirty-four years younger than Masaryk, and still only fifty-one when he became President. When he returned to Prague after four years in exile in September 1919, he was an unknown quantity for the Czech politicians. He had written a few obscure essays on sociology before the war; and a not entirely original study of the French national character; he had taught sociology at a technical college and then, from 1912, at Prague University as well. He had moved from a political position which was sympathetic to the Social Democrats to membership of Masaryk's party. The Realists were probably the only organization suited to Beneš's tastes: all his life, he regarded himself as Masaryk's pupil.

He might have become a good university teacher. He was a diligent person, who probably would have written a number of monographs on sociology. They would have been notable for their methodical construction, their careful treatment of facts and their lack of originality. But they would have been appreciated by other academic sociologists, and his students would have been wise to use them. 'The gift to inspire by word was his only to a small extent' was the opinion of one of Beneš's contemporaries, who had observed him at close quarters over the years. Occasionally, in his speeches or political articles, or in his memoirs, he fought abortive battles with words, and his listeners or readers could often watch him losing them. At his worst he could be didactic, smug and dull. Beneš had written before the war because writing was one of the more easily accessible public activities for the Czechs in Austria-Hungary. The war then opened up new horizons to Beneš: his ambition became apparent to the politicians who came from Prague to meet him in Geneva in September 1918. Beneš's driving ambition was contained in a small physical frame. He was just noticeably taller than a dwarf.

There was often sparkle and humour in what Masaryk said and did; Beneš's industry, his huge capacity for work, required no such distraction. The main part of Beneš's work was concerned, for some twenty years, with the administration and execution of Masaryk's ideas; the putting of flesh on skeletal structures. That work required the drafting of state papers and of minutes; receiving and convincing people; relentlessly pursuing and implementing ideas which were sometimes casually thrown out. In that sense, Beneš was a man of action: an intellectual who preferred action to words as a means of expression.

And in all Beneš's actions there was much method. He preferred the orderly, the expected side of life. For the same reason, he disliked party politics. The organization of men's desires and passions was not for him: he could devote himself to the structures of treaties, the ultimate abstractions of political life. Masaryk, especially the Masaryk of the later years, say, after 1912, was a politician through and through. He did not mind receiving and dealing out the body-blows of politics. He even enjoyed their untidiness, the unexpected turns of the wheel of fortune. He was a totally unsentimental person, his nerve-ends well hidden under the skin. Beneš understood the usefulness of being like that, but he never quite learned the trick. On major questions – such as the election of his successor – Masaryk could be grandly firm, magnificently obstinate. When Beneš was obstinate, he appeared to be petty.

He may have been attracted to Masaryk's Realist Party for the wrong reasons. It probably appeared to him to be the only party which conducted itself with the gravity appropriate to the serious business of politics, and which concerned itself with politics as a scientific subject. Beneš walked around political parties with much caution. When he had to choose one as the minister of foreign affairs, because otherwise he could not have remained the minister, he never took much part or interest in its activities. His main strength lay in the way he accumulated facts and his patience in using them. During the war he was simply the person who knew everything and everybody necessary for the successful pursuit of the action against the Habsburgs. When other men's zeal for the revolution was becoming exhausted, when all the grand phrases had been said, Beneš was there, in the background, in full possession of his facts. He became indispensable.

After the foundation of the Czechoslovak republic, it was said that only those rights existed which men were prepared to claim, and very few Czech politicians were prepared to claim the right to formulate foreign policy. Kramář was an exception. Otherwise, an average politician's interest in foreign affairs, it was said, would start and stop at the aftermath of a Japanese earthquake. It was all too easy to go wrong in home politics, and no one dared to tread the much less explored foreign ground. Masaryk's and Beneš's right to pursue their own foreign policy was therefore rarely questioned, and foreign policy was the gate through which Beneš stepped into prominence. He never bothered much to read the minds of the Czech and Slovak politicians; instead he carefully read Masaryk's mind, putting into action those ideas which he could decipher. That was what he had done during the war, and there was no reason that he should change his habits in peacetime.

From 1918 until Masaryk's abdication, Beneš was the only member of the frequently changing governments who always remained in office; his privileged position was secured for him by Masaryk. But that position isolated him from the day-to-day political life of the country. He happened to be a member of many governments, but he never lived with them through their political trials. At the end of 1935, when Beneš took over the presidency from Masaryk, he inherited a position with which his expertise was not quite equipped to deal. Masaryk had carved out for himself a position of great power in the state, and he handed over that position to Beneš.

Masaryk's view of the powers of the president was, roughly, that a strong president would have more power than a weak one. He happened to be a strong president, his position strengthened by an almost legendary prestige. Even cynical politicians found it impossible to destroy Masaryk's prestige. Secondly, Masaryk visibly enjoyed the position into which he slipped, seemingly without any effort, after the war. He came to regard his whole life as a preparation for his achievement in 1918.

Masaryk's character, his success in the war, made it possible to keep a large share of power in the new state for himself. Some of his political quarrels, before 1914, had been forgotten. Many of his former adversaries and critics had died, and the battles had been fought over a different battleground. The unfortunate Beneš – and this is what he turned out to be – did not have even that minor advantage. Before he became the president, he had spent some fifteen years in the middle of Prague in-fighting, standing in the way of many of the shafts aimed at Masaryk. There were young politicians growing up around him who would never forgive him for what he had done to them in the past.

Nor was Beneš able to ride the tidal wave of enthusiasm for the new state which had helped Masaryk across the seas of post-war troubles. Beneš's task was much more difficult, and he was a lesser man. He had a share in the wartime monopoly of success, but its returns were diminishing all the time. After 1935, he had to prove that his expertise was useful for the state.

His achievement in foreign policy was marked by excessive caution. The hedges around some of the clauses of the Mutual Aid treaty with the Soviets, for instance, were so impenetrable as to have made the whole exercise of concluding the treaty of interest only to diplomatic historians. One of the clauses was made to depend on another one, in another treaty, which in fact did not exist. On that occasion perhaps even Beneš had failed to read the small print of his treaty carefully enough; perhaps it would have made no difference to Hitler if he had.

Throughout the times that Beneš was head of state, Hitler and the Nazi movement in Czechoslovakia tested his political skills. At first, Beneš behaved as if nothing of importance was happening in Germany or the German parts of Czechoslovakia. When Hitler's Germany left the League of Nations, the German minister to Prague reported to Berlin that Beneš said to him, almost cordially, that for his part 'he would do anything to clear away any difficulty with Germany, to avoid all conflicts and to ensure the peaceful coexistence of the two states'.[1]

Nevertheless Czechoslovakia became, for the second time in her brief existence, an asylum for refugees. After 1918 many of the Russians who had fled the country and the Bolshevik revolution found at least a temporary refuge in Czechoslovakia, and Masaryk helped them establish a Russian University in Prague. After 1933 Social Democrats and many other opponents of Hitler's regime crossed the border; Thomas Mann then became a Czechoslovak citizen. Despite Beneš's concept of coexistence with Nazi Germany, the former Nazi Party had been banned in Czechoslovakia in October 1934. Konrad Henlein's front organization emerged instead, making its mark in the elections of 1935.

At the same time the Czechoslovak Communist Party showed itself to be in a mood of cautious conciliation. It gave its qualified support to the policy of alliances with the Soviet Union and with France. At a meeting in November 1934 its central committee had launched the policy of a united front with the Czech and German Social Democrats, the Czech National Socialists, and the smallholders' organizations. The Communists however liked Beneš no more than they had done Masaryk. When Beneš visited Moscow in 1935, after the conclusion of the Soviet-Czechoslovak treaty, Klement Gottwald was living there in exile. Beneš probably did not inquire after his health from their hosts. The Communists charged the president with total ignorance of Russia, and with being a captive of France and her ideology. They had especially disapproved of his forecasts of an early end to the Soviet regime and his view that, at best, Lenin's experiment could suit only a backward country.

For many years Beneš had been entirely open about his views. On 6 February 1924, for instance, he told the foreign affairs committee in the Parliament that: 'We have been and we are against Bolshevik methods, we disagree with their foreign propaganda and with their efforts for a world revolution.' In the same year, soon after the Genoa conference, Stalin expressed the Bolshevik view of Beneš:

> The psalmist tells us that, sometimes, God reveals truth through the mouth of the babes. Should Western imperialism be God, then it is quite natural that it could not do without a babe. And so its babe appeared in the person of the not totally unknown Beneš, the Czechoslovak minister of foreign affairs, through whose mouth imperialism has announced that there is no point in hurrying the recognition of the USSR, because the power of the Soviets is infirm, and because it will soon be replaced by a bourgeois democratic government. It would be better, for the time being, to 'hold back normal relations' with the Soviet Union.[2]

For many years, therefore, the Communists had criticized the eagerness of Beneš's anti-Soviet policy, and the way that eagerness was calculated to appeal to London and Paris. They criticized Beneš, as well as Masaryk, on three other counts. In the first place, they remembered that the Allied policy of intervention in Russia became reality when the Czechoslovak troops came into conflict with the Bolsheviks in May 1918. Secondly, that Beneš and Masaryk supported the emigration from Russia, and that their support cut across an understanding with the Soviet Union. Finally, the trouble Beneš took over the Little Entente was seen, by the Communists, as an attempt to construct an anti-Soviet platform for the small states of East Europe.

The Communist adversaries of Beneš explained most of his foreign policy by his 'fear of Russia', a fear which pushed the government far to the right. Nevertheless some at least of Beneš's fear must have left him by the time he concluded the Mutual Aid treaty with the Soviets in 1935. France, of course, had concluded a similar pact with Russia a fortnight before Czechoslovakia. According to his own testimony, Beneš then reversed his view of the Soviet achievement. 'The two five-year plans have considerably changed the economic structure of the Soviet Union, to such an extent that it has become one of the biggest industrial countries in Europe. My trip to Russia between 6 and 17 June 1935 fully confirmed these views.'[3]

But even then, when Beneš reviewed his attitude to the Soviet Union, he remained suspect to the Communists. They maintained that he must have been very hard pressed to change his mind, and that in any case the change was approved by his Western allies. Zdeněk Nejedlý, who was about to complete his monumental biography of Masaryk as a young man, wrote that: 'Even so, it will always be to the everlasting discredit of Beneš's foreign policy that Czechoslovakia was the last of European capitalist states which "recognized" the Soviet Union.'[4]

Though Klement Gottwald returned to Prague from exile in Moscow in 1936, the party and its organizations remained under close scrutiny by the police. The activities of the Association of the Friends of the Soviet Union were also closely observed: in November 1936 the Prague police for instance allowed the association to use some poems at a public meeting, provided that certain changes were made; in August 1937 the ministry of foreign affairs recommended that no public collections for the association should be allowed. There were also difficulties about the celebrations of the twentieth anniversary of the Soviet state because, as an official in the foreign ministry pointed out: 'The celebration of 7 November is not at all a celebration of the origin of the state, but is a jubilee of the Soviet regime in a state which has existed for centuries.'[5]

In the funeral oration over Masaryk's grave, on 21 September 1937, Beneš made no direct reference to the Nazi threat. His only mention of Germany was contained in his reference to Masaryk as a philosopher, who 'extended our philosophy and learning, until then inhabitants of a German environment, to embrace

Western Europe and the whole world'. He then went on to describe the inheritance Masaryk had left behind him: 'He was a happy man not only in his life and triumph but also in the manner of his passing, for he went away in the firm faith that the structure which he had built was upon firm foundations, that we all jointly rule it, and that our state and all our citizens of every class and nationality are, and will be, competent for their task.' Equally indirectly, he called upon everybody, including the Germans in Czechoslovakia, to complete Masaryk's work in 'perfecting our just, firm, indomitable, evolutionary, humanitarian democracy'.

Less than a month later Konrad Henlein, the camouflaged leader of the Nazis in Czechoslovakia, came on another visit to London. He lectured to a study group at Chatham House, and told his listeners that the Germans were ready to behave as loyal citizens of Czechoslovakia, that they merely demanded the same rights and privileges as the Czechs. Privately at dinner Henlein told Sir Robert Vansittart that ninety per cent of the Germans were in favour of complete annexation to Hitler's Reich. In November 1937 Henlein was in Berlin, telling Hitler that he wanted nothing more than the incorporation not only of the German, but of the Czech areas as well, into Germany. This was precisely what Hitler had in mind himself.

Austria became a part of Germany on 11 March 1938. Of the total of 3,000 kilometres of Czechoslovak border (2,400 of which was with Germany, and only 200 with friendly Romania) 400 kilometres of completely open frontier were added to its large German sector. Nazi propagandists were then busy presenting German nationalism as an irresistible force which simply had to be satisfied; Dr Goebbels had had a lot of practice in this respect in the Saarland, and then in Austria. The Germans were asking for no more than self-determination for their people: a just demand, which Beneš and the Czechoslovaks resisted.

There was no way in which Beneš could win against Henlein and Hitler, unless his friends stood by him. They did not. The French and British governments had decided to capitulate to Hitler some time before they signed the Munich agreement. Finally, in a few days in September 1938, Britain, France, Germany and Italy decided that Czechoslovakia should not exist in the geographical extent in which it had been established nearly twenty years before.

Czechoslovakia was excluded from the negotiations, and so was the Soviet Union. Under extreme pressure from his former friends and allies, Beneš (he had been producing one 'plan' after another, to pacify the Czechoslovak Germans, often to the embarrassment of his friends and always to the joy of his enemies) accepted the Munich agreement, and the greatly diminished state. The agreement was signed during the night of 29–30 September; Czechoslovakia was ordered to hand over her border territories to Germany, starting the following night. The takeover was to be completed by 10 October. The treaty, which established a precedent in international practice, was unusual in its conception as well as in the speed of its execution.

In the evening of 27 September Mr Chamberlain made his famous point, in a broadcast speech: 'How horrible, fantastic, incredible it is that we should be digging trenches and trying on gas masks here because of a quarrel in a far away country between people of whom we know nothing.' In Prague, on 30 September, Kamil Krofta, Beneš's mild-mannered, scholarly successor at the foreign ministry, told the British, Italian and French ministers of his government's acceptance of the Munich agreement made 'without us and against us'.

The Munich crisis touched on the most sensitive spot of Czech national consciousness. It was another disaster to be added to the many calamities of the past. It concerned the viability of the state as well as the reliability of its friends – its domestic and foreign policies. But most of all it concerned the capacity of the nation to defend the state. Beneš and his government decided to give in, and by doing so, they confirmed the expectations of their enemies and the worst suspicions of their own people. In effect Beneš and his government said that the state would not be defended, and that it was not worth defending. The troops which had been gathered together during the general mobilization went home; the border fortresses fell into enemy hands. Some months later, in March 1939, Hitler's troops marched into Prague, and the Czechoslovak state ceased to exist in any form whatever.

During the Munich crisis the Germans had been intercepting telephone conversations between Beneš in Prague and Jan Masaryk in London. As an act of courtesy, Goering passed them on to the

British ambassador to Berlin. On 23 September, Jan Masaryk told Beneš that:

> The old Lord [Runciman] has rung me up. He has been deceived as much as you.
> BENEŠ: The Lord who was with us?
> MASARYK: He has been slighted in the most shameful manner.
> BENEŠ: I felt it.
> MASARYK: Yesterday he still thought that we would have to cede only up to 75 per cent [those districts where the Germans had at least a three-quarter majority]. I told him about the 50 per cent. He collapsed and wept.[6]

Beneš had sent Jan Masaryk to London in 1925. In 1935 Masaryk began to commute between the two capitals, as tension in Central Europe was growing, and his father's health was worsening. The summer of 1938, a year after his father's death, was the most difficult for him. He was dedicated to Beneš. In this dedication, he was a dutiful son. Before his death, his father said to him: 'You know, Beneš understands me and understands us. Work with him.'[7] Such obedience had not always come naturally to Jan.

Jan was born on 14 September 1886, four years after his father came to Prague to teach, and at the height of the manuscript controversy. His brother and sister, Herbert and Alice, had been born in Vienna, and as long as the Masaryks lived in Vienna, the children spoke either German or English. In Prague Czech became the family language. All the children's names were chosen by their father: Herbert was named after Masaryk's friend, Josef Herbert; Alice after the heroine of a now forgotten novel, *Martyr of Tilbury*. (When she grew up, Alice very much wanted to read the novel, but apparently could not find it anywhere, not even in the British Museum Library.) She was called 'Elis' at home, and was sorry that she did not have a nice Czech name, like Jan.

When the children saw their new brother lying in the laundry basket in the nursery, Alice was seven and Herbert six years old. The family were then living in a villa flat on the fringes of Prague: Vinohrady, the suburb, was a comparatively new district, which replaced fourteenth-century vineyards. The house had a large garden. An astronomer and an author of historical novels were the other inhabitants. There was a good view of the surrounding countryside from Masaryk's study; the children saw him disappear there soon after breakfast, before nine o'clock. He usually spent the morning in the study, not minding when the children played around him. Sometimes he gave them a ride on an especially thick volume of Aristotle.

Their childhood was unusual, not quite conventional; and the children sometimes had unusual ways of looking at it. Alice, the most strong-minded of the Masaryk children, who remained a spinster and died in exile in America, was the only one of them to record impressions of their childhood.[8] Jan, who grew up to be a very unliterary person, talked to his friends. They saw their mother as a very gentle woman, who tried to understand her children and kept a diary about them. (Many years after Charlotte's death Alice found the diary, at Lány.) Charlotte also tried to give her children suitable interests – semi-precious stones, plants – and a lot of freedom.

The children soon realized that they were being brought up much less strictly than their contemporaries; their mother, whose parents had been very strict, wanted to give her children something she had missed herself in her youth. Two years before Jan was born, for instance, the children's American grandfather came to visit them in Prague. He was not best pleased with their behaviour. He was very keen on discipline, as it applied to children; many years later even Alice admitted that 'we, the children, perhaps had too much of that freedom'. From time to time, the children were taken by their parents to the Ladies' American Club, a social and literary club which had been founded by a Czech who had spent a few years in America, and who returned convinced that women had a role to play in society, a view which was shared by both Thomas and Charlotte Masaryk.

Masaryk's children also became aware, early in their lives, of their mixed antecedents. Their grandmother sent them a magazine called *St Nicholas* from America, and marked the passages she liked best with a red or a golden maple leaf. They were very fond of their Moravian uncle Ludvík who sometimes came to stay with them. He did not look like a Prague person at all; he wore strange clothes, and was tall and strong, with thick black hair brushed straight back. Thomas, who probably had visions of a family cooperative (he would write and his brother print), had helped him to set up as a printer in Hustopeče. But Thomas's real brother did not like being a printer; he left Moravia and came to Prague where he set himself up as the owner of a Moravian wine-cellar, which became popular with writers and painters.

As long as Masaryk's mother was alive (she died a few months after Jan's birth, in April 1887) the children spent their summer holidays in Moravia, with their grandparents. In Hustopeče there was the cottage which Masaryk had built for his parents. Alice soon came to realize how very close Masaryk was to his mother, and how he loved the sunny, open plains of his native Moravia. He loved the sun above all; one day, when he was old, after an illness, he told his daughter: 'I don't feel so sunny any longer.' The children's grandfather was a more remote and incomprehensible figure to them than their grandmother. There was something pagan about him, and he spent as much time in the open as he could. He had a small vineyard near the house, and tended it very carefully; he hated visiting towns.

From his trips to Russia, Masaryk brought the children wooden toys, a beautifully illustrated edition of old Russian legends, and an embroidered dress for Alice; they were especially impressed by a copper samovar, which stood in front of their mother's place on a large dining-room table, the glowing coals shining, the steam hissing and singing. Soon after Jan's birth, however, Masaryk's involvement in the manuscript controversy and the attentions of the press became too much for the landlord, the author of historical novels. The Masaryk family had to leave their flat. The children liked the move to the centre of the town. Their uncle Ludvík had opened a new restaurant near their flat, and the whole family used to go and have lunches there, in a private room. Herbert, Alice and Jan enjoyed eating at their uncle's; they did not regard it, as their parents did, as a labour-saving device.

In the spring of 1889 when Jan was not quite three years old and Alice was recovering from an attack of scarlet fever, Masaryk's fourth child was born – Eleanora, who died in infancy late in the summer. That autumn Thomas and Charlotte decided to move to Malá Strana. It was here that Jan started going to school, in the quarter of baroque palaces, cool, long archways, a quarter which nourished independence of the spirit and eccentricity of character. There was a stall near the Masaryks' flat, kept by a woman who was much liked in the neighbourhood. She sold a curious selection of goods: shoe laces and liquorice sticks, nuts, sweet and sour cucumbers, the daily newspaper which everyone read. She kept a bucket of water handy, which she used to pour over evil little boys, like Jan Masaryk.

Jenda, or Honza, to give the two most common versions of his name, was a lively little boy, who liked everybody. When he was still a small boy at school, the family doctor prescribed for his mid-morning break a ham roll and a small bottle of red wine. It did not do him much good: he shared his elevenses with all his friends in the class. Mr Wolf taught the children to play the piano, one after the other (with the exception of Herbert who had inherited his father's violin and learned to play it); he was a small, dark-skinned man, with a pince-nez on a black ribbon, who came from one of those Prague families for whom music was both a profession and an inheritance. Herbert and Olga (the youngest daughter, five years younger than Jan) were good at sports and interested in the creative arts. Alice and Jan had a musical gift, Jan more than Alice; he moved on to a famous teacher, Slavkovský, and went to concerts as often as he could.

The Masaryk children were used to an intellectual life, plain to the point of discomfort. The boys slept in the parlour/dining-room of the cramped flat. Oil lamps were lit in the evenings, and drinking water came from a pump in the courtyard; pails of water for washing were brought in by the daily woman. Every autumn and spring, Charlotte Masaryk shopped for clothes and linen for the family; she made expeditions to the better shops in the town centre, because she believed in paying more for better quality. She went with her children to the open-air swimming baths in the summer, to skating rinks in the winter. Alice remembered her vividly, walking up and down alongside the skating rink, in her black costume, her hat covered with ostrich feathers.

The flat was not heated until late in the autumn. Before going to bed, the children sat about on the floor, reading or talking, and wearing big blankets. They read Kate Greenaway's nursery rhymes, Czech, German or Russian fairy tales, Božena Němcová's classic, *The Grandmother*. They moved on to Dickens when they were older, and then parted company in their reading habits.

The Masaryks left Prague soon after 15 July, the end of the

school year. Year after year they went to Slovakia, perhaps with the exception of Masaryk's early years in the Parliament, when the family was rather hard up. They stayed at a farm at Bystřička, a village near Turčanský Sväty Martin, in the hills on the river Turec. The white farmhouse where they lived consisted of two wings, covered by one roof, but separated by a large passage which was paved with cobblestones and shut off by a gate on the side of the road, but open into the garden. A small ditch ran through the passage; a cart stood there, and an old-fashioned mangle. The Masaryks had their breakfasts in the passage, and sometimes their dinners; the farmer's family sat at a small table, the farm hands at a large one. This was the centre of life in the farmhouse in the summer, and the children liked the simple food, as well as the people who ate there.

After dinner the local huntsmen gathered in the passage, and sometimes Masaryk went with them; they carried guns, bags, lanterns. The children enjoyed the spaciousness of their holiday house: there were three good-sized rooms in its right-hand part, and a large room used for entertaining; the kitchen was in the other part of the house, as well as an enormous larder with iron bars in a small window. The garden was large and rich, and mysterious in parts; it contained a small, sweet-smelling hut, where fruit was dried. There was a gin and slivovice still in a smaller garden, between a stream and the road.

The Lehotský farmhouse was almost entirely self-supporting. The farmer went to town to sell his agricultural produce and, in the winter, wood; and to buy sugar, salt, machinery, instruments and woollen cloth. On his first visit there (he had relatives in the neighbourhood, and he probably chose the farm on their recommendation) Masaryk had agreed a payment of 100 gulden a month. The family had two, and later three, rooms, and they could use whatever they needed from the garden, the milk cellar and the larder. The children had never seen anything like the larder before: drawers full of flour, beans, dried peas and prunes, large loaves of goat cheese, stacked honeycombs and much else besides. They were strictly forbidden to eat between meals, and raid the larder. According to Alice, such acts of greed were unthinkable as far as the children were concerned.

There were three resident children at the farm, two girls much older than Alice and Herbert, and a boy about their age. Alice and Herbert started helping the farmer on the fields and around the house straightaway; Jan and then Olga also made themselves useful in due course. As a little boy, Jan used to drill his friends in the village as firemen (they were then the only organization in Slovakia under Slovak command); later, he became very fond of farm work, and was even allowed to plough the fields. For the girls work in the flax and hemp fields was unusual and exciting: they put on fresh aprons and scarves and they sang, while they carefully picked the plants by hand.

One summer night there was the inevitable and tragic fire in the village. When Alice started wailing with the other women her father sharply stopped her: 'You won't help like that!' Apart from fire, bears did the greatest harm to the villagers: they started coming down to the fields when the oats were ready to be harvested, sat on the edge of the field, and stripped the corn with their front paws. They played havoc in the small fields; the men, including Masaryk, guarded the fields against bears at night. As they were about to leave late in the evening, the children noticed a certain solemnity in their preparations.

The only bear shot in all those years when the Masaryks spent their summers in Byştřička, was shot by Masaryk himself. The bear jumped up unusually high after his shot, and disappeared in the undergrowth. Early the following morning, the hunters went to look for him. They put the dead bear on a cart, and announced their arrival in the village with a shot. The bear was decorated with flowers, in the ears and the mouth, and little Jan was sat down on him. Then the bear was hung from a tree, and the villagers came to admire and mock him. Masaryk was given the bearskin for his study. The incident was indelibly printed on the minds of the children. Masaryk himself remained fascinated by bears. When the legionaries returned from Russia, they brought back with them several bears which lived in a moat at the Prague Castle, during Masaryk's presidency.

After holidays in Slovakia, a break for the children in their Prague routine devoted to education and other intellectual pursuits, the family would return to Prague on 14 September, Jan's birthday; he thought himself short-changed on that day. But even in town, in their small and uncomfortable flat, the children were surrounded by a grand landscape which teased and extended their minds. The windows of the flat overlooked the Wallenstein Square with its Renaissance palace; from another side of the flat, the children often watched the spire of the castle cathedral, with the Czech lion at the top, through a telescope.

Sometime in the early 1890s the children's American grandfather, who had recently been widowed, set out on another trip to Prague, accompanied by his daughter Evelyn. He died on his way there, in Vienna. The New York house was sold, and Charlotte received her share of the inheritance; she used the money to furnish the 'salon', the living- and dining-room, which became the boys' bedroom at night. The Masaryks, we know, moved several times before the war, but they never left the area surrounding the castle. That was their part of Prague: two of the surviving children, Alice and Jan, later lived there, and two grand-daughters of Masaryk still do.

From time to time Jan had differences with his father. In his early youth they mostly concerned the ownership of a dog. Masaryk would not have a dog in a town flat; one of the reasons he gave was that a dog had once bitten his mother in the face. One day Jan brought back a dachshund. In the end his father agreed that he could keep the dog only if it waited for him outside the school the following day. Jan arranged for the dog to do that and kept it till it ran away.

Of all the children, Jan was the most lively, talkative and musically gifted. Every time he came home, he was full of news: the ice on the river was at last breaking, he had seen the poet, Neruda, being helped up the street by a servant, and so on. His life was full of incidents. When he was about twelve years old, he wanted to go to a fancy dress party at the skating rink. His mother said that it would cost too much. But Jan made his own fancy dress, and went. He turned his coat inside out and put patches on it; he put a feather in his father's old hat; he made a tail out of the flowers meant to decorate Alice's summer hat. The flowery tail was too much for his mother though, and she forbade him to wear it.

Masaryk enjoyed the company of his children, but he did not talk to them very much. He was severe with them, perhaps to compensate for the gentleness of his wife, and the freedom she gave them. He was disappointed in Jan, whose academic achievement at school fell well below the average; it became apparent that there would be little point in sending Jan to a university. Jan complained that his father beat him over and over again. Jan's restlessness, his resistance to any form of discipline, repeatedly challenged his father. There were times of great coolness between them. His parents were perhaps slightly afraid of him, of his excessive emotion; for his part he was a bit bored with their puritanical habits and intellectual conversation. It used to keep him awake when he was small; he could not go to bed until conversation in the living-room stopped. When he was older, he took every opportunity to escape from such evenings altogether.

In 1904 it was decided that he should travel; Jan sailed to America with about $100 in his pocket, which his father had given him as a parting present. He remained abroad for nearly ten years, keeping any form of intellectual life, except music, at a safe distance. By the time he arrived in New York he had no money and took the first job offered him. For some months he ran errands and filled ink-wells in an office. He met Charles Crane, the wealthy manufacturer of sanitary equipment and his father's friend, by chance in the street; Mr Crane found a job for Jan in a Bridgeport brass foundry. He played the piano in movie houses to supplement his income; gambling and girls were his two main interests.

The years Jan spent in America were his lost years; he never liked talking about them.[9] He kept away from his American aunts and cousins, and from the Crane family; he even may not have seen his father when he came to lecture at Chicago University for the second time in 1908. He worked and roamed around America; sometimes he taught immigrant workers English, and from Bridgeport he sometimes visited the Metropolitan for an evening of music. Most of all he wanted to be independent, until he had had enough of that kind of independence.

Whatever the differences with his parents had been, they became a fading memory during his years in America. After all he had lived for nineteen years as a member of a very close-knit family. As a little boy, he had sat on a bear decorated with flowers; watched his father fish for trout in fast Slovak streams; had been glad of the welcome by his mother after his escapades. Despite their inclination towards plain living and high thinking, his parents were

powerful personalities, and the family had marked the children
for life. Jan was a sentimental person, and must have missed a
lot the life he had been used to. He returned to Prague in time
for the outbreak of the Great War.

A few months later, in December 1914, Masaryk and Olga left
Prague for their wartime exile. Charlotte said goodbye to her husband and younger daughter at home; it was a dull, grey December
day, and Alice walked with the two travellers as far as the Kramář
villa, in a park on the edge of the inner town.

Alice was a schoolmistress, who had taught in the country before
the war; she moved to Prague to look after her mother. Herbert
was married, and Jan was in the Austro-Hungarian army, with a
desk job in a Hungarian regiment stationed in Poland; he was
recommended for a decoration. Alice was arrested in the war
and spent over a year in prison. Her mother depended on her
friends in Prague for support and company, and on Jan. According
to Alice, having Jan in the country during the war was tremendously
important for their mother, and Jan was very careful and protective
of her.

Soon after Jan's return to Prague the family split up, and
rearranged itself. Olga, the youngest of the children, who had been
very close to her father, went abroad with him. She did not return
to Prague after the war, marrying a doctor in Switzerland. Alice
and Jan grew nearer to each other during the war, and their relationship survived until Jan's death.

There was some uncertainty when Masaryk returned to Prague
in December 1918 as to what should happen to Jan. His qualifications were diverse. He had picked up languages easily and, apart
from English, spoke German, French and many of the Slav languages. Like his father and grandfather, he was a good horseman,
though he was otherwise physically lazy. A very good pianist and
an accomplished improviser, he was also a talented story-teller.
There was something of the showman about him. Above all, he
could not stand office work in any form.

A place was in the end found for him in the diplomatic service,
in Beneš's foreign ministry, and he was left to find his own feet.
Beneš was then busy creating the Czechoslovak foreign service
and it had to be built from the foundations. When he was still at
school, Jan's father had very much wanted to become a diplomat;

diplomacy was then a preserve of the Austro-Hungarian aristocracy, though there had been a few Czech members of the Habsburg consular service at the end of the war.

After 1918 foreign service was a new form of employment for the Czechs and the Slovaks, much more so than the other branches of the civil service or the army. Appointments were being made fast, and there was a scramble for the top posts by men who had no qualifications apart from their participation in the anti-Habsburg movement. Much acrimony arose out of the scramble: Beneš's methods and personnel policy were criticized, and the ranks of his enemies started to grow.

Jan was sent to Washington as chargé d'affaires. At the turn of the year 1919–20 he was transferred from there to London, where he stayed until 1922 as counsellor at the Czechoslovak legation. He returned to Prague the following year, and started acting as a link between the diplomatic corps and the government. There were difficulties on both sides. Beneš could be remote and tactless at the same time, and his relations with the foreign diplomats were indifferent; many of the diplomats, on the other hand, regarded the new regime as one run by upstarts, and preferred the company of the old aristocrats, despite their diminished fortunes and departed political influence. Jan Masaryk investigated and dealt with the diplomats' complaints, and made peace as best he could. His stay in Prague was probably the best training in diplomacy he could get.

The American and English ministers to Prague knew President Masaryk well, and no difficulties arose in that quarter. Sir George Clerk had met Masaryk, on official business, early in the war. Richard Crane was Charles Crane's son. He was richer than the other ministers in Prague, and bought the Schoenborn Palace for the legation. Jan Masaryk was often entertained there, and he also spent a lot of time with Bruce Lockhart, the commercial secretary at the British legation. Lockhart's previous post had been Moscow, where he had been sentenced to death by the Soviet government; a diplomat and writer, who loved fly-fishing and whisky-drinking equally, he often accompanied Jan Masaryk on expeditions to Prague night clubs.

It was at this time that Jan Masaryk gained his reputation as the Playboy of the Western World. He was perhaps taken less seriously than he would have wished to be, finding himself uncomfortably placed between his reputation and his ancestry. He tried marriage. Frances Crane Leatherbee, Richard Crane's sister, became his wife in 1924. She was a widow with three children; the marriage was not a success, and lasted less than five years. Jan Masaryk never repeated the experiment.

In 1925 Beneš appointed Jan minister to the Court of St James's, where he stayed until the Munich crisis. With or without his wife, Jan was a good and popular diplomatic host. The legation, which was then at 8 and 9 Grosvenor Place (one of the houses was the legation and the other the minister's residence), was never far from the centre of diplomatic life in London. Jan Masaryk had his father's friends – Seton-Watson, who held the Masaryk Chair of Central and East European History at London University and Wickham Steed, the former editor and foreign editor of *The Times*, who started teaching Central European history at King's College in London in 1925 – to help him across the difficult patches of London political life. He became a frequent visitor to the diplomatic gallery at the House of Commons. He was tolerated by the Foreign Office, 'which looks coldly on unconventionality, but likes diplomats who give no trouble'.[10] Jan gave no trouble.

However he was a person of volatile moods, and he did not have the kind of self-confidence which comes of proven and unaided achievement. He said in London that: 'Beneš makes the policy and my job is to sell it.' He did more than that. He made Czechoslovakia known, establishing, in his own words, that 'it is a country and not a contagious disease'; he succeeded in making the country popular. Czechoslovakia and her first and second presidents did, on the whole, get a good press in the West, and some of the credit for it must go to Masaryk.

But his popularity in London could not stop Britain sacrificing Czechoslovakia to Hitler. He witnessed Chamberlain's announcement to the House of Commons of impending peace with Germany, and the joy with which it was received. Even after his return to London, and after the outbreak of the war, Masaryk kept away for a long time from the diplomatic gallery. Those of his friends who caught a glimpse of him after September 1938 scarcely recognized him; his pallid face and sunken eyes made him look years older. From then on he started putting on a lot of weight.

In Prague Beneš decided to leave the country in October 1938. To his mind going into exile was an honourable thing for the Czechs to do. But Thomas Masaryk, many years before, had left Austria-Hungary, a state with which he was bound by no ties of loyalty and which it was his intention to destroy. In 1938 Beneš left the state which he had helped to create and failed to defend. He had ignored the telegram from Berchtold Brecht: 'Fight and those who vacillate will join you'; he had stopped the army, fully mobilized, from defending the state. Jan Masaryk never once referred to Beneš's decision to surrender, and there was not a breath of criticism by him of that decision, either in public or private.

Masaryk had a tremendous respect for Beneš's intellect and for his judgement, and he had been asked by his father to remain loyal to Beneš. Though he was only two years younger, he treated Beneš with a 'boyish deference'. He could not argue with Beneš any more than he could betray him. In any case, Jan was a post-poner of decisions, and of confrontations. During the war, when he had an unpleasant message to give to Beneš, he would ask other people to do him the kindness of passing it on.

It may be that such a personal loyalty was harmful to the state, and that it diminished the usefulness of Masaryk to Beneš. It may be that Beneš was an opinionated person, who would have accepted advice from a Masaryk. During his playboy years in London Jan had acquired firm personal loyalties. In the first place his loyalty to his father. Since the end of the war he had been drawing closer to his father. Ten years in America, and four in the Austro-Hungarian army had probably shown him that there are worse things in life than having intellectual parents. He came to regard his father as a 'saint and scholar'; when he moved out of the legation towards the end of the year 1938, he took down the picture of his father with his own hands. By then Thomas Masaryk had been dead for over a year, and Jan transferred much of his respect and admiration to Beneš.

Despite his deep disappointment with the policies of Chamberlain's government, Jan retained his liking for the English and American way of doing things: he was not affected by Munich in the same way as Beneš. Masaryk did not turn away from the Western Powers: many other Czechs and Slovaks did. Munich revealed to them the flaws in the foreign policies of pre-war Czechoslovakia. In London Jan had been partly sheltered from the direct impact of the Munich decision; he had developed, over the years, a strong preference for England over America.

Jan Masaryk, who sounded to the English like an American, would admit that America had many advantages: the ability to learn from past mistakes, her riches and her future. But he could not stand the attitude, as he put it, of 'business, business *über alles*'.[11] In a more flippant and a more concise way, the son echoed the criticism of America made by his father in his war memoirs. But Jan had spent many years in London, and his affection for England was based on two comparisons: with America, and with Central Europe.

He liked England because his daily woman left her hat on when she scrubbed the floor; because a plumber would offer him a cigarette. He liked the Cockneys. He loved it when he heard a pregnant woman say to a man in a bus queue, 'Mind the child, mister,' and when he smiled at her and said, 'Which child, mother?' she patted her stomach and said, 'D'you think I've been stung by a wasp?' Masaryk liked conversations like this, which reminded him of the gentle vulgarity of his native town.

He enjoyed reflecting on the similarities and the differences between his native country and the British Isles. He said on one occasion that the sea around the isles explained a lot about the kind of lives the English led. They did not speak much, but observed a lot; they did not like planning – what was the point of planning when the sea was calm? They improvised and relied on their captain; they left politics to a few hundred people at Westminster. They did not bother as long as all went well; but they became alert when the captain sailed into dangerous waters. Then they bought the captain a house on the mainland, sent him to the House of Lords and found another one.

'They are tremendously obedient people,' Masaryk said. 'Tremendously disciplined. If the captain says that from tomorrow, at twelve, everybody must start collecting fat-rings off their soup, fat-ring collecting centres are at once set up, and it becomes unimaginable that a single fat-ring should get lost.' And life in ships also taught people to think in global terms: Masaryk thought that the legendary ancestor of the Czechs, who had chosen the place for them where they have lived ever since, should have made his tribe walk a bit further; they would have come to the sea shore and they could never be provincial again.

Jan Masaryk took a close look at the English over many years. He was certain that they could not run a revolution, because they had a deep respect for each other. A happy country, it had gone through many bloodless social changes, and Masaryk was convinced that there were more on the way.

A revolution in England? That would be, my friend, a very orderly affair, and the police would have no reason to interfere. Someone would have to make a proposal; someone else would have to second it; and then a far-ranging debate would take place. The effect of the revolution on the price of tobacco would be considered; on the import of eggs and bacon; on dog-racing and other matters of vital importance. The Archbishop of Canterbury would be consulted, G. B. Shaw, Agatha Christie, the BBC brains trust, George Formby and the captain of the winning team of the Cup Tie. The views of the Council for Civil Liberties would be taken into consideration; of the Association of Old Maids; of the Anglican Church and the management of Battersea Dogs' Home; of the vegetarians, the esperantists, the firemen and St John's Ambulance. I may have left somebody out. It is certain that before the end of all the debates and consultations Saturday would come, and the Chelsea-Arsenal match. Revolution would have to be postponed until Monday, when the debate would be continued in the correspondence columns of *The Times*. Sometimes I think that English Communists must feel like Solomon, who sang that all is vanity.[12]

'The English are the most equable people in the world. In spite of what they did to us at Munich, I think that they are more reliable than anyone else. For me, the English are the opposite of the Germans. I can't help it, I like them.' Masaryk said this during the war. At the end of 1938 he had left London for a lecture tour in America. During that tour he never spoke a word critical of Britain. 'I want nothing better for the world than that all countries should have the same qualities as these islands of Britain,' he told his American audiences, at a time when it was popular to say the opposite.

By the outbreak of the war in September 1939, both Beneš and

Masaryk had returned to London from the United States. Beneš then lived in a suburban villa in Putney, in respectable and obscure exile; Masaryk in his flat at Westminster Gardens. Czecho-Slovakia, the creation of Munich, had ceased to exist. The events of September 1938 had unnerved the people and soon their state started falling apart. Beneš had abdicated on 5 October 1938, and left the country on 22 October. The day before his abdication, a right-wing government had been formed. Its policy was not to cross Hitler. The new foreign minister, František Chvalkovský, the former minister to Rome, went to see Hitler and Ribbentrop on 13 and 14 October. He was mercilessly bullied, and in the end assured Hitler that the Prague government would do its best to please him. Before the month was out, Hitler issued secret directives on the scrapping of the 'remnants of Czechoslovakia'. The remnants survived another six months, until Hitler's army entered Prague on 15 March 1939.

The Slovaks had claimed autonomy for themselves on 6 October 1938 and on 14 March 1939 their National Assembly approved the creation of a separate state. The Hungarian army moved straightaway into that part of Carpathian Ruthenia which it had not occupied before. Masaryk's republic was dead. Members of the middle-class parties agreed to run anything that the Nazis would let them run. The local fascists had let loose a campaign against the remaining members of the 'castle' group, a campaign which was singular in its vituperation. One of its main targets was Karel Čapek, who died in December 1938. The Communist Party which had been resolutely opposed to the Munich agreement was banned soon after the conclusion of the agreement.

In America and then in London Beneš and Jan Masaryk were waiting for the outbreak of war between the Western Powers and Hitler's Germany, the war which was to lead to the restoration of an independent and united Czechoslovak state. Beneš insisted on the continuity of the state in international law: if Munich was invalid, he must have reasoned, so was his own resignation. Beneš's memories of his first exile, during the Great War, also affected his conduct in the second exile. There was an uncanny similarity between Beneš's and Masaryk's work abroad.

But Beneš was no Masaryk. In many respects his position was unenviable. He was followed into exile by personal and political differences, and by many men who had opposed him in Prague. He was probably more steadfast in his defence of the continuity and integrity of the pre-Munich state than any of his opponents. When, from time to time, he departed from that position, he returned to it faster than the others. The German question, the Slovak question, the social question, all the problems of pre-war Czechoslovakia were in many cases the only thing the politicians brought with them into exile; now that they had no country to rule their differences became more acrimonious.

Two Slovaks presented the most serious challenge to Beneš: Milan Hodža, the pre-war premier, and Štefan Osuský, the former minister to France. Until the fall of France the French government was openly hostile to Beneš, and manipulated Osuský against him. The British were reserved, letting Beneš live in peace in his Putney villa. 'The West is much worse than I imagined,' Beneš had said on the night when the British and the French ministers informed him of the results of Munich.[13] Throughout the war, his relations with the Western Powers were shot through by suspicion on his part. But in 1938 Beneš had not only condemned the West but also his own foreign policy. A year later he was living in London, hoping for war to break out.

A few days after the outbreak of the war Jan Masaryk was asked by the European service of the BBC to give talks to his home country. They became the most popular programme in the occupied area, the unlovely, colonial Protectorate of Bohemia and Moravia. Even when the short-wave circuits were taken out of the sets, and the death penalty was introduced for listening to foreign broadcasts, the Czechs went on listening to Jan Masaryk. His talks were direct, simple and peppered with occasional coarseness. His achievement and recognition as a broadcaster gave Masaryk a self-confidence which he had hitherto lacked.

Masaryk's first talk was broadcast on 8 September 1939, and he said: 'By the name I bear, I declare to you that we shall win this fight and that truth will prevail.' On 28 October, the twenty-first anniversary of the foundation of the Czechoslovak state, Masaryk returned to the memory of his father and his faith in 'good Czechoslovak people and their future. He knew that our aim must be a good, honest and honourable democracy. He knew that Czechoslovakia is a part of Western culture, and for ever bound up with it. He believed in social justice and the freedom of the individual. He believed in the Slav ideal as well as the European ideal.' The name, therefore, was important. It became the symbol of the continuity of the state, and of resistance to German occupation.

When Masaryk's broadcasts were reprinted in Prague after the war, in 1947, the whole edition of 60,000 copies was sold out in a few weeks. The talks were a matter of historical record then. Though they had lost their immediate emotional appeal, they contained a number of memorable Masaryk sentences: 'There are clouds gathering over Hitler's head, and much German blood will pour from them'; or 'the British people know anxiety; they do not know what fear is'; or, speaking of the collaborating minister of education in Prague, Masaryk said, 'Now we must all pull at one rope – and later we shall hang Moravec on it.'

The partnership between Masaryk and Beneš began to emerge early in the war. Apart from absolute loyalty to the president and his intimate knowledge of British life, Masaryk's contribution was human touch and warmth. They were all qualities which Beneš badly needed in his second exile. He had been programmed to deal with matters of foreign policy. Though Masaryk became Beneš's minister of foreign affairs, Beneš kept the control of foreign policy, and much of the detailed work, for himself. Czechs and Slovaks in exile needed a leader: instead they came to be led by an administrator.

Beneš adopted a plan of action very similar to the one Masaryk had adopted in the First World War. He established a National Committee which would eventually be converted into a government; he set out to organize an army in exile; he kept in close touch with Prague; and he assumed that the Czechs at home would do nothing which would upset his plans. There was some conflict, early in the war, between Beneš's two main concerns. Beneš had used every opportunity to insist that Jan Masaryk must be co-opted to the Committee. Then the question arose of the co-option of two members of the Protectorate government, who had escaped from Prague. They had been in contact with Beneš, and Beneš argued that there existed unity between the government in Prague and the movement in exile; that the 'government at home and resistance abroad are mutually complementary'.[14]

It may have been a useful argument for the recognition of the National Committee by the British government. Nevertheless Beneš's view of the situation exacerbated the differences between the exiles, and further strengthened the original right-wing composition of the Committee. There had been resistance on the Committee to Beneš's proposal that Masaryk should be co-opted; in the case of the co-option of the two ministers, Beneš was warned, by one of his supporters, that it would be 'badly received by our people at home, because they will see in it a return to the old system'.[15] No socialists were represented on the Committee at the time; no Slovaks; no Germans. Both the French and the British mentioned to Beneš their view of the Committee, that it was too narrow and exclusive for their liking.

Later Beneš experimented with a parliament in exile, which was to be more comprehensive and satisfy those politicians who did not get a place on the Committee. The Committee itself was jealously guarded by Beneš, without a trace of magnanimity or political leadership. In the spring of 1940, for instance, the question of German and of Communist representation on the Committee came up. As far as the Germans were concerned, Beneš himself had nothing against their participation. He was less welcoming to the Communists. 'Should this question be posed at all,' Beneš wrote, 'it could be solved only in agreement with the French and the British government.'[16] The Molotov-Ribbentrop non-aggression pact was of course still operative then. Though Beneš regarded it as a way of buying time by the Soviets, it had immobilized the Czech and Slovak Communists who were bound by party discipline to regard the war as an imperialist conflict, and take no part in it.

Meanwhile Masaryk as well as Beneš was irritated by the slow progress of their work in the West. On 20 December 1939 the British government agreed that the National Committee should organize the reconstruction of the Czechoslovak army in France. In his broadcast, Jan Masaryk hailed the exchange of letters between Lord Halifax, the foreign secretary, and Beneš as a recognition of the National Committee by the British government, drawing the inevitable parallels with the First World War. This was the middle of the 'phoney war': Poland had fallen, and there was no fighting going on anywhere in the West. In April 1940 the war got going again after the initial hesitation. Denmark and Norway were invaded by the Germans that month; in May, Holland, Belgium and France. Some 3,000 Czechoslovak troops were among those evacuated from Dunkirk. Then the Battle of Britain began, and over 500 Czech airmen were killed in it.

After the fall of France the British recognized Beneš's National Committee as the government, but the recognition was provisional, and the Czechs were not invited to become one of the Allied governments. Jan Masaryk was foreign minister; this procrastination by the British irked him. He signed himself, when writing to his friends, 'Provisionally yours', and he asked whether the Czechoslovak airmen who were killed flying over Britain were provisionally dead.

The disenchantment, however, was mutual. The ideal 'new Europe' planned by Thomas Masaryk and his friends in Britain had never come into being; the weakness of post-war Europe, especially in its central and eastern parts, had become a contributory cause for the Second World War. The Foreign Office was then considering various schemes for federation – ghosts of the Habsburg Empire? – keeping the exiles in their places, without taking much notice of their advice.

Nevertheless Czechoslovaks abroad proved themselves to be reliable and useful allies, and full recognition was not denied them for long; Beneš was also confirmed in his office as president, a confirmation for which he and Jan Masaryk had worked very hard indeed. The Czechs were gratified when Eden replaced Lord Halifax as foreign secretary in December 1940. Jan Masaryk was enthusiastic, and expected him to move fast in the Czechoslovak interest. But Eden went away on a long mission to the Middle East, and nothing happened for a few months; the Czechoslovak government remained provisional.

Finally, on 19 April, Churchill reviewed Czechoslovak troops at Leamington Spa; they sang 'Rule Britannia' for him rather well. The same evening Churchill wrote a terse note: 'I do not see why the Czechs should not be put on the same footing as the other Allied governments. They have deserved it.'[17] On 18 July 1941, Eden gave Jan Masaryk the British note according the Czechoslovaks full recognition, and recognizing Beneš as their president. Though the British still did not concede Beneš's point about the legal continuity of the republic, Jan Masaryk broke down;

on the way out of Anthony Eden's office, he kissed his old friend and the British representative to the Czechoslovak government, Bruce Lockhart, on both cheeks.

By now, however, the war between Germany and the Soviet Union was four weeks old. Beneš and his government had new problems to deal with. Beneš insisted, we know, on keeping in touch with Prague. In one respect, his insistence brought him considerable dividends. Colonel Moravec, head of Czech army intelligence, and several of his most important colleagues, had joined Beneš in exile. They brought with them their key records, as well as the control of a considerable net of agents; Colonel Moravec's unit kept in touch with the resistance movement in Bohemia and Moravia, which specialized in collecting military and other intelligence.

Moravec had a unique asset in Paul Thümmel, one of the most curious and high-level double agents of the Second World War. Thümmel had worked for the Czechs since 1936, for rather high fees. He was transferred from the *Abwehr* (German military intelligence) headquarters to Prague, where he was finally arrested, in the spring of 1942. For six years Thümmel had been the prime source of intelligence for the Czechs. He remained active longer than he should have done, considering the risks he took. He had the advantage of being protected against the suspicions of the Gestapo, by Himmler himself, who had known Thümmel's family well before the war. In London therefore, Beneš, who kept in direct touch with Moravec, was one of the best-informed exiles; and the services of Moravec were useful for the British and their allies as well.

Nevertheless since the outbreak of the war a strange peace had descended on the Protectorate of Bohemia and Moravia, a peace which disturbed Beneš and his government in exile. Not only did the politicians, the civil service and the police collaborate with the Germans, but businessmen and labour did as well. Active resistance was limited to a handful of former professional officers and, after the attack on the Soviet Union in June 1941, the Communist Party activists. In a way Jan Masaryk's broadcasts from London reflected that situation. They contained no exhortation to the Czechs to resist the forces of occupation, or instructions on how to carry out such resistance.

The first strong reaction to events in Bohemia and Moravia took place in Jan Masaryk's broadcasts from London in October 1941, a few days after Reinhard Heydrich became protector in Prague. Heydrich, chief of the Reich security head office, was making preparations for a Europe run by the German master race. He set out straightaway to eliminate any potential political leaders of the Czechs. The workers and the farmers were, for the time being, to be given enough to eat. He intended to bend the Czechs, not to break them.

In Prague, General Eliáš, the prime minister who had been in touch with Beneš in London, was put on trial for treason, by a special court: its proceedings lasted a few hours and resulted in the death sentence. His defence speech contained an element of self-sacrifice: General Eliáš said that he would bear his punishment gladly, if this made the Czechs co-operate sincerely with the Germans.

Nevertheless Heydrich's campaign of intimidation against the Czechs continued in full public view. Beneš asked Masaryk to tell their compatriots in his broadcast on 1 October 1941: 'We lived through similar times with Masaryk in the last war, when they imprisoned our families and executed our soldiers. And yet we won our holy fight and those who had then acted in the roles of murderers and thieves, perished miserably, paying a physical and moral penalty.' Perhaps Masaryk thought of his own First World War experiences while he was delivering Beneš's message. He may well have wondered whether Beneš was right. The Nazis were a different enemy from the Habsburgs: not only were they more ruthless, but also much more hostile to the Czechs than the old Austro-Hungarian administration had been.

Nevertheless Beneš, through the mouth of Jan Masaryk, again advocated caution to the nation: 'Be cautious, maintain calm, do not be provoked. But at the same time we promise that we shall do everything, together with our allies, to bring the day of reckoning nearer to avenge ourselves completely.' The 'maintenance of calm' was soon to become a grim joke phrase in occupied Prague.

In fact Beneš was as embarrassed by the passivity of the Czechs as the Germans were pleased by it. He started planning to shatter that calm, in which the continuous humming of the Czech armaments industry was the only clearly audible sound. Beneš knew that his chief of military intelligence, Colonel Moravec, had been sending parachutists to the country to maintain links with the underground. Sometime towards the end of 1941, Beneš suggested that a spectacular action against the Germans should be devised, which would wipe out the stigma of passivity and stimulate resistance.[18]

Towards the end of the year 1941 Beneš also abandoned the position he had held since the outbreak of the war: that the governments in Prague and in London were acting in unison. The open hostility between the two Czech governments probably made the decision on a spectacular assassination easier for Beneš: Reinhard Heydrich presented himself as the obvious target. The assassination was to be carried out by two parachutists, a Czech and a Slovak, who had been trained by the British special operations executive. The action against Heydrich was carried out in Prague on 27 May 1942. The *Reich Protektor* was seriously injured by a bomb, and died in a hospital a few days later.

Beneš had been warned, on at least three separate occasions, against the method of political assassination. There were two urgent coded messages from the underground organization on 9 and 12 May which recommended that the operation be cancelled; the head of Czech military intelligence in London had told Beneš that the action would be extremely costly in lives. But Beneš was not to be convinced, and insisted, as supreme military commander, that the action should be carried out. There is no evidence that Beneš consulted his cabinet; Jan Masaryk was then away on a long trip to America, and there had been no opportunity for him to discuss the matter with Beneš.

As a publicity device, the operation was highly successful. At the heart of the action against Heydrich was the personal bravery of the two parachutists, and it was also a considerable technical achievement. 'Czechoslovakia received world wide attention and in the delicate matter of our contribution to the war effort we had been responsible for the execution of the action.'[19] But it failed in its primary objective: it did not stimulate Czech resistance to Nazi occupation. On the contrary. The secret organization which had been set up by the parachutists was smashed by the Gestapo, and so was the remnant of the local underground organization. In addition all the top functionaries of the illegal Communist Party were arrested, and several of them executed. As a postscript to the Heydrich affair, the Germans destroyed the village of Lidice.

After the war Beneš tried to disclaim responsibility for Heydrich's assassination. He had planned the operation secretly, with his chief of military intelligence, and with the knowledge of a very limited circle of military personnel. Most important, the operation went ahead without any preliminary consultation with the Czech underground. It was imposed on it by Beneš, with disastrous consequences. Beneš wanted to prove himself as a leader of decisiveness, a worthy successor of Thomas Masaryk in the Second World War; but he faced a much tougher and more resolute opponent and himself confused firmness with obstinacy.

Jan Masaryk's father was a more thoughtful strategist than Beneš. He saw a broader range of political options, and kept them open as long as he could; he was more flexible about his choices. The parallel with the First World War, and the ways in which Beneš drew on Masaryk's and his own experiences, cropped up in the most unexpected connections in the Second World War. When replying to the request from Prague that the order for Heydrich's assassination should be cancelled, Beneš insisted that there existed a danger of compromise peace with Germany. A memory of the halfway point in the First World War must have helped to set off that reaction in him, as there was no real justification for it in the spring of 1942. It should be added here that, though there was a jubilant broadcast in Czech from Moscow on the occasion of the assassination of Heydrich, the Communists had no occasion to be pleased with Beneš and his role in the near destruction of their underground organization. Nor did they take to the technique of political assassination. They opted instead, when the opportunity arose, for the partisan form of resistance against the German forces of occupation.

It has been said that Jan Masaryk questioned Beneš's policy only with regard to Czechoslovakia's relations with the Soviet Union. But even here his hesitation was more 'psychological than rational'. In any case, as he put it himself, 'I would rather go to bed with Stalin than kiss Hitler's behind.'[20] It is true that Jan Masaryk did not suffer the same shock and revulsion against the Western Powers as Beneš did after Munich, and that he probably did not feel the need for an alliance with the Soviet Union as keenly

as Beneš did. There was certainly room for differences between
the two men.

Munich undermined the certainties on which Beneš had constructed his whole policy. Even before Munich Beneš had added
the Mutual Aid pact with the Soviet Union to the range of diplomatic instruments which were meant to protect his country. But
the alliance of the East with the West against the centre of Europe,
the alliance of the First World War, did not materialize straightaway in the Second. Beneš and his policy fell betwen two stools.

Beneš's distrust of the West led him, according to the Soviet
ambassador to London, Maisky, 'to set out on a direct course for
the East'. The place of France was then taken by the Soviet Union
in Beneš's calculations. In a conversation with a messenger from
Prague, as early as 31 January 1939, Beneš expressed his belief
that: 'Russia will have a lot to say with regard to central Europe . . .
we shall have a common border with Russia. This is no panslavism.
A law of geography. . . . Then they will respect us. . . . Hitler will help
us to become Russia's neighbours.'[21]

At that time, Beneš had no appreciation of the effects such
a policy would have on his relations with the Czech Communists,
relations which in any case had never been very cordial. Beneš
was too much of Masaryk's pupil for that; despite his deep disappointment with the Western Powers, he chose London, and not
Moscow, for his place of exile. Both Bruce Lockhart and Maisky
said, in different ways, the same thing about Beneš. Lockhart
remarked that Beneš's policy was based on the hope of an understanding between the Western Allies and the Soviet Union. Maisky
wrote that:

> When I first met him he was a split personality. His soul there,
> his reason here. He understood that the future of Czechoslovakia
> could be secured only by close co-operation with the Soviet
> Union. He understood that, rationally. . . . In order to secure the
> independence of Czechoslovakia in the future, he was prepared
> to swallow the bitter pill of Soviet-Czechoslovak rapprochement.[22]

The key to Beneš's attitude to the Soviet Union lay in his relations
with the Czech Communists, and especially with the exiles in
Moscow. The Communist deputies and senators in London (they
had left for their places of exile in the West with the agreement

of their central committee) kept in touch with Beneš, who probably thought that he was on better terms with them than was actually the case.[23] The Communists, before and after the conclusion of the Molotov-Ribbentrop pact, held against Beneš his behaviour during the Munich crisis, the composition of his National Committee, even the choice of his residence in exile.

The reaction of many of the Communists who came to London was not one purely of relief: '... and then we saw the proud walls of Whitehall, the beautiful parks and gardens, palaces reaching out to the sun and the expressions on the faces of the people who entered them, getting out of luxury cars; we felt that we had arrived in a world in which the sorrows, ambitions and fate of our people were as distant as the earth is from the sun.'[24]

On one occasion early in the war, on 10 October 1939, Beneš met Šverma, a former Communist deputy, in Paris; Šverma's friend, Vlado Clementis, was unable to attend the meeting because he had been arrested by the French police. Šverma had conducted negotiations with Beneš in 1935, before his first presidential election; now, in October 1939, he tried to persuade Beneš to leave London for good, and come to Moscow.[25] Beneš replied that he would not leave the West until the Soviet Union entered hostilities, and that for the time being he was most interested in working for the unity, 'at any price', of the Czechoslovak movement abroad.

Šverma argued that the situation in the West would push Beneš far to the right and that he would become alienated from the Soviet Union. Beneš said that this would not be so, that the running of the movement in the West could not be left to people like Hodža and Osuský, and that the 'correct progressive, all-national unified line, and of course global eastern and western conception at the same time' would have to be carefully tended in the West.

Again Beneš's way of looking at the Second World War as if it were the First is striking. Like Thomas Masaryk, Beneš would stay in London, working for the cause and for the unity of the movement; he would go to Russia only when it was absolutely necessary, to sort out the situation there; would play both sides of the alliance, East and West, rather than stake everything on one side alone. But Gottwald was no Dürich; he was the leader of a highly disciplined party, who had observed Beneš's policies and actions in his Western exile carefully, and without full approval.

Klement Gottwald, whose performance in the Czechoslovak Parliament before the war we have had occasion to remark, was younger than Beneš; he was only forty-three years old on the outbreak of the war. He had been apprenticed to a carpenter in Vienna, served in the Austrian and Czechoslovak armies, and became one of the founder members of the Communist Party. Its secretary general since 1929, Gottwald was also a member of the executive of the Comintern. He had left Prague for Moscow after a decision of the party's central committee in November 1938.

He was joined in Moscow by Zdeněk Nejedlý (the biographer of Thomas Masaryk) and by many other leading members of the Communist Party. Until the conclusion of the Soviet-Czechoslovak treaty in December 1943 there had been little contact between the emigrés in Moscow and the London government. For instance, in a letter in April 1940 (well before Russia's entry into the war) Beneš wrote to his brother Vojta, an embittered anti-Communist who lived in the United States: 'The Communists are of course playing havoc in our ranks, because even if Russia will now be restrained, the Comintern will go on being active. I tell them: the duty of us all is to fight against Nazism. If you don't want to go along with us leave us in peace, or go to Russia – there, you can make propaganda.'[26]

The key, we have suggested, to understanding Beneš's attitudes to the Soviet Union lay in his relations with the Czech Communists. But Beneš himself would not have agreed. He never brought those two parts of the equation properly together. He wanted better understanding with the Soviet Union, but he was unable to improve his own relations with the Communists. Underneath Beneš's often penetrating analysis of the international scene, there was an almost total lack of understanding of the hidden forces beneath. Beneš was scrupulous in not letting his personal feelings affect his foreign policies, and he assumed that every sensible man in public affairs would more or less share that habit.

The Communists did not. Nor, for that matter, did Jan Masaryk. He had been spared any direct involvement in the pre-war hostility between the Communist and the middle-class parties. The Communists had probably regarded him as a playboy adjunct of the establishment, who was out of sight most of the time. Masaryk had often talked to his father about pre-revolutionary Russia, and remembered the emphasis the old man put on two points: that spiritually Tsarist Russia did not really belong to Europe, and that it was a great power firmly based on imperialism.[27] He told a friend that he always tried to refer the Russia of the 1940s to the picture of Russia drawn by his father. And he found that: 'For me, the Russians will always remain Asiatics. But that is not the worst of it. The English also have a different way of thinking from us, and the Americans as well. And yet we can live with them in peace and co-operate with them, respect each other and be like brothers.'

Russia remained an imperialist power for Masaryk, though: '... socially, much has changed in Russia after the revolution. In politics, radically, very little. At least in foreign politics. The *muzhik* is free. Very important. Perhaps it was worth all the bloodshed. But free for what? To become an instrument of imperialism.' Masaryk regarded Stalin as a kind of Bosnian, Balkan patriarch, and he thought that he detected a touch of humanity in him. But he came to dislike the Russian diplomats. He thought it incredible that before the war there had existed Soviet diplomats who, with a glass of vodka in hand, were very good company. Masaryk had known Litvinov in Geneva and Maisky in London. Perhaps it helped, he thought, that they were Jews. They were the last Soviet representatives with any sense of humour. Molotov then started the deadly serious school of diplomats. Gusev, Bogomolov, Zorin: Masaryk shuddered. They were, as far as he was concerned, the hard-nosed lot. Every time he went to see Molotov, Masaryk said, he had put on an extra vest.

As in every other respect, Masaryk remained loyal to Beneš and his Soviet policy. He himself took little part in the formulation of that policy; nor did he have any alternative to offer. On 18 July 1941, the day the British recognized Beneš's government while stalling on the point of Czechoslovakia's legal continuity, the Soviets recognized both, and more. They concluded a treaty of alliance with the Czechoslovaks, and Masaryk had signed the treaty before he went to see Anthony Eden at the Foreign Office. He referred briefly to that eventful day in his broadcast on 23 July:

... the tiny quislings at radio Prague were ordered to attack the signing of the Soviet-Czechoslovak treaty – and they will therefore raise hell against the bolshevik-plutocrat-Jewish-masonic democrats. You and we shall however understand it. You know that President Beneš, a friend and ally of Britain and Russia, is making your own, honourable Czechoslovak policy.

Though Beneš considered inviting the Communists into his government, and finally did so during his Moscow visit in December 1943, they joined a government consisting of the representatives of both the London and Moscow emigrés only in April 1945. By then the Red Army had entered Czechoslovak territory. Throughout the war, however, Jan Masaryk had been 'instinctively suspicious of the Czechoslovaks in Moscow',[28] and especially of Zdeněk Fierlinger, the Czechoslovak minister to Moscow, who had been asked by the Soviets to leave Moscow in January 1940, and who returned there in the summer of 1941. In July 1941 Masaryk strongly opposed Fierlinger's reappointment.

But Beneš would not change his mind on the appointment. Fierlinger was a professional diplomat, and one of the first employees of Beneš's ministry in 1918. He had served in the Czechoslovak legion in Russia during the war. He joined the Social Democrat Party in 1924, became the minister to Moscow in 1937, and returned to Moscow in 1941. As far as Beneš was concerned, Fierlinger had performed his duties in Moscow well: he replied to telegrams and reported in detail on the attitude of the Soviets to matters of interest. It was generally known that Fierlinger had taken the left position in the Social Democrat Party, and that he was in favour of co-operation with the Communists.

Masaryk did not like Fierlinger's type – thin-faced, unemotional; for Masaryk, he belonged to the Molotov school of hard-nosed diplomats. Fierlinger had worked for Jan's father during the First World War while Jan served in the Austro-Hungarian army. He had risen in the diplomatic service as fast as Jan, and during the war he made as frequent appearances on Moscow Radio as Jan did on the BBC. But Fierlinger never gossiped about the Czechs in Moscow and Masaryk resented his reticence. Their similar careers in the Czechoslovak diplomatic service established no bond of trust between the two men.

Beneš took no notice of Masaryk's reservations on questions of policy and personnel, and briskly proceeded with his own version

of Thomas Masaryk's travels in the First World War. He was perhaps so absorbed in his balancing act that he did not notice that
he travelled the other way round: to America first and after that
to Russia, twice. Beneš discussed his trip to Washington with the
Soviet ambassador, Bogomolov, and later reported that Bogomolov – another hard-nosed diplomat according to Masaryk – came
to see him in April 1943, visibly 'joyful and moved'.[29] Beneš could
have his treaty with the Soviet Union, Bogomolov said, if he really
wanted it.

The following month Beneš came to Washington where, according to his own testimony, his magic worked once again:

> In Washington, I found straightaway complete understanding for
> our policy towards the Soviet Union, and Roosevelt as well as
> Cordell Hull and Sumner Welles agreed with it in principle.
> The North American government saw, in our treaty with the
> Soviet Union, an example of what the other neighbours of the
> Soviet Union should do, in order to secure their independence
> and respect for their internal situation and social structure.[30]

Beneš had intended to go to Moscow immediately after his
return from Washington, but he was moving too fast, especially
for the British. In the end he went to Moscow only after the meeting
there of the three foreign secretaries – Hull, Molotov and Eden – in
December 1943. By then plans for a Polish-Czechoslovak federation
had been quietly dropped, and the London Poles had broken with
Moscow. There had also been some complications about Jan
Masaryk's talks with the Foreign Office about the treaty: the Soviets
protested that the treaty concerned Russia and Czechoslovakia and
no one else.

The Czechoslovak-Soviet treaty was signed by Molotov and
Fierlinger on 12 December 1943, the day after Beneš's arrival in
Moscow. It confirmed and extended the treaties of 1935 and 1941,
and was to remain valid for twenty years. While Beneš was away
in Moscow, Masaryk attended the foundation meeting of UNRRA
in America. He was very tired when he left for New York; and
full of gloomy thoughts. He may have feared disappointment for
Beneš in Moscow; he was sorry for him, and for his loneliness in
England. About that time he said to a friend of his: 'If anything
happens to me, look after Beneš. He means so much to us and

he has so few friends here.'[31] Meanwhile in Moscow Beneš met
Gottwald and other members of the Czech colony there. He invited them to join the government, but they refused the invitation.
Beneš replied: 'I accept your attitude. I must admit that in some
respects it will make my position in London easier.'[32]

The differences between the London and Moscow exiles, hidden
until then, started coming into the open. They did not appear
insuperable for the time being, as they did in the case of the Poles.
Beneš had six long discussions with the Czech Communist leaders
in Moscow, ranging over both the past and the future. Beneš again
defended his Munich policy; the Communists told him that 'Russia
would not have lost', had the war started at the time of Munich.
This was a criticism of Beneš's foreign policy rather than a statement of historical fact. Gottwald and his comrades questioned
Beneš's policies which reached out for alliances in the West as
well as the East. They had watched him fall between two stools
before, and they were indirectly offering him a different solution.

There were also sharp differences between Beneš and the Communists on the Slovak question: Beneš maintained that only a
'Czechoslovak' nationality existed, whereas the Communists argued
that the Czechs and the Slovaks were two separate peoples, and
that they should be treated as such in the post-war state. Other
differences emerged after Beneš's return to London.

Beneš carried with him Klement Gottwald's letter to the Czechoslovak Communists in Britain which pointed out that: 'The
Czechoslovak government in London, as a belligerent government,
is responsible for the initiation and organization of the war effort
of the country, a duty which the government has so far fulfilled
in an unsatisfactory way.'[33] That reference embraced a number of
criticisms, from the inactivity of the London government with regard
to the situation in the Protectorate, by way of Beneš's one-off action
against Heydrich, to the broadcasting policy of the Czech section
of the BBC.

The matters raised in Gottwald's letter of 21 December 1941,
with its comprehensive programme for the organization of post-war
Czechoslovakia, received at first scant attention in Beneš's cabinet.
Nevertheless Beneš had been favourably impressed by the Czech
Communists in Moscow. He reported to his cabinet that: 'The
situation there is good, and better than in London ... they have to

work somehow ... they do not quarrel.'³⁴ Beneš was then ready to support the Communist demand for partisan warfare on the German armed forces, and to license experiments with new groupings of political parties. The 'socialist block' in London was one of them. It consisted of the leaders of the Communists, the Social Democrats and his own party, the National Socialists. The experiment contributed little to political peace and amity. One of the toughest disputes within the block concerned the organization of post-war local government in Czechoslovakia.

Early in 1944 Beneš probably started having serious doubts about the policy of alliance with Russia, a policy which he had tested, rather inconclusively, before Munich, and which he tried so hard to resuscitate during the war. What were the implications of his Eastern policy for the post-war organization of Czechoslovakia? Had he gone too far in Moscow? Some of his ministers were certain that he had. Feierabend, the minister of finance, for instance was convinced that the Soviet treaty was to blame for his lack of success in obtaining credits for Czechoslovakia in the United States.

The Communists, on the other hand, contrasted the negotiations and agreements the London government had achieved in the West with its comparative neglect of the Soviet Union. Throughout the year 1944 only two minor agreements were concluded with the Soviet Union. Beneš concluded his wartime memoirs with his visit to Moscow in December 1943. Their last chapter, written sometime in 1946, analyses in a rather desultory manner Czechoslovakia's position between East and West. It is impossible not to feel sorry for Beneš, when reading those pages of hesitant prose, in the way Jan Masaryk felt sorry for this small, hard-working and friendless man. It is difficult not to admire the tenacious way in which he pursued his lonely presidential ambition.

He did not ask any of his senior ministers to accompany him to Moscow. He was going there to sign a treaty with the Soviet government in the first place and then, after official business, to talk to the Czech Communists. This may have been a tactical and psychological error, perhaps a very important one. The Czech Communist leaders did not trust Beneš; his order of priorities in Moscow could have been seen as a calculated snub for them. He also badly needed a second opinion on his talks with the Communists in Moscow:

he had none available, when he returned to London. And while
Beneš was in Moscow, Jan Masaryk was engaged in the UNRRA
negotiations in America, of which the Moscow Czechs were, initially,
highly suspicious.

Meanwhile the Slovak uprising took place late in the summer of
1944. A few months later it became clear that the Red Army would
reach Czechoslovak territory first. Beneš started to negotiate a new
government with the Communists and then with the other parties.
In February 1945 it was decided that a political delegation – not the
London government – would travel to Moscow and discuss a united
government with the Communists there. The negotiations took place
in March 1945. Jan Masaryk left London in a mood of controlled
pessimism.

The Yalta Conference had taken place between 4 and 13 February: no decision on the Eastern or Western allegiance of Czechoslovakia had been made there, or at any other Allied conference;
no precise demarcation lines had been laid down for the advance
of the Allied armies on Czechoslovak territory. Jan Masaryk went
to see Winston Churchill immediately after his return from Yalta,
and then reported to the cabinet: 'The three of them will rule and
they rely on bayonets. Churchill told me: the three of us will make
the decisions and others will have to follow the lead.... It is obvious
that the three are determined to make ruthless *Machtpolitik*!'[35]

The Czechoslovak delegation to Moscow filled three RAF bombers.
Beneš was in the first plane, with his wife and two nieces, his
personal doctor, maid, butler, the officials of his chancery, and
Jan Masaryk; the second plane contained the political delegation;
the third civil servants. It was shortly before ten o'clock in the
morning of 9 March 1945 when the planes took off; spring was
early in London in the last year of the war, and the day was very
warm. The delegation was seen off from the airport by most of
the Czechs and Slovaks in London.

At lunchtime the planes landed at Toulouse; after a short stop
they passed Sardinia and climbed above the clouds. The expedition
landed at Tripoli for dinner and the night. The following afternoon,
as they were flying over the endless desert, one of the Catholic
priests, a member of the political delegation, brightened the bore-
dom of flying by remarking that he at last understood why Christ
was able to resist the devil when he offered him the world. They

spent the second night at Shephards Hotel in Cairo, and dined
with the Czechoslovak minister. Two of the planes had to wait in
Cairo for three days for Beneš's plane which had been delayed at
Tripoli.

On 14 March the planes flew over the Persian mountains; the
travellers were offered oxygen masks. In the afternoon they landed
at Teheran, where the Czechoslovak ministers to Moscow and
Teheran were waiting for them at the airport. The Czechoslovaks
transferred to Soviet planes, and left for Baku on 16 March; they
arrived in Moscow the following day in the afternoon. Gottwald and
other Czech Communist leaders welcomed them at the airport. In
Moscow controversy about the distribution of government offices
lasted until 28 March: the ministries of the interior, education,
information and agriculture went to the Communists, while Gottwald became the deputy prime minister; Zdeněk Fierlinger, the
minister to Moscow and the man Jan Masaryk could not abide,
became prime minister; Masaryk himself retained the ministry of
foreign affairs.

Three days after the composition of the new government had
been agreed, on Saturday 31 March, its members and many others
left Moscow by train for the Czechoslovak territory which had been
liberated by the Red Army. The government finally reached Prague
on 10 May 1945. Jan Masaryk was not on the train; he did not
return to Prague via Slovakia with the new government.

The last months of his exile had been especially trying for him.
He was haunted by the subject which had previously fascinated
him: the relationship between the great powers and the small
nations. He feared the application of cold ruthlessness in that
relationship. Above all he wanted the Czechs to avoid the fate of
the Poles: the harsh division of their politics into two streams, with
one group doomed to remain in exile for ever. He could find no
consolation in the fashionable theory that Czechoslovakia would
become some kind of a 'bridge' between the East and the West.
He knew that bridges were misused: they got blown up in wartime
and in peacetime animals fouled them up.

From time to time Masaryk expressed strong views on a personnel
matter, especially when it concerned the appointment of a Communist to an important post. (Masaryk for instance advised against
Ludvík Svoboda, the commander of the Czechoslovak army in the

Soviet Union, being made one of several top-ranking officers in the Czechoslovak army.) Otherwise Beneš's grand conception of foreign policy was never questioned by Masaryk. He remained, in his relationship with Beneš, deferential, devoted, even admiring. And yet Masaryk was only two years younger than Beneš: it was as if the younger man thought of the gap in their ages as being much larger; as if he insisted on being an unequal partner.

There were also private sorrows in his life. One of his two nephews – the half-Swiss sons of his sister Olga – had been killed flying for the RAF; the other, a gifted musician, died of TB in February 1945. Masaryk would have liked children of his own: the loss of his two nephews during the war was a very heavy blow to him. Apart from Jan, they were the last male descendants of Thomas Masaryk; Jan himself was so ill and exhausted in February 1945 that he retired to a nursing home. He left it in time to accompany Beneš to Moscow; he then went to San Francisco, via London, to another meeting concerning the United Nations.

The Internal Exile

WHEN Jan Masaryk returned to Prague in the summer of 1945, some time after the other members of the government, he was a stranger in his own country. He had been away for almost ten years, in America, before the First World War, and he spent the best part of the war in the Austro-Hungarian army, in other parts of the Empire. Then there were the years in the diplomatic service between the two wars, and then exile. It had become Masaryk's habit not to live in Prague.

On 11 April 1945 he made his last BBC broadcast: 'It is a curious fate. I am going to Prague from London, via Moscow and London and San Francisco. Yes, to Prague. Thank God. But I am very glad that I have had the honour and the pleasure to visit Moscow, the Slav metropolis, talk with Soviet leaders, and find that they and the Russian people like us, know about us, and see in us their faithful allies.' Soon after his return to Prague from San Francisco, on 5 August 1945, Masaryk said in another broadcast: 'For seven years, I have looked forward to a Czechoslovak microphone. I have had more than enough of foreign ones. At last, it has come off.' And speaking of the San Francisco conference, he said: 'The basis of our policy, that is close co-operation with the Soviet Union, proved to be working very well at the San Francisco conference. Co-operation with the Soviet delegation took place every day, and was intimate and friendly.'

In 1945 Czechoslovakia was different from the country Jan Masaryk's father had known. Even its shape had changed. Its province furthest to the east, Carpathian Ruthenia – the unexpected gift to the first republic from the peace conference in 1919 – was incorporated into the Ukrainian SFR by a treaty of 29 June 1945.

Czechoslovakia therefore acquired a common border with the Soviet Union, losing her pre-war border with Romania in the process. The ethnic structure of the country changed as well.

Though Czechoslovakia had not been directly involved in the hostilities, losses in her population were estimated at 360,000. Article xii of the Potsdam agreement of August 1945 on 'The Orderly Transfer of the German Population' was implemented in the main by the end of the following year. More than three million Germans, almost one-third of the population of the Czech lands, left for the various zones of occupation in Germany; the Hungarians of Slovakia were also to be transferred.

Beneš had insisted that the transfers take place. There were to be no minorities or minority rights in the new Czechoslovakia. The Jews had either died in concentration camps or left the country; now its Germans and Hungarians were about to leave. They had all left behind them their history and their dead, and most of them what they used to call their property. After the war the Germans left behind them their farms and their factories, and it was not easy to find enough Czechs to slip into their jobs and their ways of doing things. Consumer industries were especially hard hit; the attention paid by governments, especially by the Communist governments after 1948, to heavy industries was not always a matter of choice.

The Prague Jan Masaryk returned to was dusty and very hot, and full of Red Army troops. Nights were often turned into days by army flares; there was no other use for them any more, and they were set off in exuberance that the war was over. Masaryk moved into the Czernin palace, the building near the castle which housed the ministry of foreign affairs. He was looked after by an old butler, Příhoda, who had served his father.

Masaryk's flat was on the second floor of the palace, a set of rooms of which he used only one. It had three large windows and a brass bed at one end, a sofa and a few armchairs at the other and a writing desk under the middle window. The Loreta church stood on the other side of the square; its bells played a lovely carillon on the hour, the opening bars of a hymn based on a folk song. It was the Masaryk part of town. A few minutes' walk and to the north of the castle the Masaryk family had lived, on one side or the other of the castle, for many years. Even now his sister, Alice, had a flat in an ancient house near the ministry. At night when he first moved into the room, Masaryk cried and cried.

In a few weeks Jan Masaryk would be fifty-nine years old. He was over six feet tall, and rather fat, but he walked lightly, often on the balls of his feet. He was small-boned, and used his neat small hands a lot in conversation: his father used 'to mould his ideas with his hands'. He had an irregular, lived-in face; his eyelids drooped a lot; his nose was long, beaked and asymmetrical; his eyebrows were mobile. He had his father's eyes: black, lively, deep. He often wore a black hat of no particular shape. He was fond of food and drink, and smoked a lot of Players' cigarettes. He had been married once, for five years. His closest friend was Mrs Marcia Davenport, the American novelist whom he had met in New York a few weeks before Pearl Harbor in November 1941.

After his return to Prague, Masaryk frequently visited Lány, where his parents were buried in the village cemetery. His father's former country residence was at the disposal of President Beneš (he preferred his own house at Sezimovo Ústí). Masaryk's room at Lány was left as it had been when the president died. A plain iron bed, book cases, pigeon holes which Masaryk used instead of a filing cabinet. There were a death mask and a cast of Masaryk's right hand in glass cases. There were Lippizaner horses in the stables, as before the war. The familiar, distant coal mine was visible from several places in the large park.

In the last two years of his life Masaryk increasingly sought refuge in the past, and in withdrawal into his private world. He was becoming more introspective than he used to be. His moods changed even faster, and the present was sometimes impossible for him to bear. A solitary person who feared loneliness, Jan sought out the company of Marcia Davenport as often as he could. However the two had decided that they would lead their own lives, and meet only on special occasions. Mrs Davenport thus had her own existence, and her own novels to write. Then forty-three years old, she was very fond of Jan, and was prepared to commute between New York and Prague for his sake. But he preferred her not to be dependent on him emotionally and socially and she could not be for Jan what Charlotte, another American woman in the family, had been for Thomas Masaryk.

She left a valuable, impressionist record of their relationship.

H

Written many years after his death, it is a record from the outside of two lives marked by the ineluctable realities of the post-war world. She had to guess at the ways Jan was affected by them. In public, for instance, he was full of optimism about the San Francisco conference, saying that it had gone well, as had his common work with the Soviets. Mrs Davenport's view of the way in which the conference had affected Masaryk was quite different. It was 'the first of the series of unrelenting public humiliations at the hands of Molotov and the Red block, including the Communist robots among the Czechs, which were visibly to tear him apart'.[1]

There was no one, it seems, to whom Masaryk could talk openly about the extent of either his public insincerity or his private humiliation. And yet in the optimistic summer of 1945 there was perhaps little need for such a doom-laden retrospective view of Masaryk's political and personal problems.

Marcia Davenport spent a month in Prague in the early spring of 1946, most of it with Jan Masaryk. He then left for the Paris conference of twenty-one states, which negotiated peace treaties with Italy, Romania, Hungary, Bulgaria and Finland. By then, the wartime alliance had clearly and visibly broken up, and the growing tension between Stalin, determined to consolidate Soviet gains in East Europe, and the English-speaking powers had resulted in sharp diplomatic skirmishes. They concerned Iran and south-eastern Europe; the status of the Danube and Italian reparations; the administration of Trieste and the territorial gains of Greece. In most of these problems Czechoslovakia had no direct interest, but on many occasions Masaryk and his delegation voted with the Soviets.

Though the Russians had been demobilizing fast, their military intentions were not above suspicion in the West, while to the Russians, US monopoly in atomic weapons looked no less threatening. In the post-war situation Beneš's and Masaryk's policy was becoming less and less viable. Differences between the years after the First and Second World Wars started emerging with a clarity which was displeasing to many Czechs.

Again Germany was defeated, but this time, it lay in ruins which it would take a generation to repair. Again an East-West alliance

had defeated the centre of Europe, but this time Germany had
failed to beat Russia before being defeated, in its turn, by the
Western Powers. After the Second World War there were visible
reminders of Russia's strength in most parts of Central Europe.
Though the Red Army left Czechoslovak territory in November
1945, it was drawn up in Germany on the river Elbe; the Soviet
occupation zone in Austria ended far to the west of Vienna; Red
Army units were stationed in Poland and Hungary, Romania and
Bulgaria. Stalin seemed determined to turn round the *cordon
sanitaire* – the safety zone of small states between the Baltic and
the Adriatic seas, a French foreign policy concept after the First
War – and make it face the West.

In a way the situation which Kramář and his Czech friends
had prayed for early in the First World War became reality at the
end of the Second. Thomas Masaryk's political triumph had been
at least partly based on the simple fact that the Russian armies
never reached Prague. After the revolution in Russia he had little
sympathy with the new Soviet regime. One accident and one policy
decision had strengthened Thomas Masaryk's hand. After the
Second World War Beneš and Jan Masaryk were not so favoured.
The Red Army had reached Prague, and Beneš and Masaryk had
a long past behind them of disapproval of the Soviet state and
of Communism. Jan Masaryk had often used the theme of Slav
solidarity in his broadcasts from London during the war. Slav
solidarity in practice was a different matter.

He left Prague for America in October 1946 and attended the
meeting of the UN General Assembly at Lake Success. Again the
Russians showed little willingness to play the international organ-
izations game according to the rules laid down by the Americans.
By now Masaryk's private preferences and his loyalty to his
country and to Beneš had started moving apart. He left the United
Nations meetings as often as he could; he saw a lot of Marcia
Davenport and was able to relax in her company. He stayed on in
America for the UN meetings until the end of November, and then
decided to stay for Christmas.

Mrs Davenport had been lent a house in Florida. This was the
first holiday Jan Masaryk had had since Munich – something he
said that he did not mind, because the years before 1938 had been
one long holiday for him. For an articulate person, however,

Masaryk was becoming increasingly reticent about the matters which were uppermost on his mind. It is true that politics had never been a subject of absorbing interest to him, as it had been for his father, but he had often talked politics in a general, impressionist way to his friends. Now, in the last years of his life, he kept on turning to the past, and 'old memories, old flavours, glimpses of vanished worlds' filled his favourite conversations. Ancestry was another subject he talked about. He was sure that he must be Jewish somewhere, though the 'presentable story' did not say so. He thought that no one in Europe could be certain of his ancestry, not even the people who had it carefully recorded in the *Almanach de Gotha*: there, in particular, Jan thought, you got 'into the fun and games department'. Who knows whether his reference to the 'presentable story' and to his Jewish ancestry was set off by some barely remembered hint at the connection with the Redlich family on his paternal grandmother's side? Jan's view of his paternal grandfather, an easy-going countryman who was very fond of his drink, perhaps fitted the picture of the kind of person who would marry a woman much older than himself and pregnant, and then look after her eldest son as if he was his own.

Early in 1947 Marcia Davenport moved into her flat in a fifteenth-century house in Prague. The windows of all the three rooms overlooked most of the town. It was about two minutes' walk from the ministry of foreign affairs, and Jan Masaryk's sister, Alice, lived in the same house. He leant more than ever on the companionship of the two women who were closest to him.

Though some of Jan Masaryk's Western friends and acquaintances were suspicious of his political position and activities, others understood that position, and came to see him in Prague. In May 1947 Bruce Lockhart came from London to visit Jan. He found the foreign minister 'sometimes serious, but mostly cheerful and buoyant with hope'.[2] Jan Masaryk's days were busy; they usually started on the telephone at eight am and moved through the rounds of official paperwork and public engagements, sometimes till late at night. He always found enough time for his friends, using the rest of the rooms in his flat only on the occasions when he entertained them.

Bruce Lockhart's report on Jan Masaryk's state of mind in the spring of 1947 was the most comprehensive, and was written by someone who had known Masaryk for almost three decades. Leaving Prague on 20 May 1947, Lockhart jotted down the report on the train on the way to London.[3] Jan Masaryk appeared to be 'politically much happier'. This did not mean, Lockhart wrote, that he liked the Soviet leaders any better. On the contrary. He was still afraid of them, but he was also irritated by the Americans' misreading of the situation in Europe. Most of all, he feared a rupture between the Americans and the Russians. Jan retained his personal charm and mastery of words. According to Bruce Lockhart, that was where his political power lay.

It is possible that, just as Marcia Davenport had been too pessimistic about Masaryk's view of the situation in 1945, Lockhart was over-optimistic for 1947. He was however right about Masaryk's political influence. It was built on shallow foundations. In the parliamentary elections in May 1946 the Communists had emerged as by far the most powerful organization in Czechoslovakia. They had received 40·17 per cent of all votes and ninety-three mandates in Bohemia and Moravia; and 30·37 per cent and twenty-one mandates in Slovakia. Klement Gottwald became prime minister; Masaryk was glad of this change, because of his intense dislike for Fierlinger, Gottwald's predecessor.

Lockhart mentioned in his report that Jan Masaryk was not afraid of the Czech Communists, because he thought that they were on the downgrade. He apparently told Beneš that: 'You are the most popular man in the country, I am the second and David [the speaker in the Parliament], not Gottwald or Slánský, is the third.'

It may be that Masaryk made the same kind of mistake as Beneš with regard to the Communists. He underestimated them, and did not pay enough attention to them. As early as December 1943, when the final phase of the war started taking shape, Beneš had gone to Moscow to see the Soviet leaders first and the Czech Communists second, an error of tact and tactics.

In his own way Jan Masaryk also teased the Communists. Sometimes he did so in public, and without mercy. At a food exhibition for instance, he called out to Kopecký, the minister of information and a descendant of the family which ran the famous marionette theatre, 'Come here, I have the right buttonhole for you, and the right colour too!' And led him, amidst much laughter, to the red paprika stall.

Perhaps it is a mistake to be too solemn in print about a simple and innocent joke. In Prague just after the war such public horse-play would have been acceptable between men who knew each other well in private, and who liked each other. But Masaryk's relationship with Communist leaders was of a different kind. He met them at cabinet sessions and public functions, but that was all. No one could expect Masaryk to have many friends among the Communists, but it was perhaps unusual that he did not have a single one. Even Vlado Clementis, Masaryk's deputy in the ministry of foreign affairs, an intellectual, a lawyer and a Slovak, was not trusted by Masaryk because he came under party discipline. Clementis had spent the war in the West; he was soon to perish in the party purges.

Jan Masaryk was perhaps right to fear the Soviet leaders, as long as he never showed fear. He represented for them – as he did for the Czechs – the Western capitalist tradition. The Soviet leaders happened to disapprove of it. Moreover in their historical memories they would have been hard put to it to discover a single reason for remembering his father, and his activities in Russia, with affection.

On the other hand Masaryk and Beneš had little hard evidence of Western support for Czechoslovakia. They had sought an American loan without success. President Truman would not consider recommending a loan to a country which had Communists in the government as Czechoslovakia very visibly did. Neither Masaryk nor Beneš had any reason to suppose that the Western governments cared whether they themselves stayed in the Czechoslovak cabinet or not.

So far we know of no steps taken by either Masaryk or Beneš to settle with their Communist colleagues in the government their different views on Czechoslovakia's international position. It was common knowledge that the country's official policy was to have alliances in the West as well as the East, and that the Communists were critical of that dual conception.

There seems to have been a lack of contact between Masaryk and the Communists on this important matter. No one seems to have established precisely the extent of the difference and whether it

would spill over into the domestic affairs of the country. Indeed
Jan Masaryk behaved as if he had never heard of phrases like
contingency plan, irreconcilable clash, or resignation. He relied
on his charm and on his oratory – 'his happy knack of expressing
a commonplace in a highly original manner' – to give him political
popularity, and he confused this with political power. He had no
liking for the day-to-day political routine, and even less for
political parties.

In that way Jan Masaryk resembled Beneš as well as his father.
It is remarkable that the three best-known democrats in Czechoslovakia should have shared such self-imposed remoteness from
the ordinary machinery of politics. We remember how Thomas
Masaryk had solved that dilemma after 1918 by surrounding himself with people who were dedicated to him, or very powerful in
public affairs, or, preferably, both. Neither Beneš nor Jan Masaryk
was so fortunate or agile. The Communists, on the other hand,
had a powerful organization at their disposal.

There was a distinct hint of the approaching crisis in the
summer of 1947. On 5 June 1947, in a speech at Harvard University, George Marshall called on Europe to unite to achieve economic salvation. On 18 June Mr Bevin and M. Bidault invited
Mr Molotov to Paris to discuss with them the recovery of Europe
with the aid of America. Molotov came, and started arguing
points of procedure soon after his arrival. He left for Moscow on
2 July 1947, after accusing Western powers of trying to interfere
with the rights of other countries, and of dividing Europe into
two hostile camps.

Nevertheless London and Paris pressed on with the initiative,
and invited twenty-two states to take part in a conference in Paris.
The Soviet media kept referring to 'dark adventurist aims' whenever they mentioned the conference. For the second time Mr
Harold Wilson returned from Moscow, at the end of the month,
without a commercial agreement.

Despite danger signals from Moscow, Gottwald's cabinet
accepted the invitation to Paris on 4 July. After a long and
exhausting meeting, all the Communists in the cabinet, including
the prime minister, agreed that Czechoslovakia should attend the
conference. Unfortunately little is known about the cabinet meeting
that night, but taking into consideration small scraps of evidence

as well as the events immediately after the meeting the following picture emerges.

The non-Communist ministers, led by Jan Masaryk, simply convinced the Communists that their country must be represented at the Paris conference. It was a straight fight. With the Social Democrat ministers joining ranks with the non-Communists, the ayes to the conference had it, even in terms of straight numerical majority. It is not apparent that the cabinet discussed contingency plans in case of Russian objections. Jan Masaryk had won a Pyrrhic victory.

At another meeting a few weeks before Gottwald had given a broad hint as to Czechoslovakia's foreign policy. He said that in his view the Soviet-Czechoslovak treaty was the basis of common action not only against Germany, but against any other state which might become Germany's ally.[4] Several cabinet members disagreed with Gottwald, who suggested that a delegation should go to Moscow to discuss the treaty with France and other matters.

Jan Masaryk had agreed to that proposal, and found himself on a plane to Moscow, a member of a small delegation headed by Gottwald. This was on 3 July 1947, and the Marshall plan was not officially on the agenda for the Moscow talks. A few hours before their departure, however, members of the delegation had been told that Poland had refused to be represented in Paris. The following afternoon Stalin told Gottwald privately that he would prefer it if Czechoslovakia did not take part in the conference.

Later on the same day, 9 July, he told the whole delegation, including Masaryk, that he would regard Czechoslovak participation as a hostile act, and that if it took place, Czechoslovakia could no longer rely on Soviet friendship. Masaryk later told several friends that: 'I went to Moscow as the Foreign Minister of an independent sovereign state; I returned as a lackey of the Soviet government.'[5] Though several versions of the sentence were in circulation, it is very likely that Masaryk actually said something of the sort; many references were also made to Munich, a very misleading comparison.

The non-Communist members of the delegation to Moscow – Jan Masaryk, Prokop Drtina, and Arnošt Heidrich – conceded defeat straightaway after the interview with Stalin. Gottwald then telephoned Prague. He asked the cabinet to meet and accept Czechoslovakia's withdrawal from the Paris conference. He also instructed Jan Masaryk's deputy, Vlado Clementis, to tell Beneš of the decision. The meeting of the ministers opened at four am in Prague. Clementis, who had meanwhile sought out Beneš, was unable to tell him the news since he was gravely ill and unable to speak; he had suffered a brain haemorrhage. Other ministers had been trying to get in touch with him in vain. At its early morning meeting the cabinet agreed to revoke its acceptance of the invitation to Paris.

In July 1947 it therefore became apparent that there was no effective opposition in Prague to the Communist Party. The key issue of foreign policy had been resolved. The Communist Party had advocated alliance with the Soviet Union alone. The other parties saw a broader range of options. They had varied in their tolerance of the Soviet link, and regarded Western alliances as its essential counterpart. But that battle was over, and the politicians who had lost it probably assumed that their defeat would have a far-reaching impact on domestic politics.

It could have been expected that the delicate civil peace in post-war Czechoslovakia would be broken by an issue of foreign policy. Memories of the foundation of the state were still fresh; foreign policy, and foreign powers, had played a very important role in it. From July 1947 there was probably no alternative to the Communist Party taking over more and more responsibility for the running of the state.

Let us, however consider the position of Jan Masaryk. The person to whom he was absolutely loyal and whom he regarded as the major source of political wisdom was probably dying. Masaryk knew full well how grave Beneš's illness was. The president had suffered from arteriosclerosis for some time, from spinal TB and high blood pressure. Masaryk must also have noticed certain personality changes in Beneš, especially sharp fluctuations between stubbornness and weakness.[6] Was Jan Masaryk now released from the promise he had given his father? Or did that promise lead to another, more important obligation?

There was no question that Jan Masaryk could or would carry Beneš's responsibilities as well as his own. He had said, 'I wish I could be rid of it all,' to too many people: his habits were on the whole private and leisurely, but he had become a public property, an emblem of the continuity of the state, and of its links with the West.

Having become a dutiful son rather late in life, Jan Masaryk assumed more and more responsibilities, including those, in the end, of a living symbol. He was not equipped for that role. When he returned to Prague from Moscow on 12 July 1947, he knew that the symbol had no substance and that it was a complete sham. He looked ill and bloated. He had been living on nervous energy for some time; he was exhausted, and often had severe attacks of coughing in the mornings. He was stunned and nervous after his return, alternating between rapid speech and long spells of silence. Mrs Davenport wrote of that time: 'In the last year of his life the pressures on him were savage. I felt, at a range so close that it might be said to be with his own feelings, the intolerable despair and humiliation which wracked him. I felt his judgement weaken and sway and wheel from desperate hope to more desperate hopelessness.'[7]

But still Masaryk held on. There followed a period of shadow-boxing between the political parties, which sometimes turned into a real fight. There was trouble in Slovakia and in the Social Democrat Party. In September Jan Masaryk and two other ministers were sent parcel bombs, the incident which set off the fatal struggle for the control of the police. The Cominform was established in Moscow in the same month to ensure unity in the ranks of the Communist states. After the wealth tax controversy, also in September 1947, Masaryk, who had not attended the cabinet meeting where the tax was discussed, published an unusual statement which attacked the cabinet decision as well as the Communist press.

Jan Masaryk had arrived in New York on 15 September 1947. He dislocated his shoulder – an American friend told him that he must have been leaning too hard on the iron curtain – and put himself on the United Nations' sick list. He made his customary foreign minister's speech, and then attended a few committee meetings. One day he went to Washington, hoping to see President Truman or the secretary of state, Marshall. He was received by neither. As far as the United States were concerned, Czechoslovakia was apparently consigned to the other side of Europe. After July and the refusal to attend the conference in Paris, there was nothing that the Americans could usefully discuss with Masaryk. Masaryk himself did not see the situation in his own country in such clear-cut terms. He still hoped. There was to be a general election in Czechoslovakia in the spring of 1948, and he thought that it was important. He wanted to find out if anyone outside his country shared his view of the election, and what the American attitude would be to a full-scale political crisis in Czechoslovakia.

Jan Masaryk had meant to spend two days in Washington, but there was no need. He returned to New York, to Mrs Davenport's house, on the same day. When she answered the door that evening she found Jan Masaryk there looking deathly pale. They sat together in silence for a long time. Finally he 'looked at me as if I had asked a question and with a small, quick motion, almost imperceptible, he shook his head'.[8]

He may well have reflected on his father's visits to Washington towards the end of the First World War, on his father's glory and his own impotence. Perhaps he thought of some tragic flaw in his patrimony, or of the turns of the wheel of fortune. He had not yet reached the age at which his father left for exile in the First War; all the same, he was very tired. There was a curious quality about the final stages of the two Masaryks' state. The principal actors had little to say for themselves. They indulged in no dialogue and engaged in no controversy. They acted out a mime and then left in silence.

This time Masaryk did not stay in America for Christmas. On 3 December he telephoned Bruce Lockhart from his London flat in Westminster Gardens; the two men saw each other for the last time. Jan Masaryk talked wearily of the UN meetings; he praised Marshall and said, again, how much he disliked Vyshinsky, who had, as Masaryk put it, 'abuse in his blood'. He must have told Lockhart that some of his American friends had warned him not to return to Czechoslovakia, adding: 'You can leave your country twice or as many times as you have the strength to fight. You can't do it to fight your own countrymen.'[9] But Masaryk was optimistic about the spring election, and his last words to Lockhart were mockingly resolute: 'Never mind old boy. We'll beat the buggers yet.'

They did not. The formal takeover of power by the Communist Party was completed on 25 February 1948. Gottwald then presented

to Beneš the list of his new government. The Communists held
half the cabinet posts, three went to left-wing Social Democrats,
and to representatives of other parties who were ready to co-
operate with the Communists. Jan Masaryk retained the ministry
of foreign affairs. In the afternoon Gottwald visited the castle to
get a confirmation from Beneš that he accepted the new cabinet.
Beneš signed the list.

Jan Masaryk was also at the castle at the time. On his way
back to the foreign ministry, after Beneš had confirmed the list put
before him, he stopped at Mrs Davenport's flat. He sat with her
for a long time and in silence, then he went to see his sister Alice
in the same house. Early next morning his butler brought Mrs
Davenport a note: 'Am staying in this "govt" for the time being.
It breaks my heart for you to receive these shocks which you
deserve less than anybody else in the world. Do not be too sad.
Be bitter and proud – of yourself. I am very proud of you. You
believed in a decent hope – so did I. It could not be. But this is
not the end.'[10]

The note could have been written to himself. He had only
bitterness and pride to fall back on. A few days later he said that
he stayed on in the cabinet because Beneš, unable to stand his
own ground and not in full command of his faculties, also remained
in office. But such perseverance was beyond the call of duty, and
Masaryk must have known that. He could neither do what he
thought was expected of him, nor, in the same way as Beneš,
could he resist what he took to be the will of the people. Even
more than before, silence surrounded all his actions.

He no longer bothered to give reasons for anything he did. His
policies and actions were, he must have known, inexplicable in
his own terms. When he talked, he started telling people contradictory things. That he was going to stay in Prague; that he was
going to escape abroad; that he was going to kill himself. From
time to time he read the Bible which used to belong to his father
and which was sent to him by the widow of Dr Šámal, the head
of Thomas Masaryk's chancery, who had died in a concentration
camp.

His last public appearance took place in Prague, on 7 March
1948, at a ceremony to commemorate the ninety-eighth anniversary
of his father's birth. His father had died on 14 September 1937,

on Jan's fifty-first birthday. Jan died three days after his father's birthday. He was found in the early hours of the morning of 10 March, lying dead in the courtyard of the foreign ministry. His father's Bible lay open on the bedside table.

It was sufficient for the drama of that night to take place in Jan Masaryk's mind. He had fallen into the terrible habit of silence; his last hours also remained unexplained. There was no need for assassins to disturb the peace of the ancient, cavernous palace in which Masaryk spent his last night. He knew, as well as his adversaries did, that his life was at an end, and that he could no longer effectively influence the course of events in Czechoslovakia. He was the heir to an historic name, a name which was charged with historic meaning. But that meaning was not read even by all the Czechs and Slovaks in exactly the same way; and by others less so.

Notes

Introduction

1 D. A. Lowrie, *Masaryk of Czechoslovakia* (London 1937), p. 205.
2 F. Nečásek, J. Pachta and Eva Raisová (editors), *Dokumenty o protilidové a protinárodní politice T. G. Masaryka* (Prague 1953); F. Nečásek and J. Pachta, *Dokumenty o protisovětských piklech československé reakce* (Prague 1954).
3 Karel Pichlík, *Zahraniční odboj bez legend, 1914–1918* (Prague 1968).

Chapter 1 Young Masaryk

1 This autobiography was first published in Jaromir Doležal, *Masarykova cesta životem* (Brno 1921), II, pp. 1–18. There are two earlier, less complete translations into English: in W. Preston Warren, *Masaryk's Democracy* (London 1941) and in Paul Selver, *Masaryk* (London 1940).
2 For instance Willy Lorenz's essay on the Masaryks in his *Monolog über Böhmen* (Vienna 1964).
3 Jan Herben, *T. G. Masaryk* (Prague 1947), p. 16.
4 Zdeněk Nejedlý, *Masaryk* (Prague 1930–6), I, 2, p. 343.
5 Nejedlý, I, 2, p. 348.
6 Nejedlý, I, 2, p. 347.
7 Nejedlý, I, 2, p. 353.
8 Karel Čapek, *Hovory s Masarykem* (Prague 1946), I, p. 110.
9 Nejedlý, I, 2, p. 377.
10 Nejedlý, II, p. 12.
11 Nejedlý, II, p. 226.
12 Nejedlý, II, p. 32.

Chapter 2 Masaryk in Prague

1 Nejedlý, *Masaryk*, III, p. 7.
2 Jan Herben, *Deset let proti proudu* (Prague 1898), p. 36.
3 Herben, *T. G. Masaryk*, p. 92.
4 Herben, p. 93.
5 Herben, p. 135.

6 A. Bráf, *Paměti*, edited by Josef Gruber (Prague 1922), I, editor's preface.
7 Bráf, pp. 20–1.
8 Bráf, p. 22.

Chapter 3 **Masaryk and Russia**
1 Zbyněk Zeman, *The Break-up of the Habsburg Empire* (Oxford 1963), p. 16.
2 T. G. Masaryk, *Světová revoluce* (Prague 1926), p. 12.
3 Zeman, p. 77.
4 Pichlík, *Bez legend*, p. 98.
5 R. W. Seton-Watson, *Masaryk in England* (Cambridge 1943), p. 40–7.
6 For Svatkovski's and Giers's reports from Rome see *Mezhdunaródnye otnoshenie v epokhu imperialisma* (Leningrad 1931 and after), series III, VI, 2.
7 Pichlík, p. 107.
8 Pichlík, p. 117.
9 Pichlík, p. 199.
10 Pichlík, p. 200.
11 Masaryk, p. 141.
12 Masaryk, p. 150.
13 *Politische Chronik* (January 1917), pp. 73–4.

Chapter 4 **The World Crisis**
1 Pichlík, *Bez legend*, p. 237.
2 Masaryk, *Světová revoluce*, p. 155.
3 Zeman, *The Break-up of the Habsburg Empire*, p. 121.
4 Pichlík, p. 241.
5 Pichlík, p. 243.
6 Beneš, *Paměti* (Prague 1947), I, p. 335.
7 Masaryk, p. 207.
8 Masaryk, p. 211.
9 Masaryk, p. 571.
10 E. V. Voska, *Ve víru poválečném* (Prague 1922), p. 10.
11 Masaryk, p. 209.
12 *Dokumenty o protilidové a protinárodní politice T. G. Masaryka*, document 3/VII; *Berliner Tagblatt, Abendausgabe* (29 August 1924).
13 Pichlík, p. 327.
14 Pichlík, p. 341.
15 Beneš, *Dokumenty*, no. 275.
16 Milner Papers, New College, Oxford.
17 J. Kratochvíl, *Cesta revoluce* (Prague 1928), p. 639.
18 Masaryk, pp. 239–42.
19 United States Foreign Relations (1918), supplement 1, L, 818.

20 Masaryk, pp. 271–2.
21 Masaryk, p. 366 *et seq.*
22 Masaryk, p. 372.
23 Pichlík, p. 383.
24 Pichlík, p. 384.
25 Zeman, p. 220.
26 Herben, p. 350.
27 Herben, p. 351.

Chapter 5 The President

1 K. Čapek, *Hovory*, p. 175.
2 Masaryk, *Světová revoluce*, p. 383.
3 Masaryk, p. 386.
4 Ferdinand Peroutka, *Budování státu* (Prague 1933), I, pp. 461–2.
5 Peroutka, p. 494.
6 Peroutka, p. 472.
7 Peroutka, p. 474 *et seq.*
8 Peroutka, p. 915.
9 Peroutka, p. 481.
10 Peroutka, p. 1319.
11 Herben, p. 380–1.
12 Herben, p. 413.
13 Peroutka, p. 1317.
14 Peroutka, pp. 1317–8.
15 Peroutka, p. 2166.
16 Herben, p. 410.
17 Herben, p. 427.
18 K. Gottwald, *Vybrané spisy* (Prague 1954), I, 178; the first part of the passage quoted here was deleted from the parliamentary records, but was published in full in Gottwald's *Selected Works.*
19 *Dokumenty o protilidové a protinárodni politice T. G. Masaryka*, p. 96.
20 Herben, p. 459.
21 Herben, pp. 470–1.

Chapter 6 The Patrimony

1 J. W. Bruegel, *Czechoslovakia before Munich* (Cambridge 1973), p. 103.
2 L. Škornová, *Nejedlého kritika Benešovy zahraniční politiky k SSSR* (Prague 1954), p. 15.
3 Beneš, *Paměti*, pp. 10–11.
4 Škornová, p. 64.
5 Škornová, document facing p. 64.
6 Bruegel, p. 277.
7 R. W. Bruce Lockhart, *Jan Masaryk* (London 1951), p. 37.
8 Alice Masaryk, *Dětství a mládi* (Pittsburgh 1960).

9 Marcia Davenport, *Too Strong for Fantasy* (London 1967), p. 280 *et seq.*
10 Lockhart, *Jan Masaryk*, p. 18.
11 V. Fischl, *Hovory s Janem Masarykem* (Tel Aviv 1952), p. 82.
12 Fischl, pp. 78–9.
13 F. Klátil, *Beneš zblíska* (London 1944), p. 30.
14 L. Feierabend, *Z vlády doma do vlády v exilu* (New York 1964), p. 58.
15 J. Křen, *V em igraci* (Prague 1969), p. 590.
16 Křen, p. 597.
17 Lockhart, p. 36.
18 F. Moravec, *Master of Spies* (London 1975), p. 210.
19 Moravec, p. 222.
20 Lockhart, pp. 38–9.
21 Křen, p. 501.
22 *Kulturní Tvorba* (1 July 1965); Křen, p. 503.
23 Beneš, *Paměti*, p. 144.
24 B. Lašťovička, *V Londýně za války* (Prague 1961), p. 70.
25 Beneš, p. 208.
26 Křen, p. 579.
27 Fischl, p. 81.
28 Lockhart, p. 39.
29 Beneš, p. 360.
30 Beneš, p. 362.
31 Lockhart, p. 40.
32 Lašťovička, p. 309.
33 Lašťovička, p. 312.
34 Lašťovička, p. 309.
35 Lašťovička, p. 483.

Chapter 7 **The Internal Exile**

1 Davenport, *Too Strong for Fantasy*, pp. 292–3.
2 Lockhart, *Jan Masaryk*, p. 50.
3 Lockhart, pp. 62 *et seq.*
4 J. Korbel, *The Communist Subversion of Czechoslovakia* (Princeton 1959), pp. 180–1.
5 Lockhart, p. 66.
6 Davenport, p. 351.
7 Davenport, p. 353.
8 Davenport, p. 357.
9 Lockhart, p. 68.
10 Davenport, p. 365.

Index

Abbreviations used:
TGM for Thomas Garrigue Masaryk,
JM for Jan Masaryk.

J6